CASTLES
MADE OF
SOUND

CASTLES MADE OF SOUND

THE STORY OF
GIL EVANS

LARRY HICOCK

DA CAPO PRESS

Designed by Janice Tapia
Set in 12.25-point Perpetua by the Perseus Books Group

Cataloging-in-Publication data for this book is available from the Library of Congress.

First Da Capo Press edition 2002
ISBN 0–306–80945–1

Published by Da Capo Press
A Member of the Perseus Books Group
http://www.dacapopress.com

Da Capo Press books are available at special discounts for bulk purchases in the U.S. by corporations, institutions, and other organizations. For more information, please contact the Special Markets Department at the Perseus Books Group, 11 Cambridge Center, Cambridge, MA 02142, or call (800) 255-1514 or (617) 252-5298, or e-mail j.mccrary@perseusbooks.com.

1 2 3 4 5 6 7 8 9—06 05 04 03 02

For my daughters,
Reagan, Erin, and Delaney

The example of great and pure individuals is the only thing that can lead us to noble thoughts and deeds.

—ALBERT EINSTEIN

TABLE OF
CONTENTS

Foreword   ix

PART ONE: 1912–1956

The Sounds of Life   3
Swingtime   7
New York   18
Wartime   28
A Whole New World   35
A Basement Room on 55th Street   49
Birth of the Coolest   59
Behind the Scenes   74

PART TWO: 1957–1964

Miles Ahead   85
Gil Evans Plus Ten   93
New Bottle, Old Wine   96
Porgy and Bess   98
Great Jazz Standards   104
Sketches of Spain   107
Out of the Cool   116
Live at Carnegie Hall   122
Into the Hot   124
Quiet Nights   126

Time of the Barracuda   131
The Individualism of Gil Evans   135

PART THREE: 1965–1979

Re: Invention   145
Miles Davis and Company   150
Flower Power   158
Great New Moves   166
The Music of Now   195
Where the Work Is   205

PART FOUR: 1980–1988

Changing Partners   213
Reincarnation   227
Monday Nights   234
Buster's Last Stand   244

EPILOGUE

Memorial   281
Last Words from the Musicians   284

Interviews Conducted by Author   289
Bibliography   293
Index   297

FOREWORD

ONE EVENING IN 1973, I was on my way to a Jazz Composers Orchestra workshop at New York University when I spotted Gil Evans sitting in the foyer. Just a couple of days earlier, I had seen Gil's band for the first time, in concert at Lincoln Center. (His magnificent composition "Zee Zee" was recorded that day and can be heard on the album *Svengali*.) I walked over and said hello and told him how much I'd loved the concert and how great I thought his band was. He thanked me for the compliment—not with one of those merely polite but dismissive responses, I felt, but with the utmost sincerity—and I distinctly remember liking the man instantly. We talked for a few minutes, and he was most friendly. I proceeded to tell him about my radio program in Canada, and I asked him for an interview. He declined—graciously, of course—but I persisted, and finally he agreed. I would come on Saturday morning to his home, a loft in Greenwich Village. I would take my bags with me so that I could go from his place directly to the airport to return home.

Gil and his wife Anita were hospitable and equally charming. Before starting the interview, we sat over coffee at the kitchen table and had a very nice little chat. I soon realized that Gil was a gifted raconteur. Not wanting to miss any of his stories, I immediately brought out my tape recorder. But when I reached to turn it on, Gil stopped me. "We'll get to that later, let's just talk for a while." Gil seemed as interested in hearing about my life as I was about his, which, as I've since heard from many other people, is typical of Gil. My visit lasted several hours, and we talked about all kinds of things, within music and far beyond. Yet each time the subject turned to music, or to his life, and I went for the tape recorder, he'd stop me again. "Aw, you don't want to record this, we're just talking right now."

Gil had lived through and experienced firsthand almost the entire history of jazz; he had worked with and befriended most of the great innovators of the past thirty years—Benny Goodman, Lester Young, Charlie Parker, and dozens more; he himself was hailed a legend solely on the strength of his work in the 1950s with Miles Davis; and he was witty, insightful, and eloquent, if not mesmerizing. Clearly he had a great deal to say, and of course I wanted all of it on tape. But somehow, the more we talked, the less important that became. It began to dawn on me that, without the tape recorder on, the conversation remained on a personal level—something that he clearly preferred and seemed to be enjoying. Taping the conversation would turn it into an interview, which was not only less intimate but also something Gil associated with business—a publicity hustle, a vehicle for promoting the next tour or the latest record. Business, I soon learned, was not something Gil cared to talk about unless he absolutely had to. In point of fact, Gil was just then in the midst of completing *Svengali,* his first major-label album in several years; he needed all the publicity and media exposure he could get. Indeed, we also talked at length that day about touring. I was convinced that this new band, with its unique mix of jazz and rock and its exotic array of acoustic instruments and electronics would appeal to a far wider audience than most jazz groups. I went so far as to propose looking for a date or two in Canada, and I suggested that I could perhaps organize a radio broadcast to defer expenses. Gil appreciated the gesture, but instead of pursuing the matter, he went to great lengths to talk me out of it. Rather than consider the potential benefits that he stood to gain, he chose to persuade me not to waste my time on such a dubious venture as a big band tour.

Then off we'd go again to a more pleasant subject—like rock and roll bands: Which ones did I like? Who did I listen to? Gil was sixty years old at the time, nearly three times my age, yet it was not our differences that struck me so much as the interests we shared. I could relate not only to his musical tastes (Jimi Hendrix, Sly Stone, Aretha Franklin, Stevie Wonder) but also to his lifestyle—his funky clothes, his long hair, his very cool loft—and more than anything else, his cheerful and uncannily youthful outlook. At one point I asked about his synthesizer, a Minimoog, which was set up in the living room area; I'd never seen one up close, I told him. Gil jumped up and turned it on, looking now like a little boy showing off the nifty features on his new bike. He showed me how it could be programmed to make different sounds, and he talked about all the new "colors" he was exploring. Colors? Voicings? At the time, I knew nothing about what arrangers did, and I had no idea what any of these terms meant. Seeing the blank expression on my face, the little boy in Gil now gave way to the wise and kindly elder. Colors, he told me, that's his thing—the pure and simple tonality of an instrument, and the one-of-a-kind colors that different people can produce—like the sound of Miles Davis's trumpet compared to Louis Armstrong's. Then there are the colors you get by blending certain instruments together. That's what "voicing" is, basically, like when you mix a French horn and a tuba with a couple of electric guitars and a harp—like a blues harmonica or a great big string harp or maybe both of them together, yeah. And, now there's the synthesizer—Gil's eyes lit up and there was the little boy again—an incredible new instrument and a whole other set of colors, and wow, isn't that just amazing? I marveled at the way Gil could be so excited and yet so calm at the same time.

And so the morning went. I looked at my watch and was startled to see how long I'd been there.

I told Gil that I had to leave or else I'd miss my plane home, and he turned to Anita—"The kids aren't home till tomorrow, right? We've got room for him here"—and then he invited me to stay longer if I wanted to. I declined that offer, and many times since then I've wondered what that weekend might have been like had I stayed. And when I left Gil's that day, after spending some three or four hours with him, I realized that not once had I turned on my tape recorder. Years later, I read an interview in which he described himself as something of an artful dodger, and I immediately thought back to that Saturday morning. That's what happened to my interview, I thought, smiling. It had been dodged by the master himself.

Our paths crossed briefly thirteen years later, through a mutual friend, Glen Hall, with whom Gil had recently worked. By this time I was no longer involved in jazz broadcasting, but I had agreed to write the liner notes for Glen's subsequent CD release of the music he and Gil had recorded. In talking with Glen about that project, and especially his experience in working with Gil, I was soon intrigued, and once more it was the man, as much as the music, who fascinated me. Here was a project that had little prospect of generating much attention, let alone profitability, yet Gil had not hesitated to sign on, after only a couple of phone calls with Glen before they'd even met. This, too, I would hear later, had happened to many other people, including musicians whose playing Gil had never heard but whom he hired on gut instinct.

Gil had brought his band to the Toronto Jazz Festival in June 1987, and after the concert, Glen and I went backstage to say hello. Gil certainly looked older—gaunt and rather frail, in fact—yet in his eyes, his smile, and especially the lyrical tone of his voice, he seemed as vigorous and youthful as he did when I first met him. What was his secret, I wondered, and where does it come from? If the music business was really so vile and nasty, as he himself had told me, how could such a gentle soul survive it? If the jazz life was such a hard struggle, why did Gil Evans always seem to look so relaxed—so happy? There is great sorrow in much of his music—this is one of the most fetching qualities of his writing—but it is not anger or bitterness we hear in it, but rather the cry of love, and it is passionate and beautiful. I wanted to know more about his artistry, how he made such fine music, and I was drawn, too, by his idealism.

And so began the adventure that turned eventually into this book. In February 1988, I wrote to Gil proposing to work with him on a documentary film. He and Glen Hall had been talking about a new project—they were hoping to get Elvin Jones involved, among others—and I wanted to film the whole process from start to finish. Surely, I wrote, there could be no better way to experience the magic of Gil Evans than to see it and hear it as it began to grow and take shape. I do not know if Gil even saw my letter. He went to Mexico within days of its mailing, and it was there, in Cuernavaca, on March 20, that he died. Glen Hall's album, and now my film—and, as I later discovered, perhaps a half dozen other projects—were not to be.

I continued over the next several months to try to develop a documentary film, but I lacked the necessary resources and experience. Then in January 1989, I heard that Lee Konitz was in town, playing at a Toronto jazz club. I went to see him play, and he agreed to meet the next day for an interview about his work with Gil. Suddenly, almost by accident, the journey had begun. I could not do a film without Gil, I reasoned, but I knew that I could write a book about him. And what better way to approach it than as an oral history—not as a formal, critical study (beyond my capacity and indeed my inclination) but simply through interviews: Gil Evans as musicians knew him, the story of his music and his career as told by the people who were right there with him. Even Gil himself might read such a book.

‡   ‡   ‡

It has taken much longer to finish than I expected or even imagined, but I am happy to report that the original game plan has essentially remained unchanged. The core of this book is comprised of original interviews, as listed in the appendix. Most of these interviews were conducted in person between 1990 and 1993—in Toronto, New York, Boston, and Montreal—and the balance were conducted by telephone. I have organized the stories thus gathered into chronological order, and in the narrative I have attempted to provide an accurate picture of the context in which Gil's life unfolded. I regret, and accept full responsibility for, any errors or inaccuracies in this account.

I am deeply indebted to all of the people who found time to speak to me about Gil; without their generosity, I would have no story. I am especially grateful to the following individuals: Jimmie Maxwell, without whom I would have no direct link to Gil's work dating from the 1930s, and who spoke to me on three separate occasions; Gerry Mulligan, George Russell, and John Carisi, for doing two interviews each (one in person and one by phone). My interviews with Tony Williams, Joe Beck, and Wallace Roney are not quoted in the book; their input was nevertheless helpful and is appreciated. I wish also to pay my respects to those who contributed to this story who have since passed on: Gerry Mulligan, John Carisi, Tony Williams, and Red Rodney.

None of this would have happened had I not received that first, fateful telephone call from Glen Hall. "No, no, no," he told me from the very first. "You have to understand. There are people who are one in the million, but Gil Evans is one in a billion." After drawing me into the world of Gil Evans, Glen was my closest advisor and a tireless supporter ("Aren't you done yet?"). Anita Evans has helped me more than any other individual; she gave her time freely and generously in two lengthy interviews and in numerous telephone calls about this or that person, place, or event. She linked me up, directly or indirectly, with perhaps half of the people I interviewed, and more than one of these would not have talked to me without her blessing. Gil's sons, Noah and Miles Evans, have also helped greatly, at the very beginning of this project and at its conclusion, with interviews, fact-checking, and photos, all done with great enthusiasm.

After completing the interviews, but before very much of the book manuscript had taken shape, I turned my attention to the development of two radio documentaries about Gil Evans—the first, a series for CBC Radio Canada in 1998, and the second, a segment for National Public Radio's Jazz Profiles series. For their help in sharpening the editorial focus and clarity of these productions, I wish to thank CBC executive producer Anton Leo and series producer Li Robbins, and Jazz Profiles executive producer Tim Owens and assistant producer Madeleine Smith.

Among the key resources for my research, I wish to acknowledge three main books: Laurent Cugny's book, *Las Vegas Tango: Une Vie de Gil Evans,* which

I read as best I could using a French-to-English dictionary, and whose discography I found to be the most comprehensive and reliable; Jack Chambers's *Milestones*, the definitive Miles Davis biography, whose pages I've worn to tatters in the process of cross-referencing and verifying the details of the many activities Gil undertook with Miles; and finally, *Miles Davis: The Autobiography*, written with Quincy Troupe, which provided insights on Gil and their music that only Miles could provide, in words and images that only Miles could conjure. I also thank Dan Morgenstern and his colleagues at the Rutgers University Institute of Jazz Studies for providing copies of several interviews and magazine articles that would otherwise have been difficult or impossible for me to locate. Rutgers also provided a transcript of an interview with Gil done in 1972 by Helen Armstead Johnston, from which I have drawn extensively.

In closing, I wish to express my gratitude to former Da Capo editor Michael Dorr, with whom the discussions about this book began. Fortunately for me, my relationship with Michael's successor, executive editor Andrea Schulz, has been every bit as productive and rewarding as I had hoped. I thank Andrea and her assistant editor Jane Snyder for making this book far better than it was before they did their superb editing magic.

✝   ✝   ✝

Gil Evans was born in Canada, but he lived more than half his life in New York, mostly in Greenwich Village, where Anita and Noah Evans still live today, no more than a stone's throw from what is now called Ground Zero. The greatest music, the closest friendships, and the best experiences of Gil's life all happened in New York. Not surprisingly, I associate all of the best experiences of putting this book together with New York as well—except, that is, for one: The process of editing this manuscript began with a telephone conversation I had with Andrea Schulz on September 10, 2001. In respect of the tragedies of that following day, I wish to pay tribute to Americans everywhere and in particular to the people of New York City.

—LARRY HICOCK, 17 DECEMBER 2001

PART ONE
1912–1956

So much of what happened in jazz, from the '20s particularly, was determined not by bandleaders or people whose names may be on the record, but it was determined by the arrangers. The arranger is a much underrated but very important factor in the whole development of jazz. Gil, as an arranger, fits right into that very important lineage.

—GUNTHER SCHULLER

THE SOUNDS OF LIFE

WE CAN BE CERTAIN at least of his name: Ian Ernest Gilmore Green—though his friends used to call him Buster, and he settled later on Gil Evans. He even made it legal, in 1968—after nearly fifty years without any actual Evans-inscribed identification—and he only got around to it then at the insistence of Anita Saye Cooper, his second wife. We know, too, that he was born on May 13, 1912, in Toronto, Ontario, Canada, to a British mother and Australian father, just after they emigrated from Australia. Beyond this, much of the family background of this otherwise quite particular gentleman remains open to speculation.

During his childhood, his only real family was his mother. His father died a few months after Gil's birth. He had a half-brother, born in New Zealand, and a half-sister, born either "in India or Africa, I forget which," Gil said, but neither of them had lived at home during his childhood. He remembered meeting his half-brother only twice, many years later in California, and he didn't meet his half-sister until 1960, in her home near Toronto, just a year before she died. He said that, actually, his mother had had four children from a previous marriage, but two of them had died before Gil was born.

His father, a doctor but also an inveterate gambler, had died penniless, and Mrs. Green was soon out working to support herself and her newborn baby. Finding jobs came easily to her—and so did quitting them. Consequently, as a little boy Gil traveled far and wide with her as she went from one job to the next, working her way from one end of the continent to the other. Gil was self-effacing and modest to a fault, but in a rare interview in which he actually talked about his childhood (to Helen Armstead Johnston, in the NEA-sponsored Jazz Oral History Project, through the Smithsonian Institute, in 1972), he described Julia Green (née McConnachy) as a wanderer, an attractive and very independent woman, and "really a flirt. She was still flirting when she was ninety—and men were still proposing to her." By Gil's account, Julia was married five times, first when she was fifteen, then again at seventeen. She was forty-five, and in her third marriage, when Gil was born. "She's the one you should be writing about, not me," he told Johnston.

Gil recalled that when he was four or five years old, he lived with his mother in Florida, where Julia ran a little hotel near Lake Worth. "It was still pretty wild down there," he said. "I can remember waking up at night and hearing the wild horses running by. There were alligators around, and rattlesnakes—my mother would scream when she'd find one in the closet. A few little things like that I remember. And there were some counterfeiters in the hotel, making counterfeit money." In Florida, Julia was married again, briefly, to a man named Gustin. By 1920 she had married once more; husband number five was a miner named Evans.

Two *more* marriages? In such quick succession? And so long before the dawning of liberalized divorce laws and social attitudes? Anita, for one, was inclined to suspect that Gil's mother stretched the truth now and then, if not to protect her own reputation, then perhaps for the sake of her boy's. Indeed it appears Julia was prone to alter her personal history. I was told by Gil's first wife, Lillian Grace, for example, that Gil's mother had told her that it was *she* who came from Australia, not his father, and that Gil's father was actually from South Africa. She'd married him there, not in Australia, and they'd lived briefly in England before settling in Canada. What's more, he was not a doctor but a furniture salesman.

Why two different stories? Both versions came ultimately from the same source, but which one is really true? Is either of them true? Whatever his mother's legal marital status was, from that point her son would be known as Gil *Evans,* even though the new name was never registered officially.

From Florida, they moved out west and traveled constantly, for Mr. Evans, like Julia, made a practice of drifting from job to job. Their first home on the coast was in Nelson, British Columbia, where at the age of eight Gil started grade school. Before long they moved back to the United States; within the space of two years they lived in Spokane, Seattle, and Odessa, all in the state of Washington, and from there they went on to Oregon, Montana, and Idaho. Julia continued to work, too, as a housekeeper and a cook, mostly in mining and lumber camps or on farms. She was usually up by three in the morning to start breakfast for the crews and seldom had time to spend with her son before five or six in the evening, after she had fed and cleaned up after the workers. So young Buster spent the better part of his youth in the company of miners, farmers, and lumberjacks. If it wasn't his maternal influence that first engendered in him a strong sense of self-reliance, it may have been these long hours and days on his own. He grew up quickly in this rough environment, developing something very much like the survival skills acquired by today's big-city street kids. Gil remembered taking his first drink when he was ten years old. It was a homemade concoction called "white mule," and it made him terribly sick: "A lot of kids were drinking it, though, in this town I lived in, a little town in Idaho called Berk. There were no other drugs of any kind except alcohol, so I grew up on alcohol, in that respect. It was an alcohol culture, really."

None the worse for wear, Gil apparently gained more from his nomadic childhood than he lost. Life in the wild west taught him a great deal, even at this tender age, about independence and resourcefulness. And what better lesson could he have learned from his mother than how to change course at the drop of a hat?

BERK WAS IN A VALLEY between two mountains, and the valley wasn't any more than, well, say one block wide; that's all it was. And the road and the railroad, the people, everybody all went up that one street. One day a fire started about three or four towns down and it started blowing up that valley. I came running to my mother and said, "There's a fire in Mason! I think it's going to hit this town—we'd better pack our stuff and get out of here!" So we packed up all my mother's sheet music and her mandolin and stuff and got out of the rooming house we lived in—that's where my mother was working, it was like a rooming house and beanery. Anyway, the fire started coming up sure enough, and it hit Berk, and we all went down in a mine. They took us down in this mine and people brought all their belongings down there. Somebody salvaged a barber's chair, and I can remember, I had so much fun down there, sitting in that barber chair pumping it up and down. The next morning we came out and there was no town. People were poking around looking for things and there was nothing left at all.

✛   ✛   ✛

Apart from his mother's mandolin and a few records on the wind-up Victrola, the music Gil heard was mainly of the time and place: "hillbilly" or "old-time" music, as it was then called, and it aroused no spirits within him. That would come later, after he and his mother had packed up again and moved to Stockton, California. Once more the two of them were on their own; by 1922 Julia's fifth (and final) marriage had ended.

In the comparatively civilized atmosphere of Stockton, a small town eighty miles east of San Francisco, Julia had no difficulty finding better-paying, less-strenuous employment. She had retained her beauty despite long, hard years in the work camps, and apparently she could charm anyone with her elegant British (Australian?) manner. She was hired as a nursemaid for the McCormick family, heirs to one of the largest farm machinery companies in America. It was a live-in position; while she stayed at the McCormick's mansion outside of town, Gil lived in boarding houses, attending school and acquiring, even in his adolescence, all the skills and habits of bachelorhood. It was here, while he was at Stockton High School, that Gil made some friends who happened to collect records. He was introduced to jazz—more precisely, to the recordings of Louis Armstrong. "I learned how to treat a song and all that from Armstrong," Gil said in a 1986 interview with writer Ben Sidran:

> THE FIRST ONE I BOUGHT was called "No One Else But You," and it was him and Earl Hines and a band with an arrangement by Don Redman. It's great. Even now. The rhythm section sounds old-fashioned, but the arrangement is something else. I bought every one of his records from 1927 till around 1936. From then on, he repeated and became more of an entertainer. But for those ten years, he was a great creative artist. Even though he never had any special arrangements. But in every one of those three-minute records, there's a magic moment somewhere. Every one of them. I really learned how to handle a song from him. I learned how to love music from him. Because he loved music, and he did everything with love and care. So he's my main influence.

In 1927, the same year he bought his first Louis Armstrong record, Gil and a friend went to San Francisco to see Duke Ellington play. The music he heard at that concert, and on that first Armstrong record, confirmed exactly the direction he wanted his life to take.

SWINGTIME

WHEN JIMMIE MAXWELL met him in 1933, twenty-one-year-old Gil Evans was co-leader of the local ten-piece dance band. Gil was then attending Modesto Junior College, holding down a day job and taking classes in the evening; both occupations interfered with his music, however, and neither was to last longer than a few more months. The band played proms, weddings, graduation parties, and the occasional ballroom dance, primarily for young, upscale audiences in the surrounding area. When Gil decided to add a second trumpet to the band, young Maxwell, still attending high school in nearby Tracey, auditioned successfully for the job.

Jimmie Maxwell would become best known for his work with Benny Goodman (1939–1943) and later as an accomplished studio player and teacher. As a boy, he had aspired to be a priest, then considered going into medicine, before finally opting for a career in music. He had played since he was four years old (cornet before trumpet), and by 1932, primarily as a result of seeing Duke Ellington's band, he'd fallen in love with jazz. But it was the experience of working with Gil Evans that turned out to be pivotal.

During the few short years since Gil first heard those Armstrong recordings, he had immersed himself in music—Armstrong (always at the top of his list), Ellington, Red Nichols and his Five Pennies, and Fletcher Henderson, among many others. As Gil told Ben Sidran, it was by listening to the records and radio broadcasts of these and other bands that he taught himself how to play the piano and to read, write, and arrange music:

I WAS REALLY RAISED on Don Redman, Duke Ellington, The Wolverines, McKinney's Cotton Pickers, The Casa Loma Band . . . I heard them all. I bought the records. Radio was a big thing then, in the early thirties. Every day you'd hear a band from New York. Duke would be playing from some supper club. And Don Redman had a great band, wow! He had a big band but they were packed together tight. Three trombones, three or four trumpets, four saxophones, they're all bunched up together. Don Redman was the original arranger, big-band arranger, of jazz.

Apart from the inspiration of this music, what made Gil's rapid development possible was his remarkable ear. As a kid, Gil said, he had always been fascinated by the sounds of everyday life. With his back turned, he could identify the make of the cars passing behind him just from the sound of their motors. He learned his craft the same way, with no formal training or instruction, by picking out notes from his records. As Gil told Helen Johnston, "It's the same thing as going to school to learn it. If you hear it on record and want to know how it's done, if the score is available, you go and get it. If the score is not available, then you copy the record yourself—you know, just play it over and over again until you get every note of it." Jimmie Maxwell told me that he had learned to play Louis Armstrong solos the same way, and he and others in the Evans band frequently copied out dance tunes from records. But Gil Evans was the only man Jimmie ever met who could transcribe a song right from a live radio broadcast. "That's how I learned really to arrange," Gil explained, "and how I learned to read, really, and to write the notes down—by listening to the record and then painstakingly putting down on paper what I heard. At first it was slow, and then it gradually got to where I could do it readily. When you say you're self-taught, you really don't mean that you learned all by yourself without any help. I got all the help of everybody I ever heard play. And all the writing I ever wanted to read, to see how it was done, I got from the library."

Gil's influence over Maxwell extended beyond music. For all the time he and his mother spent in mining camps and lumber mills, in his adolescent years Gil nevertheless became quite the young gentleman—broad-minded and even worldly in his attitude, in Maxwell's view:

IF ANYONE IN STOCKTON could be considered cosmopolitan, I guess you could say Gil was. I thought he was very elegant. I considered him my best friend, in the sense that best friends influence each other. I was from a small town and had small-town attitudes, and he sort of broadened my attitudes in that way. I thought he had style—like his attitude about money, being very carefree about money. Well, I took that attitude on.

He was a fairly deep thinker. He was probably the first person I ever met that you might classify as an intellectual—in a favorable sense. Normally that is a pejorative term for me, but in his sense, I thought he was a very deep-thinking person. Some of the books he read interested me, and got me going in that direction. I recall that he had *The Seven Pillars of Wisdom,* which he seemed very fond of, and a strange book called *Genius,* which perhaps was appropriate. Later on, he had that book *A Generation of Vipers,* which I think was the first book to start criticizing modern American civilization.

But he used to frustrate me in some ways. I was a fairly devout Catholic at the time, and he liked to torment me, telling me that priests were all homosexuals. He used to like to tell me things like that—asking me what did I think the Pope really thought about when he was alone at night. Gil told me all kinds of obscene stories, trying to make my life miserable. I had to confess every week that I had listened to these awful conversations. He seemed to get a lot of pleasure out of this. He'd sort of grin, get this look, and fix one of his eyes on you to see what the reaction was.

✝   ✝   ✝

There had been two bands in Stockton—Gil's group and another led by bassist Ned Briggs—that merged in 1933 to become the Briggs-Evans Band. When Ned Briggs left in 1935, it again became the Gil Evans Orchestra. Like most small-town groups, its function was to perform the latest dance hits, preferably the closest possible approximation of the original source. In Gil's band, it was *jazz* dance music they played, based on charts copied from records of the best bands in the country—Isham Jones, Jimmie Lunceford, Earl Hines, Duke Ellington. The *sound* of Gil's band, however, was influenced heavily by the Casa Loma Orchestra, a popular white dance band, originally from Detroit, that was heard regularly on coast-to-coast radio broadcasts from New York. This was probably the least jazz-oriented of the bands that Gil listened to on the radio or records. Casa Loma had initially played "hot" dance music, but their real success came when in the early 1930s they started to feature soft, distinctively arranged romantic ballads. Gil loved those arrangements, particularly the ones written by Gene Gifford. Like many other musicians (blacks as well as whites), he was also attracted by the band's unique instrumentation. Gil's copying of the Casa Loma tunes affected more than the sound of his band; the desire to recreate their polish and sophistication also influenced Gil's early development as a meticulous arranger and orchestrator. Jimmie Maxwell described how this evolved:

> THE ARRANGEMENTS IN THOSE DAYS, the stock arrangements you could buy, were pretty dreadful, so whenever it was possible, generally the piano player would sketch out little arrangements for the band, which were always a dozen times better than the stock arrangements. Aside from that, stock arrangements cost money. They were a dollar, a dollar seventy-five or something, which at the time was a pretty big bite. Casa Loma was a wonderful orchestra. It was the first dance orchestra that I know of to use doubling, use interesting arrangements, harmonies, and that kind of thing—so Gil started copying their music. And also, we had two or three very talented guys who could double on other reed instruments—or who bought them outright and *learned* to double on them. So he started out of necessity, because the stock arrangements were so terrible. And the arrangements of the Casa Loma band were so beautiful that he wanted to do the same thing for his orchestra. Going from a case of necessity, it grew to more of a passion for writing.

During 1933, the band mostly played one-night stands at the country clubs and fraternity houses around Stockton, for which the musicians each earned between two and five dollars a night. At first, a good deal of that money was spent on outfits—gray slacks and navy blazers with the band's signature initials embroidered on a side pocket—which bore a striking resemblance to the Casa Loma wardrobe. In 1934, the band was hired to play at Lake Tahoe for the summer, its first steady out-of-town engagement.

> WE PLAYED UP THERE for twelve dollars a week and board and room. It was a chalet that was built out over the water, Globen's Chalet it was called. We got our meals, which consisted of creamed turkey necks and turkey wings every night. And we slept up in this sort of an attic room up above the ballroom. Most of us put our beds up in the rafters, because of the rats.

It was not as bad as it sounds. We had a wonderful time. The music was good. We had very poor crowds, though, because there was a place nearby, the Cal-Neva Club it was called—it was built halfway in California and halfway in Nevada—and a very popular band there at that time was Dick Jurgen's band. It was a copy of the Ray Noble band, and later became a big hotel band on the West Coast and did very well. They outdrew us because they were more of a dance band, whereas we leaned . . . while it *was* dance music, we did lean to the jazz side.

After Lake Tahoe, the band looked for more work out of town, Jimmie Maxwell recalled, but they soon ended up back in Stockton. "We tried to get a job in Sacramento, and we hung around there for a couple of weeks. The union wouldn't let us work the clubs, and when you go without food for four or five days, it gets a little rough. We'd all try to think of girls we knew in Sacramento and get invited over to dinner—and then say, 'Well, how about bringing my friends?'"

The next meaningful job came later that fall, at Stockton's Dreamland Ballroom. Here, the band played five nights a week, and each man was paid twenty-five dollars. For a while, they also had a steady Saturday night gig in Manteca, another little nearby town. Then in the summer of 1935 the band was hired to play the Rendezvous Ballroom in Balboa Beach, about thirty miles from Los Angeles. This job was steady enough, and far enough away from Stockton, to require an actual move, and thus the band left home base for the first time. They rented a house together and settled in for what turned out to be an extended stay. "We played in the summer and we'd each get about fifty dollars a week," said Jimmie Maxwell. "And in the winter we'd get twelve dollars a week. We'd play Friday, Saturday, and Sunday in Balboa, and then during the week we'd play at some ballroom up in Anaheim, owned by the same people."

The Balboa work gave the band a permanent new base and a steady income. It also brought the players close enough to Los Angeles that they could drive up regularly on their days off. Many of them would take a music lesson in the afternoon, then they'd all meet up at night to go hear some music. The biggest jazz club in L.A. was the Palomar Ballroom, where they could see people like Tommy and Jimmy Dorsey, the Casa Loma Orchestra, and the hottest attraction of them all, Benny Goodman.

‡   ‡   ‡

Benny Goodman's appearance at the Palomar in August 1935 was the event that effectively launched the swing era. Almost overnight, Goodman's buoyant new sound began to change the face of American pop music. Countless existing bands revamped their style—from here on, all dance bands would come to be known as either "swing" or "sweet"—and new bands sprang up everywhere, so strong was the demand for the new Goodman-inspired music. Without totally abandoning his sweeter side, Gil went with swing, too, adding several Goodman tunes to his book, including "Sometimes I'm Happy," "King Porter Stomp," and "Blue Skies" (all arranged for Goodman by Fletcher Henderson, whom Gil had admired long before Benny hired him).

Like hundreds of other band leaders in the country, Gil copied all of the new Goodman records as soon as they came out. But there was a difference: with the growing proficiency of Gil's band, and of his writing for it, the results were more impressive than might have been expected from just another local knock-off band. "Apparently we were pretty good at it," said Maxwell. "Because when the bands would come to the Palomar—like Benny Goodman, Artie Shaw, Jimmy Dorsey—they would all come down to Balboa Beach to hear *our* band, and they were tremendously impressed by it."

Benny Goodman was especially interested, not only in the music but also in Gil's players. He came to hear the band in Balboa in 1936, during his first return to the Palomar since his breakthrough there a year earlier, and he immediately hired saxophonist Vido Musso out of Gil's band. "We took Benny one night to see Lionel Hampton," Maxwell recalled. "Vido, Gil, and me. And all of us sat in—Vido and I sat in, anyhow—and at that time Benny hired Lionel and he hired Vido." Apparently, Maxwell added, Benny had also been impressed by Gil's clarinet player, Ruel Lynch: "Actually he copied some of the things that Ruel played, because I heard him do it on records—things that Ruel had played."

RUEL DIED VERY YOUNG, he was a drunkard. He wanted to be a priest and he was always going into the seminary and then getting drunk and leaving. Finally he had all his teeth pulled out so he couldn't play anymore, theoretically, but actually he could, so he came back and he still played with the band. The only thing was, he'd get a little drunk and he'd clown around. He'd come down to the mic to play a solo and he used to like to let his teeth fall out. Which didn't make Gil too happy, but it *was* funny.

Notwithstanding Benny Goodman's self-serving image in the business (Maxwell knew him to be far more generous than his reputation suggested), he can be credited with trying to help Gil's band get its first serious break. Goodman got the band signed by Music Corporation of America (MCA), at that time the country's largest booking agency. Then he got Gil his first record contract, with Victor Records. With MCA, the band should have expected to play all the best hotels and other prime dance spots, while the record deal would have provided national exposure. It was not to be so. Jimmie Maxwell remembered:

> WE USED TO GO UP to L.A. every week and talk to Norman Doyle at MCA—he was our personal manager. We kept asking for a good job— you know, "When are you going to put us in a hotel?" And Norman would say, "Well, you think you guys are ready?" We'd say, "*Sure* we're ready"— and Gil would say, "Well, no, we're not really ready yet." Gil was always saying we weren't really ready yet. Same thing with that record contract—we never made a record ever. Gil still didn't think we were good enough. We'd argue with him and yell at him and every other damn thing. But . . .

Put simply, Maxwell explained, it was a matter of Gil's standards. He just did not want the band to be recorded unless it was at least as good as Goodman's or Dorsey's or the Casa Loma Orchestra. There may have been a degree of insecurity involved on Gil's part, either toward himself or the band, but more than this, it seemed to Maxwell and the others in the band that it wasn't so much a case of Gil's lack of confidence as his lack of business skills. Gil lived for his music and for his band, but he seemed unwilling or unable to come to terms with anything to do with its finances, promotion, bookings, or any of the other facets of the business. "He was very casual. He was perhaps the most relaxed person I ever knew—he was infuriating. They call it 'laid back' now, or 'cool' or something. I didn't know those words then; he was just a pain." If he was working and the band was getting by, Gil was happy, and for the most part, Maxwell told me, so were the rest of the players.

> WE NEVER TALKED ABOUT making money. It wasn't a law or anything; it's just the way it was. We were all deeply devoted to our music and to Gil's band. What made it a good band was the enthusiasm of everybody in the

band. If they didn't have it, they didn't stay in the band. We didn't always make that much money, so you really had to love what you were doing and have a lot of faith in the band. So we generally had the best musicians locally. Even when we went down to southern California, we got surprisingly good musicians to fill in when he enlarged the band a little bit—surprisingly good considering we didn't offer very much money.

But also I think it was Gil's . . . I was going to say his personality and his drive, but that would give you the wrong picture of him. He wasn't a go-getter like Knute Rockne—"Let's get in there and fight, boys." He was always kind of laid back and snickering at us. He'd say, "Well, look, if that's the best you're going to play, we're not going to amount to much." But he was still able to get everybody's loyalty and everybody's desire to please him. I can certainly speak for myself, I was always anxious to get his approval.

Gil's opinion was still of the utmost importance, Maxwell told me in 1992, some sixty years after working with Gil: "I must confess, to this day I find myself thinking, 'Boy, I wish Gil could hear what I just played.'"

Gil was not as tyrannical as many bandleaders were, but he also was not altogether reliable when it came to keeping the band gainfully employed or simple general baby-sitting duties. There were times, Maxwell recalled, when Gil would drop everyone off in L.A. and then forget to pick them up at the end of the night. The musicians would have to hitchhike back out to Balboa Beach at three o'clock in the morning. Yet there was never any doubt about who ran the band or about Gil's priorities, "laid back" or not.

HE WAS RELAXED in his speech, and his facial expressions and body expressions—but he was iron-willed about what he wanted. There was no question of it, and there was not really much need for him to even say so. Everyone knew it. In what he wanted to do, he went straight ahead. Nothing could stop him. He would move in on anybody and live with them till they threw him out—as I had to do, later—but all he was interested in was finding a place where there was a piano and he could work on his writing.

After a second season at Balboa Beach in 1936, the band is known to have played at least three other dates in early 1937—the Trianon Ballroom in

Seattle, Washington; the Uptown Ballroom in Portland, Oregon; and at Jantzen Beach, near Portland—for in that year there appeared the band's first published review. In *Tempo*, a West Coast music magazine, the group was described as "a promising band modeled somewhat after the formalized swing style of Goodman. [Evans] has pushed his way steadily into the front ranks of West Coast bands." But after these and perhaps a few other occasional dates, the band returned for another season at Balboa Beach, where they ended up spending the balance of the year—"dying on the vine," as Jimmie Maxwell put it—as the work gradually slowed to a trickle. At the very height of the swing era boom, Gil Evans could not keep this highly talented band employed. He could work day and night perfecting his charts, but he simply could not, or would not, deal with the business of running a band.

Toward the end of 1937, MCA came up with a plan to get everybody working. Manager Norman Doyle suggested to Gil that if he would perhaps let a singer front the band, there would be a lot more work available. The man he had in mind was another of his clients, Skinnay Ennis, a drummer turned vocalist who'd become popular with a dance orchestra led by Hal Kemp. Ennis wanted to strike out on his own as a leader, and Doyle saw an opportunity to set him up with a full band, complete with its own charts. For Gil, after nearly another full year of scuffling, it came down finally to a matter of survival. MCA's offer could not be refused. As Gil explained to Whitney Balliett (quoted by Ira Gitler in *Swing to Bop*), "They couldn't get me any work at all," Gil said, "but they could get him work, so we took the job. It was my band and my library. The first couple of jobs we played, Skinnay would stand out front and listen to it. When the number would be over, he would applaud and everything, forgetting that he was the leader of the thing."

Gil was not at all happy about turning over his band to Ennis, but the work did materialize, and it was very good work. MCA got them booked into Victor Hugo's, a posh supper club in Hollywood, where they worked six nights a week in a run lasting several months. "It paid pretty good," said Jimmie Maxwell.

IT PAID SIXTY DOLLARS a week, and that wasn't close to anything we'd ever made before. The average working man made thirty dollars at that time, so you can see it was a good salary. [Victor Hugo's] was *the* night club in Beverly Hills. All the famous movie stars came there on Sunday nights. They sort of took it over and put on an impromptu show—they'd get up and do their acts. Jack Benny and Bob Hope would get up and tell jokes at each other, Betty Grable and all these people came in. Rosalind Russell—she said she used to be a girl scout and she came up and played my trumpet. Most of those movie stars were all originally musicians. Tony Martin used to sit in and play tenor sax. Mickey Rooney and Jackie Cooper used to fight with each other over who was going to play drums. So they thought it was a glamorous life. Some of us thought it was a pain in the ass. But the music was very good. It was still Gil's arrangements.

‡   ‡   ‡

The band's next big break, in the summer of 1938, was in radio, in the form of a lucrative contract in Hollywood to work as the regular band for the Bob Hope Show. Virtually from the night of its launch, on September 27, 1938, the show was an instant hit. The program made Bob Hope a radio star, propelling him to the top of the popularity polls, alongside the likes of Jack Benny and Fred Allen. The show would run continuously until 1952.

Skinnay Ennis got a lot of attention on the show, too, not only for his singing, but in particular for his part in the comedy routines and as the brunt of many of Hope's jokes. Cracks about Ennis's lankiness ("spaghetti in search of a meatball") were almost as frequent as those about Hope's nose. The band performed a whole range of musical chores, all live, from the opening theme to sign-off: cues and fills for the comedy skits, backgrounds for the commercials (Pepsodent toothpaste was the show's sponsor), and backup for musical guests and other variety acts. Skinnay usually sang one or two songs, as would the show's regular vocal group, Six Hits and a Miss.

As the show progressed, there was a need for more variety-oriented charts rather than for straight band tunes, and Ennis also wanted to see more new vocal arrangements, not the least of which were for his own features. Accordingly, he reasoned, Gil's role as the show's music director was going to have to change. "Gradually the library got changed to his kind of music," Gil told Whitney Balliett. "Skinnay had a little whispering kind of continental sound. Although he didn't sing in a foreign language or anything, he had that kind of sound—he became very popular in England and all over—so the manager and I decided he had to do that kind of music." It was also decided that a second staff arranger would need to be added, one with more experience working with singers. Gil was more than capable of writing vocal charts (his own band had almost always had singers), but Skinnay and his manager were apparently looking for a "name" arranger. As Gil explained to Balliett, "Skinnay had one of those managers who would sit back and twirl his mustache and say, 'Who is the greatest vocal arranger in the world?' At that particular time in California, Claude Thornhill had a hit record out with Maxine Sullivan, 'Loch Lomond,' so he said, 'Okay, send for him.'"

Later describing the whole Ennis-Hope period as "fairly miserable," in 1957 Gil told Nat Hentoff that he made the best of the situation, treating even the most perfunctory assignments, like backing up the tap dancers or scoring toothpaste commercials, as "an introduction to show music and the entertainment business. . . . It gave me another look at the whole picture." And indeed, if this wasn't quite the direction he had in mind for his own music, neither was the lifestyle exactly a struggle. Gil had a steady job, a roof over his head (he and his new dog, a Great Dane, shared a rented house with some of the other musicians), and lots of free time on his hands. Yet Gil was never tempted by the Hollywood high life. He could have gone to glamorous parties, dated young starlets, or rubbed shoulders with the deal makers, but instead he mostly hung out at home. "Gil hardly ever went anywhere, as far as I can remember," said Jimmie Maxwell. "He stayed home and played his music and worked on his writing."

Given his frustrations with the radio show, it was obvious that it would only be a matter of time before Gil left the Ennis band—if not of his own accord, well then, perhaps with a little push from someone else. This time, the big change in Gil's life was set in motion by Skinnay Ennis. In hiring Claude Thornhill to take over the band's vocal arrangements, Ennis inadvertently pointed Gil toward the most important musical relationship of his career.

NEW YORK

PIANIST, ARRANGER, AND COMPOSER Claude Thornhill joined the Skinnay Ennis Band in 1938, not long after the Bob Hope Show began, and he would leave less than a year later to form his own orchestra back in New York. During this brief time, however, his work put him into almost daily contact with Gil Evans. Instead of rivals or competitors, they became good friends. They found that they shared musical interests and aspirations—most notably, the desire to take a more "philosophical" and less conventional approach to orchestral music. From the beginning, Gil was impressed with Thornhill's writing ("Even then, Claude had a unique way with a dance band"), just as Thornhill was taken with Gil's distinctive arrangements and orchestrations. When they later joined forces, starting in 1941, the Thornhill-Evans partnership would produce some of the most exciting and original music of the big band era.

Unlike Gil, Indiana-born Claude Thornhill had shown early musical promise. In his teens he was already an accomplished, conservatory-trained pianist with more than a passing interest in arranging and composing. His introduction to the popular music business came through Artie Shaw, who had "discovered" him. He played piano for Shaw in Cleveland, and then he moved to New York to join Hal Kemp's band. In 1935 he joined Ray Noble and his orchestra, whose music was arranged by Noble himself and by another staff arranger, the soon-to-be-famous Glenn Miller. Thornhill left the Noble band in 1936 to pursue what became a very active freelance career. In addition to

18

his highly successful recordings with singer Maxine Sullivan, he worked with such established stars as Benny Goodman, Tommy Dorsey, and the quasi-classical orchestra of André Kostelanetz. Claude Thornhill thus had already acquired considerable radio experience, in Hollywood as well as New York, prior to joining the Bob Hope Show.

During his stint with Ray Noble, Thornhill had become good friends with Glenn Miller, acknowledging Miller not only as a strong musical influence but also an ardent supporter. In 1939, Miller, with his own orchestra on its way to becoming the top-drawing band in the country, gave Thornhill the financial backing to start his own band. It was not uncommon for successful band leaders to finance other bands and lend a helping hand to friends and colleagues—just as Tommy Dorsey had backed Glenn Miller during his earlier, struggling years. On the other hand, these leaders were also "diversifying their investments," for by now big bands were also big business. Glenn Miller, admired by many for his business acumen as much as for his musical success, had financed Charlie Spivak and, later, Hal McIntyre. But whereas he was known to impose upon these bands his own strict parameters to ensure their commerciality, Miller gave Claude Thornhill no such stipulations.

Returning to New York in September 1939, Thornhill spent about six months assembling and organizing his band, working with arranger Bill Borden to develop its book. One of the band's first engagements was back in California, however, and ironically, the date was set up through Gil Evans, who'd had so little success booking his own band. Gil had recommended the band to the management of the Rendezvous Ballroom, and Claude was subsequently hired for the summer of 1940. After this gig, during which Gil was no doubt a frequent visitor to his old Balboa Beach stomping grounds, the Thornhill band then traveled back east in the fall. Here they played a number of clubs and dance halls that were part of the "Shribman circuit," an extensive string of rooms throughout New England booked and/or operated by Cy and Charlie Shribman, considered the most effective agents in the business. Several prominent bands, including Glenn Miller's, got their first important exposure through the Shribman circuit and by way of the live "remote" radio broadcasts, also organized by the Shribmans, that were transmitted via the national networks. It was through these proven channels that the Claude Thornhill Orchestra was to be launched.

The first Shribman booking of real consequence was scheduled for March 1941, at the Glen Island Casino, the most prominent and popular dance hall on the East Coast. Situated on Glen Island, adjacent to New Rochelle on the north shore of Long Island Sound, the casino's stylish country club atmosphere made it an especially appealing summertime alternative to muggy Manhattan. It was close enough to draw much of its clientele from New York, as well as from Westchester County and the other affluent communities in the area. It was here, in 1939, that Glenn Miller's career had taken a sharp upward turn; his summer engagement, and especially the radio remotes, generated a level of excitement that had not been seen since Benny Goodman's sensational hits in 1935.

Having landed the Glen Island booking, Claude Thornhill seemed poised for certain success. To this prestigious engagement, he would also add a recording contract. He was signed first to OKeh Records and would later record for its parent company, Columbia. Even before reaching Glen Island, the band had started to build an enthusiastic public following. Thornhill's distinctively light, cloud-like sound was achieved through a formidable combination of musicianship, writing, arranging, and notably, his choice of instruments, an assemblage that was unprecedented in dance orchestra history. "It isn't exactly orthodox," Thornhill said, in a 1942 interview (quoted in George Hoefer's 1965 Down Beat article on Gil Evans). "On some arrangements we utilize six clarinets. And we have two French horns, two trombones, three trumpets, and four rhythm. The six clarinets aren't always in action. We use five saxes and one clarinet more often. The whole idea behind the band is 'lightness,' and that's why we score for six clarinets, playing the upper register, with long sustained chords behind them. We want an airy bounce, not a funeral tromp-tromp in heavy, labored accents."

Still not satisfied with the orchestra's overall development, Thornhill made some key personnel changes before the Glen Island Casino date. With his impressive list of bookings, Thornhill was able to attract some of the top musicians in their field—including the New Orleans–style clarinetist Irving Fazola, lead trumpeter Conrad Gozzo, and trumpet soloist Rusty Diedrick. "I joined the band from leaving Red Norvo's band," Diedrick told me in 1992. "And as a result of my joining Claude Thornhill's band, several other members of the Red Norvo band came over to Claude's band—including Conrad Gozzo, Ted Goddard, the guitar player Allan Hanlon."

During its two-month run at Glen Island, the band achieved success on virtually every level, garnering the enthusiasm of the public and the acclaim of critics and peers alike. The orchestra's ballads, whether instrumental or vocal, were extremely popular among the young dancers. Those who came out to listen, rather than dance, were taken with Thornhill's fresh and highly original sound—its exciting whisper-to-a-wail dynamics, the clarity and economy of Claude's "one-finger" solos, and the unique sound of the French horns and the unison clarinet lines.

Even before the band left Glen Island, the casino's management booked them for the following year, this time for the full summer season; in fact, they returned to the club several more times in 1941, including the very busy week ending with New Year's Eve. Apart from working at Glen Island, during 1941 the band toured, mainly around New England, and in early 1942, they made a widely successful cross-country trip. Also in 1941, Thornhill started recording. Among his first releases were popular hits such as the ballad "Where or When" and his own composition "Snowfall," which became the orchestra's theme song. For modern-day dancers, he offered a sprightly arrangement of "Brahms's Hungarian Dance No. 5." Another Thornhill original, "Portrait of a Guinea Farm," exemplified the depth and wit of his writing and his great finesse as a pianist.

The band's one remaining weak spot, to some ears, at least, was its lack of real jazz material. What was needed was more rhythmic excitement, more *swing*. "They didn't call them 'jazz' bands so much in that era," said Rusty Diedrick, "but Basie or Benny Goodman—*they* were more swing bands. In Claude's band, the emphasis was not totally upon swing. Naturally it did swing, but that wasn't the main thrust of the thing. It wasn't an out-and-out hot jazz, swing-style band, which I was more accustomed to with Red Norvo's band." Like Diedrick, many of the other musicians were fully capable of playing stronger jazz. The lack of swing was a result, partially if not primarily, of Thornhill's own disposition, for he had never really considered himself a "jazz" player. It might also have been due simply to a shortage of charts. Arranger Bill Borden told the *New Yorker* jazz writer Whitney Balliett, "When I joined the band, in December of 1939, it hadn't settled into a groove. Sometimes it sounded like Jimmie Lunceford, sometimes like Bob Crosby. Claude said he had started out with sixty arrangements, but I suspect it was fewer than that. I suggested he get Gil Evans, who wasn't happy with Skinnay Ennis." Gil, in the meantime, had been after Claude constantly, "writing and pestering him for a job" since he left Hollywood. Finally, in mid-1941, Gil got the call. Prompted at least in part by the departure of Bill Borden, who had enlisted in the army, Thornhill offered to take him on.

"Gil Evans joined the band at Glen Island," Rusty Diedrick recalled. "We were working there, and I remember his pulling in. He had an old convertible, a Model A Ford or something, and he had driven in from California with a Great Dane dog sitting by his side. At that time, Claude and Bill Borden—and to some extent, I—were doing the arrangements. And then Gil came along, and of course he became the foremost arranger for the band." Later recalling that occasion to Whitney Balliett, Gil said, "I arrived at the casino in the evening, just before the band hit. I was told that Claude was sick and I would have to take his place. Well, he wasn't. It was one of his practical jokes. . . . But he wasn't much at *taking* jokes. Once, I set an alarm clock to go off on the bandstand just as he was playing his tinkly piano on 'Autumne Nocturne.' He didn't think it was very funny."

Apart from all of its other accomplishments, then, this early version of the Claude Thornhill Orchestra also heralded the arrival of this "new" arranger, just in from the West Coast and seeking a niche in the flourishing New York music scene. The move represented all that Gil might have hoped for: a promising, innovative band to work with, one that was situated in the very center of the jazz world—and not a juggler, joker, or tap dancer in sight. Best of all, his new employer's view of Gil's place in the band was far different than Skinnay Ennis's. Only weeks before Gil set out for the east, *Music and Rhythm* had quoted Ennis's exuberant but nonetheless telling remarks: "Lots of my boys are good jazzmen. And our arranger! His name is Gil Evans—a former terrific jazz arranger. It's taken me several years to tone him down to my speed." Claude Thornhill represented Gil's ticket out of Hollywood, away from Skinnay Ennis and all that, in Gil's mind, he stood for. Instead of "toning him down," Claude Thornhill provided Gil the opportunity, and the vehicle, for getting *up* to speed.

The Thornhill orchestra became a kind of workshop in which Gil was able to experiment freely with new ideas, not only without interference from the leader but in fact with his full support. In essence, Gil used the band's established sound as his own starting point. He described the process in 1957 to writer Nat Hentoff for *Down Beat*:

AT FIRST, THE SOUND of the band was almost a reduction to an inactivity of music, a stillness. Everything—melody, harmony, rhythm—was moving at a minimum speed. The melody was very slow, static; the rhythm was nothing much faster than quarter notes and a minimum of syncopation.

Everything was lowered to create a sound, and nothing was to be used to distract from that sound.

But once this stationary effect, this sound, was created, it was ready to have other things added to it. The sound itself can only hold interest for a certain length of time. Then you have to make certain changes within that sound; you have to make personal use of harmonies rather than work within the traditional ones; there has to be more movement in the melody; more dynamics; more syncopation; speeding up of the rhythms. For me, I had to make those changes, those additions, to sustain *my* interest in the band, and I started to as soon as I joined. I began to add from my background in jazz, and that's where the jazz influence began to be intensified.

Apart from what Gil was about to contribute, it should be noted that he readily embraced many of the characteristics of Thornhill's existing sound. He favored Thornhill's symphony-oriented approach to instrumentation to such an extent that, in later years, many continued to associate this and other aspects of the sound with Gil rather than with their originator. It was Thornhill who first used French horns in a dance band and later, the tuba—not for the rhythm section, as in the New Orleans tradition, but as a new voice, a new color. Gil pointed this out often and clearly acknowledged Thornhill's influences upon him: "Claude deserves the credit for the sound. My influence, such as it has been, was really through him. His orchestra served as my instrument to work with. That's where my influence and his join, so to speak." It was within Claude's imaginative orchestral context that Gil Evans was to find his stride. Notwithstanding the importance of Thornhill's innovations and his development of this unique sound, the fact remains that it's what Gil *did* with his orchestra that provided many of its most enduring and endearing qualities.

The first Gil Evans works recorded by Claude Thornhill are dated 1942. Two of these, "There's a Small Hotel," a charming vocal ballad, and "Buster's Last Stand," an up-tempo swinger written by Evans and Thornhill, demonstrate Gil's already impressive versatility. Beyond filling the orchestra's jazz gap, he added greatly to the band's overall sense of style—with rich new tonal colors, which he produced by uniquely blending instruments together, and with his exciting new dynamic conception. Gil did not supplant Thornhill's popular material. Indeed he wrote more of it, but he also gave it his own unique signature. Discerning listeners were struck immediately by his voicings, by the elegance and verve of the new material. Yet Gil did not alienate the band's dance crowd, even in his most sophisticated arrangements. Rather, he gave them more danceable music than ever and a much wider selection of moods and tempos, with none of the usual clichés of either sweet *or* swing bands. Finally, it was the musicians themselves who were most impressed by Gil's work—those who came out to hear the band and, especially, those who played his music. Rusty Diedrick recalled:

> WE LOVED PLAYING his arrangements; he became my favorite arranger. Claude did some writing, and he knew how to get the band to play well— he had his own little methods all his own—but Gil's influence on the band was the most outstanding and the most predominant factor.

Most of Gil's work, and indeed most of the other Thornhill material of this period, went unrecorded. This music was destined, like many other musical jewels of the period, to be lost in the tide of events that together spelled the decline and fall of the big band era. Big band music would remain a lucrative, if not always thriving business, for some years yet, but it was in 1941, very much at the height of its popularity, that the first cracks in the foundation appeared.

+   +   +

It began with a 1941 radio ban against the American Society of Composers, Authors and Publishers (ASCAP), which was imposed by the radio networks during one of many financial disputes with the royalty-collecting organization. Unable to agree upon a new fee schedule by which songwriters and publishers would be paid for performing rights on copyright material controlled by ASCAP, the networks banned ASCAP-held music from the airwaves and looked instead to their own organization, Broadcast Music Inc. (BMI), to supply them with new music. The ban was a serious setback for big bands of every stripe. During the ten months before it was finally lifted, their recordings got no airplay at all, and the bands were prevented from performing ASCAP material on their live radio broadcasts. They had to replace virtually all of their music, including the hits and theme songs for which they were best known. Thornhill's "Hungarian Dance No. 5" was one of the non-ASCAP songs that could still be played during the ban; many bands were scrambling to find other public domain songs, classical or otherwise, and to write new material that they could register with BMI.

Even more damaging to the bands was the recording ban of 1942. This time the dispute was between the major record companies (mainly the "Big Three": Columbia, Victor, and Decca) and the American Federation of Musicians, headed by the militant Chicago-based president, Jimmy Petrillo. Petrillo had announced that the AFM's contract with the manufacturers was to be terminated on August 1. Until the companies agreed to meet the union's demands concerning the establishment of a trust fund for aiding unemployed musicians (to be financed by the record companies), no union musician would work in a studio. The strike went into effect as scheduled, but it had been anticipated by the record companies, which had stockpiled as much new inventory as they could. It took over a year before Decca and Capitol signed new contracts with the union, and then another full year—in November 1944—before the strike ended completely, when Victor and Columbia finally signed with the union.

Like the "ASCAP wars," which took many years before and after the 1941 radio ban to be fully resolved, the AFM strike was part of the union's ongoing battle with the record companies and broadcasters. At first, it was a largely futile attempt to forestall the loss of union jobs resulting from the replacement of live music by recordings, juke boxes, and "canned music" radio programs. After that it turned into a prolonged fight for getting the musicians a bigger piece of the action. Few today would argue the importance of the AFM's struggle to see that its members were fairly compensated for their contribution to the increasingly profitable recording industry, but at the time of the 1942 strike, Petrillo's defiant measures prevented a lot of musicians from getting their music onto records and into the marketplace— and none were hit harder by the strike than the big bands.

Apart from the loss of exposure and direct income from recording, the strike also led to the emergence of a new threat to the dance bands. During the strike, the record companies had turned their attention to singers (who at the time were not part of the union) to supply them with new product. These recordings usually took the form of a lead vocal backed by an a cappella chorus. Despite their obvious limitations, these records had the effect of acclimatizing the public to vocal rather than orchestral music, and they provided an early glimpse toward an era in which singers, rather than band leaders, would become the biggest stars. It could well be argued that the big band era was already on the wane and that the public was ready for something new. But even if the strike didn't directly cause the shift in popular music tastes, it did nothing to soften the blow and quite a lot to hasten the demise of the big bands.

Many big-band leaders surely saw the writing on the wall, particularly the growing popularity of the singers. But in 1942, most of the big bands were disrupted far more by the effects of the World War II. When the United States entered the war in December 1941, a majority of young men were drafted or enlisted. Fewer men were at home to take their dates out dancing, and dance gigs became smaller and less frequent. Then came the shortage of young musicians, most of whom were also in service. The remaining players, too old or otherwise ineligible for recruitment, were able to command much higher salaries; many went quickly from one band to the next as the bidding accelerated. At the same time, however, the band leaders were faced with shrinking dance audiences and, subsequently, lower revenues. Thus the hardships of the radio ban and the recording strike were compounded by a serious economic squeeze. This was the first real financial setback in the big-band business after nearly a decade of virtually uninterrupted prosperity.

Claude Thornhill was not around to face these problems. He enlisted in the navy in October 1942 and spent the next three years in the South Pacific. According to jazz writer George Simon, Thornhill declined an offer (including a Chief Petty Officer ranking) to join a band in the Coast Guard. His intention was to stay away from music in order to contribute more directly to the war effort. He saw little action, however, and ended up spending most of his time in the service playing in various shows and dance bands, among them a popular group led by his old friend Artie Shaw. A month after Thornhill enlisted, in November 1942, Gil Evans entered the army, too, by way of the draft. Asked what he did during the war years, Gil replied, "Tried to keep out of the infantry, mostly—tried to keep from being shipped overseas." (See the next chapter for more on Gil's war years.)

Thornhill would re-form his band shortly after his return to civilian life in 1945. Gil, and in fact almost all of the members of the "pre-war" band, would also join him once again. But by then it would be a different world in almost every way. For musicians, especially those working in New York, the changes taking place during their absence were nothing short of revolutionary. Jazz was never again to be synonymous with popular music, as it had been throughout the swing era. Some musicians would fail to regain their footing but would cling nevertheless to the old ways, buoyed at first by their die-hard audiences, and later by the perennial, if at times faddish, appeal of nostalgia. Others, either by choice or of necessity, would leave the swing-band business to seek out new directions, if not within the emerging "modern thing" (also known as bebop), then into the more conventional (and far more lucrative) milieu of recording, broadcasting, and commercial entertainment. For Claude Thornhill, the remaining years of the decade would provide the greatest but, alas, the final meaningful chapter of his musical career. To Gil Evans, on the other hand, it would be another beginning, a time for laying the foundation for his own master works and for those of a new generation.

WARTIME

"SMITH."

"Here, sir!"

"Jackson."

"Here, *sir!*"

"Green."

"Green!"

No reply.

"Ian Green! Is there an Ian Green here?"

"Oh, that's *me.*"

"How come you didn't answer the first time, Green?"

"Well, you see, that's not really my name—it's Evans."

"Evans?"

"Yes, sir, Gil Evans."

"So why does this say 'Green'?"

It was a long story, this "name thing." Until his draft notice arrived, Gil had not felt the need to formalize his status with the government, and now that it became a requirement, he found it would not be all that straightforward a task. To begin with, he was still a Canadian by birth. He couldn't prove this, though, because his only official records had been lost; the hospital in which he was born in Toronto had burned down. Then there was the matter of why his current name was unregistered. Gil explained his situation to the U.S. authorities, and a "temporary" solution was reached. Because his natural father's name was Green, and since, officially, his mother still went by this name, too, it was decided that he should become Ian Green once again—and, simultaneously, he became a naturalized American citizen and also a private, first class, in the U.S. Army. Should he wish to change his name to Gil Evans, he was told he would have to do so on his own time, and at his own expense, through the proper legal channels. (This was to happen some twenty-six years later.)

So it was that in November 1942, Ian Ernest Green found himself stationed at Fort Lewis, Washington, playing bass drum in the official band. "You know how those traditional things are," he told Helen Johnston. "They are very slow to recognize anything but a military instrument. I only play the piano—that's why I had to play the bass drum." Proudly, and slightly wryly, he added, "Guys told me I was a fine bass drummer."

During the war, Gil stayed close to his own preferred brand of music by way of his beloved record collection, which he carried around in a little metal case. Soon enough, though, he found that his music, almost all of it by black artists—"race records," as they were then called—won him few friends among his new brothers-in-arms. Indeed, his records provided Gil's early introduction to a kind of racism by association:

> IN THE ARMY I had a hard time. A lot of people didn't like my records. Most of those records were of Duke Ellington, Louis Armstrong. I had some very very close calls with some soldiers, some draftees—they couldn't stand it. I never even thought about that in those days because, actually, there were no black people at all over in Stockton—none. In mining country it was all full of Swedes. And out in Stockton, the people that got picked on were Filipino. I really didn't have any Afro-American friends until I moved to New York.

One black musician Gil had befriended, just before he left California in 1941, was the great tenor saxophonist Lester Young—"the President," Billie Holiday called him, then simply "Prez." Lester had formed his own small group that year, after leaving the Count Basie Orchestra, and he spent more than a year working on the West Coast. The ultimate individualist and free spirit, he gained prominence, notably during his time with Count Basie, for an unorthodox tone and playing style that were to influence countless generations of musicians. Young was also the definitive hipster, inventing his own dress code (dapper suits and ties and, famously, the always-present porkpie hat) and even his own language ("I feel a chill" signaled the presence of racists). Earlier, in his touring days, Young had come face to face with the blatant, often brutal racism of the American South, and he had vowed never to return. It was obvious, given his attitude and lifestyle, that Young would have difficulty conforming to army life, but he had even greater trouble coping with its segregationist policies, particularly once he was posted in Alabama.

Gil met Lester again in 1945, just after he was transferred to Augusta, Georgia. Young had been inducted in September 1944 and was stationed at Fort McLellan, Alabama. Just four months later, he was charged for possession of marijuana and barbiturates and sentenced to ten months in the stockade at Fort Gordon, Georgia, just ten miles from Augusta. Occasionally, Young was released to play at staff dances on the base, and it was in this band that Gil got to play with him. Gil once told writer Dan Morgenstern that one of the only things he learned during his otherwise uneventful army stint was how to smuggle four quarts of whiskey into the jailhouse, which is what he did for Lester. The two were close during the most debilitating months of Young's life. Before that, however, Gil had seen and heard him at his very best. It is hardly conceivable that the master would not have left a deep impression on Gil. Nor could one imagine anyone better than Gil to help see Lester through his prison ordeal. Quite apart from his respect for Lester and his music, it was Gil's natural inclination to do whatever he could, without hesitation, for a friend in need. During their visits over at Lester's cell block, perhaps as they reposed over a little taste from the latest haul of contraband, these unlikeliest of soldiers developed a warm and enduring friendship. In later years they talked often about working together. A recording project was in the works when Lester died in 1959.

It is certain that before joining the army, Gil would also have been catching Lester's band in New York at every opportunity. After Young returned to New York from California in 1942, he reigned supreme over the new jazz scene—not much more than an underground clique at that point—that was emerging in the obscure, often tiny clubs. The first ones were in Harlem (Minton's Playhouse, Clark Munroe's Uptown House), then in Greenwich Village (Village Vanguard), and finally, along a short strip on 52nd Street, soon to be known simply as "the Street." Here, at clubs like the Half Note, the Three Deuces, Kelly's Stables, the Onyx Club, and many others, you could hear the giants at play. You could hear Lester Young, Coleman Hawkins, Billie Holiday, Art

Tatum—often appearing on the same night, just a few doors apart—each of them holding court over spellbound audiences comprised largely of young musicians. It was these younger musicians, more than the established masters, who would soon bring 52nd Street its real fame and notoriety, with the revolutionary music that came to be known as bebop. The leaders of this new movement were black—Charlie Parker, Dizzy Gillespie, Bud Powell, Thelonious Monk, to name the best known and most important among them—but within their following there were also many whites, and few of these were more zealous, or more attentive, than Gil Evans.

Max Roach, who as a young drummer had advanced to the front ranks of the bebop revolt, pointed out that, ironically, it was racism that had contributed initially, if indirectly, to the jazz scene's move from Harlem down to the Street. In March 1941, the "March on Washington" movement was initiated by a prominent black activist, A. Philip Randolph, a founder of the Negro American Labor Council in the 1920s and a powerful political organizer through to the early 1960s. The protest was, specifically, against pay inequity between blacks and whites in war-related factory jobs, but it became the focal point for venting frustration over a whole range of injustices. Blacks in the armed forces could die for their country, for example, but they were refused such privileges as admission to the USO clubs. The march never happened, for its threat alone—and the massive publicity it generated—was sufficient to elicit government action. The organizers agreed to cancel the march, scheduled for July 1, when on June 25 President Roosevelt issued an executive order forbidding employment discrimination in all defense and government industries. This was only a partial victory for the movement, however, because the government stopped short of ending the country's segregation laws, in the military or at home. Racial tensions would continue to accelerate, often erupting into violence. "That had an effect on the culture," Roach told me, "because whites stopped coming to Harlem. Minton's Playhouse and all those places were the joints where the music prevailed, but when [the violence erupted in Harlem] then the music moved downtown, to the white areas, and that was 52nd Street." If it was the desire to reach white audiences (the paying gigs) that prompted the shift out of Harlem, the resulting interaction with white musicians also added to 52nd Street's unique character. Max Roach:

CHARLIE PARKER AND Coleman Hawkins, all that group, moved down to the Street, and naturally that's when we began to meet white musicians, of the ilk of Gil and Claude Thornhill. When I hit 52nd Street, it was 1942, '43, and everybody was flocking around at that time because it was the first vestiges of integration—in New York City, on the Street. It hadn't reached the country yet, but when I came to 52nd Street, black and white musicians *did* work together, jam together, things like that. Prior to that, there were a few who would come to Harlem—like Goodman spent some time in Harlem, Georgie Auld, folks like that—but it wasn't really that highly visible. Because segregation still existed, which was a serious thing at that time. It was *serious*, it wasn't something that we just talked about—it was the law.

One of the other great ironies of bebop's emergence was the impact of another law, a new government tax. On one hand, it had a devastating effect on big bands, and on the other, as Max Roach explained, it created an ideal situation for small groups like the beboppers:

WHAT HAPPENED WITH US on 52nd Street, at that time in the States we had the twenty-percent entertainment tax—during the war all this happened. That was levied on top of your federal tax, on top of your state tax, and if you were an entrepreneur in a city like New York, you also had a city tax. If an entrepreneur had a singer on stage, if he had tap dancing or vaudeville of any kind, if there was public dancing—and big bands play for *dancing*—he had to pay twenty percent tax. If it was just *instrumental* playing, you didn't have to pay the extra twenty percent tax. So naturally, for us—instrumental musicians—it was like a godsend in a sense, because that meant now *we* had the spotlight for that brief moment. And there was no dancing, so people began to sit down and *listen* to the music, in these small clubs on 52nd Street. It's like concerts now. So naturally, you had to be the kind of virtuoso player that arrested the attention of the people, and very few people did that at that time. So out of that—of course, bebop was *about* virtuoso playing, that's what it was about. The Tatums, the Charlie Parkers, the Dizzys, the Roy Eldridges—they're the people who prevailed on 52nd Street. It was like—play your horn, play your instrument. That was our credo: play your horn, play *hard*.

Of course, that was a real rich period for instrumentalists. We would work from nine to three downtown, in the "legitimate" houses, and then pack our gear up and work uptown from four until—whatever time. It would be daylight when we'd come up out of Clark Munroe's Uptown House—and then after we finished playing the after-hour clubs at nine in the morning, we'd roam the city, we'd roam Harlem, looking for places to jam. 'Cause, you know, we never slept, we *never* slept.

Gil Evans, upon his discharge from the army in 1945, was another virtuoso who prevailed on 52nd Street, in a capacity different than, but nonetheless respected by, the instrumentalists up on the bandstands. "Gil was a dominant figure, because of his writing," said Roach. "He was already established as an orchestrator during that early period."

WHAT ATTRACTED US—amazed us, I guess—about Gil's work was the instrumentation that Claude Thornhill had—that was totally different from the big band format. 'Cause he had French horns and tuba, and the *sound* was just *rich* to us. These other instruments gave a new timbre to the sound of the music. So Gil was part of the fabric of 52nd Street. Gil was always interested in the improvisational things we were doing. I always had the feeling he was really fascinated with the *lines* of the things that Dizzy played and Charlie Parker played.

Those melodic lines—even more than the harmonic and rhythmic innovations that set bebop apart from all other jazz forms before it—were of central importance to the maturation of Gil Evans's work. Even as bebop fell in and out of favor, and even as Gil's own direction shifted dramatically, bebop would remain part of his musical vocabulary. In a 1987 interview with CBC Radio Canada, Gil told Katie Malloch, "Bird used to say, 'Music is yes, yes, no, yes, yes, yes, no, no, yes, yes—real fast. When you're improvising, you have to make those split-second decisions. . . . What goes on in playing those notes is dozens and dozens and dozens of rejections, right? Split second, like that—boom, you play that note, and—like Bird said— Yes, yes, yes, no, no." Gil would emulate the nimble improvisations of Bird and Dizzy in his writing (right through to the 1980s), and as an arranger and bandleader he would gravitate to the best soloists of the day—Miles Davis, Lee Konitz, Steve Lacy, Cannonball Adderley, Wayne Shorter, David Sanborn, and countless others.

Another factor in Gil's music during the post-war years was his increasing interest in the classical repertoire. Even earlier, back in California, Gil

had shared Claude Thornhill's affinity for the French impressionist composers Ravel and Debussy, and Gil also explored the music of the Spanish
impressionist Manuel de Falla. "That's where I learned most of my harmonic
language and most of my orchestration," he told Dave Solomon in a 1961 interview. "Actually, though, the classical composer that impressed me most
was Ernest Bloch. He inspired me—I like the blues quality, his harmonic
language, too, which has carried me farther than the impressionists. As a
matter of fact, I think *Schelomo* is one of the most perfect compositions ever
written."

By the mid-forties Gil had taken his studies considerably farther afield,
looking as far back as J. S. Bach and to works as current as Béla Bartók's ("I
like him next to Bloch") and Igor Stravinsky's. Gil told Solomon that he first
encountered Bach's *Well-Tempered Clavier* in 1945: "I just came out of the
army, and I started playing music. I spent a few weeks playing nothing but
that. I realized how easy it would be to spend my life playing it, but it wasn't
what I wanted to do, like writing my own music." He also cited the Russian
composers as another influence—Mussorgsky, Stravinsky, Prokofiev,
Tchaikovsky, Borodin, Rimsky-Korsakov.

Claude Thornhill's classical background was deeper, if perhaps more conservative than Gil's. He welcomed Gil's experiments with advanced harmonies and orchestration, particularly those drawn from the impressionist
composers, but on the other hand, he was less enthusiastic about Gil's for-
ays into bebop, a form of jazz for which Thornhill had little interest. Thornhill nevertheless continued to give him free rein—and Gil would take full
advantage of his generosity. The result was that between 1946 and 1948, Gil
would create the collection of new and innovative works for which the
Claude Thornhill Orchestra is still best known, and for which Gil Evans
would earn his first niche in music history.

A WHOLE NEW WORLD

CLAUDE THORNHILL RE-FORMED his orchestra in April 1946. Most of the pre-war members returned, including both of his arrangers, Gil Evans and Bill Borden. There were new faces, too, to add further strength to this most promising of orchestras. Many people expected Claude to pick up where he left off and, at long last, gain his rightful place among the country's top-ranking bands. Even though it was clear that the salad days of big band music were over, the prevailing wisdom among aficionados was that if any band could still succeed, it would be Thornhill's.

As for the returning musicians, few of them were as concerned about the money as they were about once again playing in this marvelous organization. "There's no one there that probably couldn't have gone on to some other name band and maybe made more money," Rusty Diedrick suggested. "But they stuck with this because it was more gratifying, satisfying, fulfilling. I guess everybody liked to *play*. I know they did. You get inside of people's minds when you work with them for a period of time. Like I did with the nucleus of that band—it was from Red Norvo's band and I'd been with them a couple of years before being with them through the Claude Thornhill band. They just wanted to play. And this was an opportunity. The chance was there to play music—*good* music."

One of the new additions to the brass section was trumpeter Louis Mucci, who later became one of New York's top session players and then a teacher at Boston's Berklee College of Music. He joined Thornhill shortly after completing a six-month stint with Benny Goodman. "The Thornhill band was really an education for me. I should have paid *him*. I think that was the greatest experience that I'd had, in spite of the fact that I'd worked with many many bands before that. Of course, we used to listen to Thornhill, pre-war, and it was a beautiful band. *All* musicians, that I knew, anyway, *loved* that band. Everybody listened to it when it came on the radio."

Claude resumed his role in the band as leader and pianist, but from this point he relied on Gil, and to a lesser extent on Bill Borden, for virtually all of the new arrangements. Gil told writer Ira Gitler, "After the war, [Claude] never really got writing again. He leaned on me, though he didn't want to. I let him, because I wanted the experience." Claude and Gil still worked well together, and neither lost respect for the other, even when their musical goals began to conflict. Their relationship continued to produce formidable results, which both men found immensely rewarding. Rusty Diedrick:

> THE BAND SOUNDED like it rehearsed day and night but it didn't. It re-hearsed occasionally, when new material would come in. Because every-body was so good—they knew what the concepts were and they just did it—it wasn't necessary to rehearse a lot. We would rehearse *after* the job. On one of these occasions, where the people had left—it was like one-thirty, two o'clock in the morning—we'd run over some new things. Gil wasn't even there—he'd gone home to California or something—and he'd sent in a chart, and Claude had to rehearse it. He had the score and he handed out the parts—and I remember Claude looking up and saying, "That's not arranging, that's *composition*." He was very impressed with it.

Gil was equally impressed with Claude's musicianship. "Gil thought the world of Claude as a pianist," Diedrick recalls. "Gil played piano—not great, but he played the keyboards—and he was always in awe of Claude because of his pianistic prowess. Man, he had the greatest *sound* on the piano. Every note was like a gem." As Gil once told Nat Hentoff, "Claude has the best sound on piano of anyone I know. I know it's a mechanical instrument, and yet it can sound so different when he plays it, the sound has a foundation when he plays. And he can *feel* a piano, allow for differences in different pianos."

Gil's increased involvement with the band also began to extend beyond writing. He started to work more frequently and more directly with the players on his new charts. He often accompanied the band for post-gig rehearsals, on road trips as well as in town. And he also started bringing new people into the fold, to add new voices and new ideas to the band—not only players but also writers and arrangers: seventeen-year-old Gerry Mulligan, baritone saxophonist and already an upcoming arranger on the big band scene; John Carisi, a trumpet player and, primarily, a composer, whom Gil had met in New York before the war; a brilliant young alto saxophonist named Lee Konitz. All three were to figure in some of Gil's best work, both within the Thornhill orchestra and later. Gerry Mulligan:

I FIRST MET GIL when Claude Thornhill's band was playing someplace in New York, and I went up there when they were rehearsing one afternoon. I was arranging for Gene Krupa then. I'd always loved Claude's band. There was a very special aura about the band, the sound of the band, and the whole conception. So I admired Gil before I ever met him, and then, because of meeting him, we just stayed in contact. I was in New York, and then I finished with whatever band I was with and went back to Philadelphia. And after a few months I got a card from him that said, "Why don't you come back to New York where everything's happening? What are you doing in Philadelphia?" So I did, and that was sort of the beginning of that whole period.

Gil got Claude to ask me to write for the band. I wrote for the band long before I played with them. At that time, the band was going through one of its expansions. And Claude was always very tolerant—I guess the word today would be "supportive" as well—of Gil's ideas. At that time they'd expanded the band up to an incredible size. Before, the band had been two trumpets, two French horns, and five reeds—and before that it had been six, because he always had two clarinet players—but then Gil started adding to it. At one point, I think they had four trumpets, three trombones, two French horns, a tuba, plus the five saxophones, with one of them always playing clarinet—so it's four saxophones, a clarinet, three flutes, and a rhythm section. It didn't last long because it was just an ungainly instrumentation. I was amazed Claude went for it anyway, but Gil wanted to do that. Anyway, the band was very very big at that point, by the time I joined. Also in that period is when Lee Konitz joined the band. And there was a lot of musical excitement around it.

Gil met Lee Konitz in 1947 and immediately urged Thornhill to hire him, too. Konitz remembers:

HE HEARD ABOUT ME in Chicago and thought that my sound would fit with the band. He was writing very lovely dance music for Claude Thornhill's orchestra. It was a dance band; it was beautiful ballads primarily. I was never really that interested in the big band scene. It was just something I wanted to do and try, and it was a steady job. It wasn't exciting, exactly, except that the music was beautiful. And it was the first major, well-known situation that I was in. I made my first record with that band. And there were some good musicians. There were some lovely, medium-tempo arrangements by Gerry Mulligan. Some of his most fetching writing was done in that period for those kinds of dance bands, with Gene Krupa, Elliot Lawrence, and even Stan Kenton. Gerry's music, and Gil's, was always my favorite music—to *play*. It was the most fun to play.

The band worked steadily for almost a year before the bookings started to taper off—no small feat given that most big bands were disappearing altogether. Thornhill was never to achieve the recognition he deserved. In fact, John Carisi told me, the Thornhill band had never been as successful as the big-name bands of that time:

No, IT WAS NO Glenn Miller by any means. *We* knew about it, the musicians knew about it. And the people, if they appreciated that band at all, it was on the road, at college proms and dances, because they played some very slow, dreamy things, just what Gil was known for—fat, close harmony chords, with that very smoky timbre. That came from Claude, and Claude got it from Debussy and Ravel. If you listen to those people, you see that that's where that comes from in the first place. Actually what Claude did, which Gil took a little further was a kind of very close, French impressionist harmony, which was great at college proms.

Trumpeter Red Rodney, another of the young bloods to join Thornhill, agreed that this band was vastly underrated. "I think it was a second-line orchestra that just happened to be better than ninety-nine percent of the other ones," he told me. At the time, Rodney was one of a select few white musicians to gain early acceptance within the bebop elite. He joined the band in 1947, replacing Rusty Diedrick. For him the job was little more than a stepping-stone, a comparatively steady gig that enabled him to stay in New York. Like Lee Konitz, Rodney had never been a great fan of big bands (Rodney told me he thought most of them sounded "corny"), but his opinion of this one—and especially of its Gil Evans charts—changed very quickly:

I DIDN'T KNOW ANYTHING about Gil Evans, I didn't know him or know *of* him. But when I got there and played that *book,* my first impression was, "Good God, this is *gorgeous.*" And I didn't play first trumpet. I was the jazz player, I was the *soloist* in the band, and, you know, when you're playing a harmony part, it's just *that*—it's a harmony part. But yet Gil had a knack of writing so that even the second and *third* trumpets had beautiful melody to them. That band, musically, was a *sensational* orchestra, it was a gorgeous, gorgeous orchestra—primarily because of Gil.

Everything he did had great beauty to it, and great melodic content, and wonderful *substance.* Don't forget, he's the *teacher,* in a sense, of great writers like Gerry Mulligan, who was also an arranger in that orchestra, only because Gil was there. He wasn't the successful instrumental star yet—that didn't come I think until '51—but Gerry was a great arranger, and to have him be *second* to somebody was quite a feat. And Gerry was very *happy* to be second to Gil Evans.

As was the case with the pre-war orchestra, while the college students danced to the ballads, musicians continued to marvel at the band's musicality. One such admirer was reed player and composer John LaPorta, best known for his distinguished career as an educator at Berklee. LaPorta had just left the Woody Herman band when, in 1948, he got the opportunity for an inside view of the Thornhill band by subbing one night for one of the clarinetists.

MY EXPERIENCE WITH PLAYING with them that night was that just reading the music wasn't enough. Because the band was so in *tune* with each other and could play with such great dynamics—you know, soft and loud, that kind of thing—that even with clarinet in the low tones, which is really quite soft, it's possible to throw the orchestra [out of balance], which is really quite remarkable. So it was not the kind of band to come in and sub, which I did. And usually I had no problem with coming in and reading the music, but it's not reading here, it's *knowing.* And if you don't know the music like they do, you're not going to be able to get your part to fit in like it should. It was a *superb* musical organization.

During this period the Thornhill band produced its greatest recordings. Many of the songs that the post-war band released between 1946 and 1948 are regarded as classics of the latter-day big band era, and much of their significance can be credited to Gil's arrangements. These recordings provide the best early examples of Gil's originality. His innovations were not in the compositions themselves, none of which were Gil's own, but in their treatment and style. The recordings illustrate his mastery of arranging and orchestration and his genius for "re-composing"—turning someone else's tune into something entirely new and original. With "Arab Dance" (from Tchaikovsky's *Swan Lake*) and "The Troubadour" (based on Mussorgsky's *Pictures at an Exhibition*), Gil showed, as Thornhill had earlier, that big-band renditions of European music need not be trite or pretentious. With "Robbin's Nest," "Anthropology," "Yardbird Suite," and "Donna Lee," he explored the revolutionary language of bebop and applied it in novel, sophisticated orchestral settings. It was these latter tunes, especially, that solidified Gil's reputation among musicians—even, and perhaps especially, among the very people Gil was emulating: Dizzy Gillespie, Charlie Parker, and Thelonious Monk. ("Actually, the only good-sounding big band I've heard in years is Claude Thornhill's," Monk told George Simon in 1948.)

Not the least of Gil's challenges with bebop was teaching the band how to play it. Louis Mucci described the process:

WE HAD TO LEARN how to phrase first, because at that time, we were used to swinging everything—you know, like the Basie band and all bands did that at that time. It was kind of strange. First he wrote lines. I remember we were at the Pennsylvania Hotel, and he came in with two lines—just melody lines, that's all, not the arrangements; he arranged them later on. He gave us the brass parts and the saxophone parts—it was a unison line. Both lines were kind of technical, so we went off on the side—we rehearsed them for a while, then we came back—and we played the line with the rhythm section, and that was it. Then he came, I don't know how long after that, he met us somewhere in Chicago or someplace, and had one of the arrangements. But that's sort of the way it happened. We kind of graduated into the thing.

"Well, it was brand new," Red Rodney offered. "For the young guys—Lee Konitz, myself, Gerry Mulligan—we fit with it, it was fine for us. But it wasn't for the older guys, though they were very good about doing it. Thornhill *may* have had some problems. He was 'Silent Cal,' he was like Calvin Coolidge, a very silent man. He never spoke. He never even counted the band off, he would just go into a tune and give us the thematic introduction to figure out where we were."

Imposing as the technical demands of this music were, an often greater hurdle to overcome was the attitude of mainstream musicians toward bebop. "They made fun of it," Louis Mucci recalled. "During record dates that I used to do when I settled in New York, it was awful. Some of the jazz players just couldn't *stand* it, and they made fun of it." The gap was not simply between the old and the young—Duke Ellington, among many other established figures, was openly enthusiastic about bebop—nor was it just about the latest change of fashion. Bebop was deeply rooted in the concept of musical art, as opposed to straight-out entertainment. Max Roach:

I REMEMBER THE FIRST TIME Charlie Parker took his band to Detroit. Charlie, of course, wrote these unusual lines, and when they would ask us to play, say, "I Got Rhythm," for the girls that were dancing—we played for chorus girls, things like that—he would play those kinds of melodies, and nobody could dance to it. Charlie Parker had a following—all of a sudden we were hired in clubs to do things—but the acts couldn't dance to the music, so they had to hire a band to play for the [show-dancers]. And we were probably the first band that became a featured act. The Charlie Parker Band would be the featured act—we would come onstage and just play our half an hour and get off—and another band would play the show. And I think that's the first time that had happened, because of Bird's music.

It's evident from this that Charlie Parker's style, even though it was artistically motivated, was nonetheless entertaining—albeit a whole different level of entertainment. "People loved it," Roach said.

HE HAD A CORE FOLLOWING that was just amazing. He had the approval of every musician. I don't care whether it was Duke Ellington, Louis Jordan, or Benny Carter—it was just a phenomenon. And it wasn't a big thing. It was almost in-house, a group of musicians who appreciated the fact that the saxophone, and improvised music in general, had taken a turn to the kind of virtuoso playing that people like Charlie Parker and Bud Powell exhibited. The critics would say, "They're not playing like Louis Armstrong and everybody else, we don't know *what* it is." But then people like [Vladimir] Horowitz would dispel that immediately—well, what are *these* guys doing on 52nd Street, you know? So that kind of gave it credibility, and that's what kind of helped turn the tide for some of us.

The music on 52nd Street—its aesthetics and the virtuosity of its practitioners—attracted the attention of many prominent classical music figures, such as Igor Stravinsky and Leonard Bernstein. Another classical musician who frequented the jazz clubs at this time was a young man named Gunther Schuller. His formal background and training, combined with a passion for jazz, were later to form the basis of a distinguished and highly eclectic career—as a composer, conductor, theorist, and educator (and then president) at the New England Conservatory of Music, author, and jazz historian. Schuller, a French horn player, was attracted immediately to the Thornhill band:

EVEN THOUGH I WAS WELL employed in the New York Philharmonic and the Metropolitan Opera, the Cincinnati Symphony and various other places, there was a part of me that always wanted to play in the big bands. And one in particular that I admired, not only because it had French horns but because theirs seemed to be among the greatest arrangements of the time, was the Claude Thornhill Orchestra. As I started listening to that orchestra—I heard on the radio, I'll never forget it, some arrangements of "Robbin's Nest," "Anthropology," and "Donna Lee"—I found out that they were arrangements made by someone called Gil Evans. And I went sort of in hot pursuit—you know, who *is* Gil Evans?—and tried to find out more. And then went about trying to get anything that he had arranged.

He was not the one who brought the two French horns to that band, but he certainly used those instruments more interestingly than anybody else had before that, even Claude himself. And the *sound* of the two French horns and the tuba, which Gil Evans knew so well how to use, just transformed that band, and therefore a certain aspect of jazz, into some whole new sound that no one had ever heard before. If you take the French horn, a medium-range instrument, the tuba, a low-range, and you add to that the baritone and the tenor saxophones, you have a low-register sound that was, for example, totally different from a Benny Goodman Orchestra sound, which was all on the bright side—or even some of the other jazz orchestras, which simply didn't have those instruments.

Claude Thornhill's own arrangements, and another fellow's, Bill Borden, also used this instrumentation very effectively, but they were not as advanced harmonically, for example, as Gil was. Gil belonged more to the new bebop, the modern jazz music that was coming in in the mid-forties. He was using all kinds of—for jazz—extraordinarily advanced harmonies and voice leadings, and then throwing in a much more interesting use of the instrumentation of a jazz orchestra. Almost all jazz writing, including with Claude Thornhill himself, was what we call block writing: You might have eight-part chords, but you divided them up between the trumpets and trombones and saxophones. Well, Gil could *do* that, I'm sure he did all those more or less conventional things, but in the Thornhill orchestra— and Thornhill encouraged him—he started to break up the instrumentation, the orchestra, the *choirs* of the orchestra, into all kinds of different combinations.

So all of that fascinated me as a composer—I mean, already a composer dealing with all kinds of advanced techniques and styles, much beyond what was happening in jazz. And here comes Gil Evans, and he's in *jazz,* but he's doing some things that are really reaching out toward this territory of [contemporary composers] Schoenberg and Stravinsky and Bartók and Ravel. And that certainly was different. You listen to those recordings, particularly "Anthropology" and "Donna Lee"—they are timeless. They are still so fresh, so innovative, that I don't think they will ever sound dated, as much of the bebop stuff *does,* from the big bands of that time. And of course the great thing about Gil, beyond that, which I heard in that band, he was a supreme orchestral colorist. He could work with timbre and sonority. The only person who did that as well, or better, is Duke Ellington. And of course, Gil was very much, supremely, influenced by Ellington.

Despite all of the daring and inventiveness of Gil's writing, the Thornhill orchestra had by no means turned into some obtuse hotbed of experimentation. Gil himself produced some of his sweetest ballads for Thornhill during this period, and these remained the favorite Evans charts of many musicians as well as dance audiences. Indeed, even his most advanced arrangements, like "Yardbird Suite" and "Anthropology," were not only accessible but also eminently danceable. The band also returned frequently to the popular tunes in its earlier repertoire—like "Snowfall," still the band's theme song—and to favorites like "Where or When" and the bluesy vocal tune "A Sunday Kind of Love." In addition to the arrangements by Gil and Claude, new charts were being written by Bill Borden, Gerry Mulligan, and others. "Gil was always very good at knowing what he could do and knowing what somebody else could do," said Mulligan. "So the three of us, our work really covered a broad spectrum, and gave some variety to Claude's band."

╬   ╬   ╬

If there was variety in the band's book, however, there was for Gil, increasingly, a serious lack of balance between the old repertoire and the new. Claude's disposition toward the former and Gil's propensity for the latter led inevitably to the end of their relationship in 1948. "My final leaving was friendly," Gil told Nat Hentoff.

> Claude gave me a fairly free hand, and our association was a good one until he began to feel there were elements being left out of his music that he wanted in there, and that elements were being added that he *didn't* want in there. The sound had become a little too somber for my taste, generally speaking, a little too bleak in character. It began to have a hypnotic effect at times. The band could put you to sleep. An example of the variation in our thinking was the tuba. He liked the static sound of the tuba on chords. I wanted the tuba to play flexible, moving jazz passages.

When Gil left the band in late 1948, Claude Thornhill's full-size orchestra was one of the last hold-outs in a fast-declining business. Thornhill continued to work sporadically—in fact, Gil continued to write for him until at least 1950—but the band got increasingly smaller and certainly less adventurous, and Thornhill's career remained in a more or less constant state of decline. He worked occasionally with name artists, including Tony Bennett and Benny Goodman. He participated in revivals of his music and those of other swing-era celebrities, on record and in concert. But he was never to regain his former stature. His last comeback attempt—a club date in Atlantic City in 1965—never materialized, for just a few days before opening he suffered a massive heart attack, and on July 1, he died. George Simon, one of Claude's earliest fans and staunchest supporters, was one of the last of his old friends to have visited him. Simon wrote that among the cards and letters Claude's wife received after his death, there was a note from Duke Ellington: "I wonder if the world will ever know what a beautiful man this was."

For many people, including Gerry Mulligan, seeing the demise of not only Thornhill's orchestra but the entire big band era was a bit like watching helplessly as your alma mater burned to the ground. Mulligan had grown up in the swing era, and he'd perfected his craft working for some of the finest big bands in the business. He had nothing but the fondest memories of that whole great era from beginning to end:

THE SCENE WAS WIDESPREAD in New York at that point. On Broadway between 45th Street and, say, 55th Street, at any given time there would be three or four functioning rehearsal studios. Three of those were quite big, and they had rooms of all sizes. Then there were always other studios opening up in the area—big ones that had a lot of rooms, small ones that were just one room—so you could wander around town, starting in the morning, and go through the day and hear one band after another. It was like a very broad society. We all knew each other, we all saw each other all the time—bands that came in and out of town, the traveling bands that were organizing, bands that were doing shows in town, bands that were starting out—and we'd all go from rehearsal to rehearsal to hear what everybody else was doing.

Having witnessed its decline from the inside, Mulligan was quick to challenge the notion that the big band era had simply fallen out of fashion.

THERE'S ALWAYS AN IMPLICATION that the public's taste changed, but I don't think that was it at all. I think it was economic factors, and almost *all* economic factors. We were in a commercial business, but the approach to the music was much more idealistic. And the fact that they could cope and survive in the commercial business was a tribute to the music—and to the audience, too. I think the audience gets short shrift in this country. Greedy commercial elements have always been out there to exploit the audience, playing to the lowest common denominator. That wasn't *always* the case. There were periods in our popular music when people were catering to the *best* possible taste of an audience.

Beginning in 1941 with the ASCAP radio ban, and the AFM's 1942 recording ban, the big bands had been hit by a barrage of changes within and around the music business. In terms of radio exposure, record sales, and overall popularity, singing stars like Frank Sinatra and Tony Bennett far eclipsed the big bands, including the bands with which they'd landed their first jobs. The federal government's twenty-percent entertainment tax, which wasn't lifted until 1951, made it increasingly difficult for all but the big-name orchestras to get steady work. General economic conditions, both during and after the war, curtailed the social lives of most Americans. Gas rationing, as just one example, made it harder and more expensive to get out to the ballrooms, most of which were on the outskirts of the cities. After the manufacturing boom of the war years, industrial output faltered. Servicemen returned from Europe and the South Pacific only to find a scarcity of jobs; labor disputes, such as a major coal strike in 1946, further aggravated the mood, if not the spending power, of the country.

Yet all through this period, the commercial music industry was booming. New technology brought improved sound quality to both records and radio sets, making "home entertainment" an increasingly popular and more affordable alternative to a night on the town. "Records came into popularity in '39, maybe '40," John LaPorta explained. "Not that records weren't being made before then, but they weren't a big thing. But by the '40s they started getting into more sophisticated technology, to produce the better sounding records. Prior to that, the radio in the '30s was more like a crystal-type thing, so they weren't very satisfactory—they certainly didn't compete with *live* music—so people would drive for hundreds of miles to hear a band."

The music industry was wholly transformed by this new phenomenon of the stay-at-home listener, and the big bands were among the first and hardest hit by the ensuing changes. Dance halls started closing down or changing to weekend-only schedules; often they did more business through private functions like weddings and socials than through public dances. Remote broadcasts fell off as the live radio shows were displaced by recorded music. The hosts of these live programs, often the band leaders themselves, were supplanted by another new creation of the media, the "disc jockey." With the loss of the big bands' radio broadcasts—for so many years the main stepping-stone for reaching and then sustaining a national following—the music of the big bands, and also the celebrity status of their leaders, dissipated rapidly. In 1947, some of the biggest of the big-name bandleaders broke up their bands, including Les Brown, Benny Carter, Woody Herman, Billy Eckstine, Tommy Dorsey, Harry James, and Jack Teagarden. If a killing blow was still needed, it probably came in January 1948, in the form of the AFM's second recording ban. This strike, over scale rates, took eleven months to resolve. Once again, for musicians in the big bands, the strike would be remembered, like the 1942–1944 ban, as yet another barrier between them and their audiences.

And if the ways people listened to music were now dramatically different, the changes in what they were listening to on their new radios and record players were even more drastic. Country and western music had risen from the hinterlands to attain major national status. By the end of the forties, Hank Williams was selling far more records than any jazz band; in 1950, the biggest-selling record (two million copies) was "The Tennessee Waltz," by Patti Page. At the same time, there was considerable growth in the other major specialty market for "race" records—the gospel, blues, and folk music of black Americans—which was renamed in 1949 by *Billboard* as "rhythm and blues."

Still considered a marginal sector by the trade, R&B was nevertheless a fast-growing market, not only because of the increasing affluence of black audiences but also because of the growing interest of young white listeners. In 1947, Louis Jordan made number one on *Billboard*'s "Honor Roll of Hits" with "Open the Door, Richard" and thus became the first black to cross over to the previously all-white national hit parade. It wasn't until a few years later, however, that rhythm and blues gained widespread prominence—and only then as a result of its adaptation (many called it theft) by white bands. This new strain of music, which also "borrowed" indiscriminately from blues and country music, got another new name, when a Cleveland-based disc jockey named Alan Freed popularized a musical term familiar to black communities since at least the 1920s: "rock and roll."

Jazz had long been included in the race-record category, even though the swing music that the general public associated with "the jazz age" was almost exclusively created by whites. This situation was already prevalent in the mid-1920s, starting with Paul Whiteman, a white bandleader who was promoted as the "King of Jazz." It continued into the 1930s with Benny Goodman, the "King of Swing," and throughout the white-dominated swing era. All this time, the music's originators—Fletcher Henderson, Louis Armstrong, Duke Ellington, Count Basie, and many other first-line exponents of jazz and swing—remained outside the media mainstream.

Obviously, black jazz musicians did not go unnoticed. Even the lesser-known bands toured constantly, and black jazz bands sold hundreds of thousands of records. Their success, however, was never realized on a true mass-market scale. The only jazz ever to achieve that distinction came from the white swing bands, whose music, for a decade or so, defined the mainstream: It *was* "pop" music. Now, jazz was losing its stature on both fronts. It was being displaced in black markets by rhythm and blues and in the white mainstream by practically anything and everything else. From this point, jazz bands—whether they were black, white, or (more latterly) mixed—would be lumped together in the same marginal little boat—sometimes close to, but never again directly at the center of, the music industry establishment.

Such was the state of the music industry in post-war America. As it grew, diversified, and prospered, it became more narrowly and conservatively focused, and its preferred mainstream products became more and more sanitized. The big bands, the long-reigning front guard of popular entertainment, were well into their descent into obscurity. The new stars were singers, not bandleaders, and the new hits seemed increasingly superficial—and an all too accurate reflection of post-war America's middle-class values: conformity, homogenization. This, as composer George Russell put it, was the dawning of the age of white-bread. "It was all Art Mooney, and "I'm Looking Over a Four-Leaf Clover," and Lawrence Welk."

If, as a musician, you were inclined toward anything beyond the grasp of the lowest common denominator—if you played bebop, for example—you could expect few opportunities to reach a wide audience. If you viewed yourself as an artist, rather than an entertainer, you had to be as persevering as you were talented. And no matter how determined you were, you were not likely to survive without the emotional, if not material, support of like-minded friends, compatriots, or benefactors. And if at that time you were in New York City, finding yourself in need of that kind of encouragement, or maybe just a place to stay the night, you probably ended up at the doorstep of Gil Evans.

A BASEMENT ROOM
ON 55TH STREET

They were very serious about their art, and I think that was the big difference between that generation of jazz musicians and the previous ones. The previous ones didn't think of themselves as artists; they thought of themselves as entertainers. But the people coming in in the mid-forties, in the whole bebop revolution, they began to think of themselves as artists as good as any of those folks on the other side of the road—the classical musicians.

—GUNTHER SCHULLER

WORLD WAR II was over and nothing would be the same, least of all the business and indeed the art of American popular music. Bebop provided sharp relief to the mainstream popular music, although few Americans knew about it. This new music was flourishing in the tiny clubs along 52nd Street. And not far from there, young musicians were also gathering together in a 55th Street basement apartment. This was the home of Gil Evans, and it, too, was a place where thoughts and ideas were shared, and all kinds of exciting new musical directions were explored.

Gil had pursued new ideas throughout his stint with the post-war Thornhill orchestra, but his most important new music would come in the next few years. It was all the result of his first collaboration with a then twenty-two-year-old Miles Davis, and it signified, among other things, the beginning of one of jazz music's greatest partnerships. The historic recordings from this collaboration eventually became known in an album called *Birth of the Cool,* regarded by many as the first expression of "post-bebop" jazz and a precursor of the "modern" jazz era. The music, which began as little more than an experiment, represents a culmination of many events and influences. It was a direct extension of the music Gil had perfected in his arrangements for Claude Thornhill's orchestra. It embraced elements of Duke Ellington's writing, and also bebop, among other styles. And it was the result of the individual and collective efforts of several contributors and participants—their common reference point being a close association with Gil Evans, and their common meeting place being Gil's subterranean apartment. During the two years he lived here, an almost endless procession of young musicians and composers passed through this apartment. Among them were some of the most prominent and influential artists in contemporary jazz—George Russell, John Lewis, Gerry Mulligan, Miles Davis, Max Roach, J.J. Johnson, Lee Konitz, and many others. All of them have acknowledged a debt to Gil, if only for just being able to drop in, hang out, and soak up the energy and excitement emanating from Gil and all of his friends, disciples, and visitors at the 55th Street "jazz salon."

‡   ‡   ‡

Gil ended up in this apartment through no initiative of his own. This time, it was his old friend, Jimmie Maxwell, who helped him out—"out" in this case also meaning, literally, out of Jimmie's *own* apartment, where Gil had been living as a guest, from the time of his discharge from the army (December 1946) for almost two months. "It was just getting impossible," said Maxwell. "He'd stay up all night fooling around on the piano, and that was the room we slept in. It didn't bother *him* at all, but it bothered us."

Maxwell hadn't worked with Gil since 1939, in Skinnay Ennis's band, back in Hollywood, when he left to replace Harry James in Benny Goodman's band. In 1943, Jimmie left Goodman and went to work in the New York studios of CBS. While Gil was in the service, he often spent his leave in New York and usually stayed with the Maxwells. "His visits were always 'exciting,' particularly for my wife," Maxwell laughed, "because she slept in the other room, the living room, and one of the great parts of Gil's visits was that we would play my collection of Ellington and Armstrong records. We'd start about ten at night and go till six in the morning. About four or five in the morning she'd [awaken], and he would give her this courtly bow and say, 'Gertrude, are we keeping you up?'

"'No, no,' Gertrude would insist." She'd turn over and try to go back to sleep, and the two men would return to their records. During my telephone conversation with Jimmie, I heard Gertrude in the background—"Here, you tell him," Jimmie said to her and handed her the phone. "You could never get mad at him, he was always so gracious," Gertrude said. "You'd want to *kill* him, but you couldn't get mad at him."

Jimmie touched on this in his eulogy for Gil in 1988. "Gil would walk into the house," Jimmie explained, "and he had a wonderful facility for taking over, and in the most charming way. You were *grateful*. He'd totally disrupt your life but you'd sit there smiling. He'd come in and he'd announce, 'All a person needs is a little watercress, a little yogurt, a handful of raisins, maybe a few almonds—that's all you need to eat. You don't need to eat like he eats—look how *fat* he is.' So we'd go out and buy watercress and yogurt and almonds—but also I would buy pork chops and roast beef and steak and potatoes, because that's what Gil wound up eating anyhow." After one of these visits, Jimmie remembered, Gil sent them a gift in appreciation of their hospitality: "He sent us a hostess present—a suitcase full of gas masks, army boots, K-rations, things he could pick up around the army post."

Occasional visits are one thing, but an indefinite stay, with no outward indication of when or if it might end, is quite another—particularly in the confines of two small rooms, one of which is occupied by a two-year-old. "Gil was a great baby-sitter," said Maxwell. "He'd have no trouble with my son David—who incidentally we named after Gil—David Evans Maxwell. We would go out and we'd come back at three in the morning, and Gil would be playing the piano, writing an arrangement, and my son would be there helping him with his pastrami sandwich and a bottle of beer. So about that time we sort of subtly hinted that we'd help him find another place to stay."

✢   ✢   ✢

Gil moved into his 55th Street apartment in 1947 and lived there until early 1949. He supported himself for most of this time, however modestly, by writing arrangements for Claude Thornhill. The apartment was in a typical midtown Manhattan brownstone—a half-flight of stairs down from the sidewalk, in past a Chinese laundry, and along through to the far end of the furnace room. It was a simple but good-sized room, with a back door leading out to a small courtyard. Exposed steam pipes ran across the length of the ceiling. The room was furnished with the barest essentials: a large bed, a piano, a record player, a hot plate, a big lamp. There was also a cat named Becky. Pinned up on one wall, Gil kept a chart showing the range that could be played comfortably in each key by woodwind and brass instruments.

From the beginning, Gil made the room a musician's home away from home, for his own benefit as well as theirs. "I was always interested in other musicians," he told Nat Hentoff. "I was hungry for musical companionship, because I hadn't had much of it before. Like bull sessions in musical theory. Since I hadn't gone to school, I hadn't had that before." The regulars included friends from the Thornhill band, in particular the rhythm section— drummer Billy Exiner, guitarist Barry Galbraith, and bassist Joe Shulman— as well as clarinetist Danny Polo. And there was a tighter, inner circle—the writers and arrangers: George Russell, Gerry Mulligan, John Lewis, John Carisi, John Benson Brooks, and later, Miles Davis. "It got to be *the* place to fall in," John Carisi recalled.

IT WAS A MARVELOUS CRASH PLACE. He was very relaxed about guys coming in—been up for X days, and saying, "Hey Gil, man, can I take a nap?" "Sure, man." People had different reasons to hang out there. Gerry and myself and George Russell, to some extent we were there because we were picking Gil's brains. At that point he was getting scores from the New York Public Library, records and scores, and studying the twentieth-century composers, seeing how they did things. So through him, we all kind of got on to that. He was one of the first guys I knew that had a library card for that reason alone, to get to go to the music library. You could get anything, right up to the latest recordings of Bartók and Stravinsky, and all the classics, like Beethoven. He really opened our ears to all kinds of things.

Gerry Mulligan, encouraged by Gil to return to New York from Philadelphia, was a frequent visitor and, soon, a permanent fixture at the apartment.

I HAD A PLACE THAT I HATED, over a building in front of the old Madison Square Garden, and finally I got fed up. He said, "Well, come stay here till you find something else." I ended up spending most of the winter there— the two of us in his room, with people wandering in and out all the time.

We used to take turns using the piano to write—it was like our lives were kind of off-center: when I slept he wrote; when he was using the bed I would write, and all the time the guys were wandering in and out. It was a great period because everybody was so totally engrossed with music.

George Russell:

It was essence-friendly. This was a common meeting ground for people of essence, people who were engaged in expressing their essence. The world has never been known to be hospitable to people [who are following their essence]—yet as humans, we had to survive in a hostile world. And that hostility impacted negatively on a lot of people; it drove many people to self-destruction, as you know. Like Charlie Parker, to name one notable case.

52nd Street was always well represented. Charlie Parker came by regularly, often just to shoot up between sets at one of the clubs, or to sleep off a bad night. In a 1983 BBC interview, Gil told Charles Fox, "Bird stayed with me for quite a long time. He came down one night and he'd been beat up by the police, and he was so outraged—not from the pain so much as the lack of dignity, lack of respect and all that. So he stayed in bed for two or three days—I fed him and took care of him." Parker stayed with Gil over a period of several months. Bird was one of Gil's most important influences, and Bird respected Gil's music as well, but the two of them did not work together during this period. As Gil explained to Nat Hentoff:

Months after we had become friends and roommates he had never heard my music, and it was a long time before he did. When Bird did hear my music, he liked it very much. Unfortunately, by the time he was ready to use me, I wasn't ready to write for him. I was going through another period of learning by then. As it turned out, Miles, who was playing with Bird then, was attracted to me and my music. He did what Charlie might have done if at that time Charlie had been ready to use himself as a voice—as part of an overall picture, instead of a straight soloist.

Parker, and others, often used Gil's place to store their "works," the needles and other hardware of their drug habit. "One time when I was visiting Gil," Jimmie Maxwell recalled, "I saw this drawer full of this stuff. I said to him, 'My God, Gil, if the police ever found this they'd put you away for *life*.' He just laughed it off, of course." Gil's drug of choice was still marijuana, which he continued to use throughout his lifetime, and he never did acquire a taste for anything harder. For one thing, he once told a musician friend, "I just *hate* needles." He told another that he'd tried cocaine, but he didn't like it either: "It made me too nervous." As for his marijuana habit, even then, according to Mulligan, it was hardly what could be considered a drug problem: "It wasn't incessant pot smoking by any means." People came to Gil's to learn, Russell emphasized, not to party. "We had 'fun' elsewhere," he said. "But 'fun' is a ridiculous word, it's a trite word, and there was never anything trite about being at that apartment. People had 'fun' in other ways—sticking needles in their arms or whatever. Sometimes that would happen at that apartment, but that wasn't the general rule. You had to be lord and king to come in and get away with that at Gil's. Bird could get away with murder at that apartment—and he did; he was a glutton for what you call fun—but it wasn't a drug den."

This group's affinity to Parker had nothing to do with drugs either. "Personally we all liked Bird a lot," said Mulligan.

> THE SIDE THAT WE ALWAYS SAW was his idealistic side, his musical side, and he was a very sweet man. He also was a split personality, so he was a lot of different things to different people. Bird was always kind of a presence, because we all admired him so much. And the effect that Bird had musically was very refreshing, because it wasn't an innovation that was totally away from what went on. It was a logical development of the mainstream that we were all involved with. And Bird had a clarity in his playing that made it very easy for us to understand.

Gil was enthralled by Parker's music, but Mulligan felt that Bird also learned from Gil.

> GIL ALWAYS BROUGHT THINGS out in Bird, I think, because Bird could approach him in a different way than he did other musicians. Bird was curious about his musical taste, for instance, and I'm sure Gil played him a lot of things—things like Debussy's *The Children's Corner*—and I think it was always very interesting to Gil to hear Bird's reaction to pieces of music.

Bird liked symphonic music very much. He would have liked to have pursued other aspects of music, but at that time in his life it was way too late for him to be a beginner.

I think, philosophically, that was one of the subjects we spent a lot of time on—when you get to a point of such incredible control, and you want to do something else, how difficult it is to go back and be a beginner. When you're an expert in the area you're in, it's not easy, and it's not something that Charlie was ever able to deal with. Had he been able to approach that, he may have been able to survive, there might have been a motivation to it. I don't think there was any motivation for him to survive. Life was too difficult for him, to go on doing the same thing, and it wasn't really a satisfaction to him. When you get to that point, you die.

In many of these philosophical discussions, John Carisi recalled, Mulligan was not only the youngest but also usually the most vociferous participant. "Man, he was an aggressive snot-nose when I first met him," Carisi laughed.

GIL WAS LESS VOCAL ABOUT THINGS. Gil and the drummer, Exiner, they were more otherworldly when they discussed things. Very often I'd listen to them and I would say, "What do you *mean* by that?" I used to challenge them—"What are you *talking* about?" And they'd give me that "Well, you know . . . "—especially Billy Exiner, but Gil, too—they would say things like, "*Well*, man, if we have to *describe* it to you, if we have to *explain* it to you, you'll never understand it." A mystical thing. [Gerry and I] were probably more pragmatic about it—"Well how do you *do* this?" or "How do you put that together?"

Gil remained aloof from religious or political dogma, but in his thinking—his acceptance of things as they are, his lack of material values—the "mystical thing" always seemed prevalent. "Spirit," he often said. "That's the main thing I look for in music. Living spirit."

He also kept his distance from the drugs, alcohol, and other excesses that were so much a part of the jazz scene, and he seemed to remain virtually unflappable by its trials and tribulations. Gunther Schuller smiled as he recalled meeting Gil (through John Lewis) at the 55th Street apartment. "He was an extraordinarily quiet person, very low-keyed—sometimes almost seeming without energy or without drive or thrust, and very accommodating to everybody. It seemed that he was incapable of getting mad or upset at anybody. I knew he'd come from Toronto, and I remember thinking once, 'My God, are *all* Canadians this quiet? This unperturbable?'" Whether it was his Canadian roots, or his California upbringing, or perhaps the influence of his free-spirited mother, there was something ethereal about Gil's demeanor that was at once disarming and attractive. His attitude set the tone and tempo of all of his personal dealings—in life, as in his music.

"Everything relates to music if you want it to," Mulligan mused.

AND YOUR ATTITUDE TOWARD MUSIC has something to do with your outlook on everything else. Even though nobody was talking about Buddhism or anything, still the tone of the discussions, the tone of the attitudes, I realized later on, was always basically Buddhist. The conversations had a deep sense of fairness—they were always about trying to understand life in the fairest way possible. Billy Exiner had started playing drums, I think, when he was in his forties. Before that he had been a merchant seaman and traveled all over the world. And Billy was a thinker, so he always stimulated this philosophical discussion around him. So he and Gil, and Danny also—there was a mystical quality about the band, and a mystical quality to the groups that formed around Gil.

While describing Gil as their spiritual leader, Gerry Mulligan, George Russell, and others also rejected the image of him as some kind of all-knowing sage. "It wasn't just Gil sitting there and philosophizing, man," Mulligan insisted.

IT WAS MUCH MORE what we like to think of as maybe the ideal university—the don or the older person, not necessarily a teacher, who attracts thoughtful young guys around him, and then it's an *exchange* of ideas. I don't think he would ever have approved of the idea that he was pontificating. He didn't pontificate. It was very much a thing of give and take. He was always *learning*. He was always finding out things that he misunderstood; somebody else would give him an insight into another way of looking at it. So I think that period was very good for him, too.

Russell concurred. "I'm sure that it *was* a growing experience for him, the 55th Street era, and that he was maturing and also pinning down *his* aim while helping other people to do that. And who better could you have for a guru than a guru who's in the process of trying to do the same thing *you're* doing? Evolving."

Typically, Gil played down his influence on the other writers. Asked by Nat Hentoff to describe his influence on Gerry Mulligan, for example, he replied, "The way we influenced each other was not of much importance. I feel we kept our own individuality through having each other as musical colleagues, rather than by having a common platform or working alone." Most of those writers would agree that they had each developed their own voice, their own artistic agenda, before meeting Gil, but they would also acknowledge Gil's role in reaffirming, and thus solidifying, that sense of individuality. For example, in 1945, two years before meeting Gil, George Russell had already struck upon the conceptual basis of the *Lydian Chromatic Concept of Tonal Organization,* his influential compositional theory on the use of modal scales, rather than chord structures, as an improvisational framework. He'd also gained recognition for his writing, at this point most notably for Dizzy Gillespie's big band. Yet Russell asserted that the time he spent with Gil was fundamental to his development. Gil encouraged him to follow his destiny, telling Russell he saw him becoming not only an important composer but a consummate artist. As Russell explained,

THIS IS SOMETHING PEOPLE don't understand. It's *not* just music, it's not just talent, that sees people through. It's not that alone—and especially for people who take on obligations that don't have anything ultimately to do with making money, but have to do with enriching the art and enriching the life of human beings. It takes more than just an innate talent, and the more essence that's involved in their project, the stronger they have to be as people. So Gil's influence on me was spiritual. Gil lit my spiritual way, and with the heat of his own essence gave me the strength to follow a certain direction.

Gil seemed to be completely *without* ego. He gave the sense of having come to terms with his life—of having accepted his life, and of dealing with it without malice or any sense of discontent. That apartment was a center, for ones centering themselves, and that was almost solely because of the calming effect Gil had on everyone. With Gil, egos fell by the wayside. You became part of something larger.

"Something larger" also meant different things to different people, but in this circle, invariably, it was about new music and the thinking of a new generation of serious, intensely dedicated people. This was a world quite removed from that of the "other" serious music practitioners, the classical musicians, but it was also a far cry from what many associated with the jazz life. Gunther Schuller, at the time a classical musician himself, as well as an avid student of jazz and jazz history, could appreciate the distinctions better than most.

MY MAIN IMPRESSION IS of how remarkably quiet, sedate, *all* these musicians were. And the kind of *integrity* they had toward their music, and the sacrifices they were willing to make in order to be able to continue to do that—they didn't care whether they starved or not. I guess they *did* care, but this was not the major issue. This was what they had to do, and their talent allowed them to do. And they saw no *alternative* than just to do that, whatever the consequences might be.

Every musician who grew up in the late swing era and then went through the modern jazz and bebop evolution, I'm sure they *all* had a sense of doing something that was important or needed to be done—but without any feeling of aggrandizement about it. And part of that comes from the fact that they *were* all starving and that they really all *had* to cling together, as a group. I think that provided a certain confidence, that they weren't alone. But they sure weren't received well. It was very controversial, and there wasn't any *money* in it.

Gil and the others in his circle did not fare any better financially than most of the bebop musicians. And although they themselves weren't playing bebop, Gil and the younger writers and instrumentalists around him were no less entrenched in their own musical pursuits. They were inspired and influenced by Bird, Dizzy, and the whole wave of 52nd Street. And like their bebop heroes, they too were driven not by worldly recognition but by the sheer exhilaration of creating something new and fresh.

BIRTH OF
THE COOLEST

There's a compulsion involved. We were relatively young guys, with a big yearning, a direction to go in—to play music, to have our music played, to be around the best people, the best players. I mean, the doing was what was important. The fact that these things got recorded was coincidental, if not accidental. We didn't think about getting them recorded; we thought about getting them played. Even before getting them played was hearing what you wrote. Somebody would say, "Hey, Gil got together with Miles, and they're going to have a rehearsal at Nola's"—and I'd run home and finish something, because we've got that rehearsal two days from now. Everybody all of a sudden came to life.

—JOHN CARISI

THE RENAISSANCE OF THE ARTS in post-war America was led by, or at least closely identified with, certain key individuals. In painting, it was Jackson Pollock; in theater, Arthur Miller and Tennessee Williams; in film, Hollywood's typical mass-market fare was contrasted by the *film noir* realism of John Huston and Howard Hawks. Jazz had yet to be accepted as "serious" music—in fact it was only in this period that it began to move from entertainment to art form—but it, too, would soon need a figurehead. Just as Pablo Picasso came to personify the whole of contemporary painting, so too the world began to associate the notion of *jazz musician as artist* not with Charlie Parker or even Duke Ellington but with Miles Davis. Others contributed as much to jazz, or more, than Miles did (just as cubism had not been developed by Picasso alone), but no one else captured the public's imagination quite like this young "Prince of Darkness."

Like his own idol, boxer Sugar Ray Robinson, Miles was handsome and debonair. He dressed well, drove exotic sports cars, and enjoyed the company of glamorous women. On the bandstand, he would not engage in idle stageside banter. When he played, he often turned his back on the audience, and after his solo he might vanish from the stage, only to reappear when it was time to play again. The more he withdrew, the closer people wanted to get. The less he said, the deeper the mystery grew and the more intriguing he became.

Miles cultivated to perfection the image of the devoted artist—a brooding, darkly romantic figure, alone against the world, yet tough as nails—but his talent fulfilled the promise of his stage persona and surpassed it. With the haunting tone and tremendous lyricism of his playing, his ballads were as beautiful and moving as anything ever heard before in jazz. On the strength of tunes like "Round Midnight," "My Funny Valentine," and "Some Day My Prince Will Come," he would produce best-selling albums at a time when "hit records" had become almost extinct in the jazz world. He had formidable technical facility with his instrument. He had been part of the cutting edge in bebop, after all, and had played in Charlie Parker's band at the age of nineteen. As a musical innovator, throughout his life Miles was to play a direct role not only in changing the *sound* of jazz, but also its direction—from bebop to cool, from chord-based to scale-based modal improvisation, from acoustic instrumentation to electric, and then to jazz-rock and fusion.

In the story of Miles's rise to prominence, and through much of his later career, his relationship with Gil Evans is pivotal. Miles established his reputation in bebop, but it was through his own work, which began with Gil in 1948, that he would emerge as a true innovator. Few would presume to single out any one person or event as the predominant influence on Miles. Parker and Gillespie, Ellington and Evans—Miles acknowledged the role of each of these people in his development, and an important part of Miles's creative vision and artistry was his genius for choosing allies. As a bandleader, Miles organized some of the most exciting ensembles in jazz history and with them produced some of its greatest recordings. His bands featured the very best players, and they gave him exactly what he required not only in their performances but also in many cases their tunes and arrangements, many of which Miles listed as his own. Most collaborated willingly, even when they were never fully credited for their work, and would continue to extol Miles's genius even as he "borrowed" their ideas. For it was his touch, however slight it might seem, that changed those notes into something greater than they were before.

Of all of Miles's relationships, none had the impact of his partnership with Gil Evans. And Miles did more than anyone else to further Gil's career. They became not only great musical partners but also lifelong friends.

✝   ✝   ✝

"I first met Gil when I was with Bird," Miles told Marc Crawford in a 1961 interview for *Down Beat*.

> HE WAS ASKING FOR a release on my tune, "Donna Lee." . . . I told him he could have it and asked him to teach me some chords and let me study some of the scores he was doing for Claude Thornhill.
>
> He really flipped me on the arrangement of "Robbin's Nest" he did for Claude. See, Gil had this cluster of chords and superimposed another cluster over it. Now the chord ends, and now these three notes of the remaining cluster are gone. The overtone of the remaining two produced a note way up there. I was puzzled. I had studied the score for days, trying to find the note I heard. But it didn't even exist—at least on paper it didn't. That's Gil for you.

Gil and Miles quickly became friends. Gil found Miles, for all his outward aloofness, to be thoughtful and serious-minded, but also extremely funny. Miles was taken with Gil's personal manner—his cool demeanor and his gregarious nature. "Gil is my idea of a man," Miles said. "Say you had a friend who was half man and half donkey, and suppose he even wore a straw hat and you said, 'Gil, meet George.' Gil would get up and shake his hand and never care what George looked like." In his autobiography, Miles recalled their first encounter:

> WHEN I FIRST MET HIM, he used to come to listen to Bird when I was in the band. He'd come in with a whole bag of horseradishes—that's what we used to call radishes—that he'd be eating with salt. Here was this tall,

thin, white guy from Canada who was hipper than hip. I mean, I didn't
know *any* white people like him. I was used to black folks back in East
St. Louis walking into places with a bag full of barbecued pig snout
sandwiches and taking them out and eating them right there, right in a
movie or club or anywhere. But bringing horseradishes to nightclubs
and eating them out of a bag with salt, and a white boy? Here was Gil on
fast 52nd Street with all these super-hip black musicians wearing peg
legs and zoot suits, and here he was dressed in a cap. Man, he was something else.

It would be another year, in 1948, before Gil and Miles actually worked
together. In the meantime, Miles joined the circle up at Gil's apartment.
Max Roach, who was also in Bird's group with Miles at the time, often accompanied him. "All the young writers at that time hung around Gil. He
was very generous with information to those people who were really interested in orchestration. And one of the most avaricious people, if you will,
was Miles Davis. He couldn't get *over* this. He saw this was another direction. That kind of sound *fascinated* Miles."

And so too it was Miles's sound that attracted Gil—the unique tone and
timbre of an instrumentalist's voice. "That's how we got together, basically,"
he told Ben Sidran in 1986. "The sound is the thing that put us together immediately, and it's always been like that. It's still the same way today."

Of course, by this point, Gil himself was already moving away from the
Thornhill band's trademark sound, and at the same time, Miles was looking
beyond bebop. It was between these polarities, the near-stillness of Claude
Thornhill and the ferocity of Charlie Parker, that Gil and Miles would begin
to explore that *sound,* what Gil saw as their common *waveform.* "Miles was
looking for something," George Russell said.

AND WHOEVER OR WHATEVER his guardian angel was, it attracted the
two of them. I don't think Miles invited *himself* to the apartment—I think
Gil was very attracted to Miles, as many people were, to his playing, and
to his sense of artistry. I think he already had the inclination to like Gil—
to be attracted to Gil and to Gil's music—and to think he could *work* with
it, which he did. Gil was a perfect match for Miles Davis because he had
the temperament to be *able* to work with him, Miles being somewhat difficult and stubborn at times.

If Miles was "difficult," working for Charlie Parker was becoming impossible. Increasingly, Miles complained, Bird showed up "just to play and pick up his money." There were nights when he didn't show up at all. There were gigs for which the rest of the band never got paid. Bird's astounding solos began, too often, to take a back seat to his stage antics. He'd make fun of the other players, singing and clowning around during their solos. In the middle of a song he'd crack jokes to the audience, or he'd start playing a different tune. All of this infuriated the serious young trumpeter and made the heady goings-on over at Gil's place even more attractive. Well before he resigned from Parker's band in December 1948, Miles had set the wheels in motion for his new collaborative experiment with Gil Evans.

+   +   +

The structure of the band that would eventually be known as the Miles Davis Nonet was in itself a reflection of some decidedly different thinking. It was conceived by Gil and Gerry Mulligan "over the better part of a winter" (1947–1948), Mulligan told me. Most of their considerations at that point, he emphasized, were less "revolutionary" in their intent than they were pragmatic:

> THAT ATMOSPHERE CERTAINLY didn't predispose you to *not* bring in new things, but I don't think it was really so much ever a question of doing something new or different just for the sake of doing it. We weren't trying to do something different; we were trying to do something *practical*. For instance, the instrumentation of the nine-piece band was a result of trying to solve a theoretical need: How can you get the density of a big band, and how can you have the interest that you can generate in ensemble playing—that's what that was calculated to do.

The intent was to retain not only the dynamic range but also the sound of the Claude Thornhill Orchestra. "We wanted that sound," said Miles. "But the difference was that we wanted it as small as possible." The magic number turned out to be nine: six horns (trumpet, alto and baritone saxophone, trombone, French horn, tuba) and three rhythm instruments (bass, drums, piano). If not for another practical consideration, there might have been ten pieces. "Actually, we intended to have the clarinet as well," Mulligan explained. "I would have liked the color of the clarinet, but we could only hear

Danny Polo doing it—it had to be somebody with that kind of sound. So we had intended to have Danny with this thing when we started writing for it, but then realized that we'd be depending on *him,* and if we could only have rehearsals when he was in town, then that really hampered our abilities. So ultimately we left the clarinet out."

The clarinet would have added to the Thornhill flavor of the band (Thornhill had used as many as six), but even without it, the sound of the six-horn front line came surprisingly close to Thornhill's. These nine instruments provided the writers with considerable latitude, which, in this band, was the whole point. The nonet's primary focus was on accommodating the ideas and interests of the writer, rather than the instrumentalist. In bebop, the written music often served as little more than a springboard from which the soloists would take flight. In the nonet, the opposite was true. Each piece in its entirety was orchestrated, literally and figuratively, by the composer and/or arranger. The solos were still improvised, but they would be enveloped in richly constructed ensemble parts.

Another integral aspect was that the writing itself was based on the nonet's instrumentation and, in many cases, the specific individuals within the band—an important page out of Duke Ellington. Thus the repertoire was affected, for example, by the fact that Danny Polo would not be available and that no other clarinetist was going to be considered, and that it was going to be Lee Konitz rather than Sonny Stitt (Miles's initial nomination) playing alto saxophone. "Oh yeah," said John Carisi. "You wrote for those guys playing those instruments. And that influenced what you wrote."

The instruments in the nonet, individually and in various combinations, provided the writers a unique and remarkably diverse choir of voices. Gil explained the concept to Nat Hentoff in a 1957 interview for *Down Beat*:

> THOSE RECORDS BY MILES indicate what voicing can do, how it can give intensity and relaxation. Consider the six horns Miles had in a nine-piece band. When they played together, they could be a single voice playing a single line. One-part writing, in a way. But that sound could be altered and modified in many ways by the various juxtapositions of instruments.

In the lexicon of bebop, "intensity" usually meant playing hard, fast, and loud; "relaxation," if the term can even be applied in bebop, usually meant playing a ballad. In the nonet, such variations in the dynamics were established at the outset—not on the bandstand, but on paper. Gil explained, "If the trombone played a high second part to the trumpet, for instance, there would be more intensity because he'd find it harder to play the notes." Conversely, even the fastest or most technically difficult passages—played softly and scored, for example, in a register *lower* than an instrument's normal range—could still sound relaxed. It was largely through the use of writing devices such as these—unusual instruments and combinations of instruments played in an unorthodox manner—that the nonet's music came to acquire the somewhat deceptive label of *cool* jazz. The dynamics resulting from this approach to writing are evident in every piece of music this band recorded, but John Carisi's tune "Israel" is a textbook example. The mood of the piece is loose and relaxed, and none of the playing sounds strained; the music never feels like an intellectual writing exercise, even though it is the most complex composition in the whole collection. Similarly deceiving is "Boplicity," cowritten by Gil and Miles (under the pseudonym Cleo Henry). This tune has an even easier, more casual tempo than "Israel," yet its melody is every bit as intricate, and harmonically (through Gil's orchestration and ensemble writing) it is every bit as challenging. Miles Davis biographer Jack Chambers wrote that when ". . . asked in 1950 to name his favorite example of his own work, Davis answered, without hesitating, 'Boplicity,' because of Gil's arrangement." Chambers also quoted composer Tadd Dameron's response to "Boplicity"—"one of the best small group sounds I've heard."

The sound of this band (and especially the predominant role of its writers) thus added a new and original twist to the definition of jazz. The nonet was neither a big band nor a small one, neither bebop nor straight swing. It embraced all of these elements, and others, within a framework in which written and improvised music were carefully, skillfully balanced. This was chamber music, garbed in twentieth-century American attire. More than simply a new style of jazz, it established a new paradigm in jazz thinking. John Carisi cited the chamber jazz approach as the band's major achievement, one that he attributed first and foremost to Gil Evans:

He chose a whole lot of harmonic voicings, of chords. I'm not even talking about voicing the instruments themselves, but just what he would pick out on the piano, and the things he would listen to—things that you wouldn't find in Fletcher Henderson's thing, much less straightforward. Some of Gil's most original compositional efforts showed up in [the nonet project]. I think one of them is his arrangement of "Moon Dreams." That's almost like a composition, because what did he do? Through the *orchestration* he did some varied things that are not just the tune alone. He takes advantage of the instrumentation, you know? And you have to play it the same way all the time. Well, that's chamber music. This was not unique in all of music; it *was* unique in a *jazz* context.

✝   ✝   ✝

"Gil and Gerry had decided what the instruments in the band would be before I really came into the discussions," Miles wrote. "But the theory, the musical interpretation, and what the band would play was my idea." To many, this might seem altogether too sweeping a claim. After all, much of the conceptual groundwork came directly from Gil's writing for Thornhill (and several other sources) and was developed further by Gil, Mulligan, and at least three other writers. Still, there was never any doubt that Miles was this band's leader and that without him, the nonet's innovations might never have left the drawing board. Gerry Mulligan:

> MILES HAD THE AMBITION to go and put the thing together. Gil and I would talk about it, we would theorize about this instrumentation, but would never get around to *doing* it. My concern with this thing was not with Miles as a leader but with the music and the instrumentation as a physical idea. Gil didn't really think like that, either. He treated Thornhill the same way—he wasn't *concerned* with the problems that Thornhill had as a working band. His concern was the music.
>
> He convinced Claude, at a time when the bands were really starting to lose their market altogether, to have this *gigantic* band—four trumpets and three bones, two French horns and a tuba, five saxophones, one of which was always clarinet, and three flutes, plus the rhythm section. Now, *that* couldn't last long, but he wrote some stuff for that instrumentation—and of course the things that Gil was orchestrating for the band, lush French ensemble sounds, it just sounded beautiful. But he wasn't concerned with Claude having to sell it or be a leader. Gil was in his own rarefied world, and he didn't want to be bothered by that kind of stuff.

While Gil continued to work out the details of their new music, Mulligan had yet to acquire the experience, let alone the inclination, to lead a band like this one. Miles, on the other hand, was the right man at the right time—

a popular and rising star, and one who'd proven his leadership skills as the de facto manager of Charlie Parker's band. He called the rehearsals, booked the studios, and made sure everyone finished their arrangements and met the deadlines. Miles also got the band its first engagement—two weeks at the Royal Roost—and it was his signature on the contract to record the nonet for Capitol Records. The nonet's theoretical depth came from Gil Evans and the other writers, and its musical polish came from an entire assemblage of superb players. But it was through Miles's determination—quite apart from his contributions as a writer, ensemble player, and soloist—that the theory was turned to practice, and that the practice was turned into music that, as Mulligan put it, had about it "a kind of perfection."

✝   ✝   ✝

The idea of the nonet came about through the initial discussions among Miles, Gil, and Gerry, but it quickly evolved into a full-fledged workshop. By the spring of 1948, it seemed to involve the whole inner circle of 55th Street and many from 52nd Street. There were the writers, notably John Lewis, John Carisi, and George Russell, and also the instrumentalists, including Lee Konitz, alto; Max Roach, drums; Bill Barber, tuba; J.J. Johnson, trombone; and Al McKibbon, bass. As the charts began to materialize, they were rehearsed in the apartment, with many of the people they'd been written for.

Max Roach, while not yet involved in writing, had already become a regular at Gil's. He sat in on many of the discussions and the jam sessions, and he was as excited about this new music as Miles was. "Bebop was just flat out *playing*," Roach explained. "And that was orchestration *plus* playing." Lee Konitz visited the apartment less frequently than most. "I've never been one to hang around too much," he told me. "I would just go there once in a while, mostly at rehearsals, the more preliminary rehearsals." There seemed to be different people at every rehearsal, Konitz recalled, but there was a definite nucleus of players, and from the beginning he was part of it. He was among the few instrumentalists who remained active from the first rehearsals through to the last recording sessions. Although he readily accepted the invitation to join the group, Konitz was never as zealous about the nonet as some of the others:

> NOT BEING A WRITER, I didn't really appreciate the significance of this. I just thought it was lovely chamber music, and I was delighted to play it, but I certainly didn't realize its significance. The writers, of course, had a better

perspective of what was happening, what might happen. Composers are a different breed of people for me. So I was pleased to be part of the scene, but I guess I had more of almost a periphery position. I liked the guys and everything, I felt friendly with them, but I was in no way part of the organization of that thing. I was just a player in the band.

Konitz proved to be an ideal soloist. Since this was a writer's workshop, his unique, light sound would not only complement the style of the music but also influence its direction. As Mulligan put it, "I just wrote with the players in mind, so it was a very particular sound because of the sound of the players being a very *individual* sound. It's very much like the Duke Ellington idea. His ensemble, the sound of it, was organic, in that it sounded that way because of the people playing it."

Most of the players worked on the nonet project on the side while they continued to play their respective gigs, and like Miles, many of them were busy people. This often made it difficult to organize rehearsals and continued to pose problems throughout the nonet's brief existence, both on the bandstand and in the recording studio. On its recording sessions for example—two nights of radio broadcasts and three one-day studio dates—the nonet would use no less than three different bass players, two drummers, three trombonists, three French horn players, and two pianists. Only Miles, Gerry, Lee, and tuba player Bill Barber were present on each of these occasions.

Despite all the personnel changes and scheduling problems, let alone the demands posed by the music itself, the nonet succeeded in producing a consistent, polished sound. Certainly by design, but also in part by accident and circumstance—who was in town and available, who got their charts finished—the nonet developed a character all its own, made cohesive by, and yet independent of, all of its individual members and sometime contributors. No single individual dominated any aspect of this project, even among the writers. This fact in and of itself is a remarkable achievement. Of twelve songs recorded by the nonet, there were listed no fewer than five arrangers. Each of the nonet's tunes—regardless of the writer, arranger, featured soloists, or orchestration—sounds unmistakably like this band alone. On the recordings, the improvised solos are divided evenly; again, no single voice stands above the others. What binds everything together is a kind of collective consciousness, in which everyone participates but no one predominates.

Gil Evans never took full credit for the nonet's accomplishments, nor should he have, yet clearly it was his aesthetic, his approach to writing, that set the direction of the music. Gil had created the Thornhill sound after which the nonet was modeled, and it was his ability, more than anyone else's, to transpose the many concepts—fusing together not only Thornhill's music but bebop, Duke Ellington, and the whole chamber jazz approach—that gave the nonet its character. For evidence, one need not look further than the Thornhill arrangement that had so impressed Miles, "Robbin's Nest," in which Gil's ensembles retain his low-key blues mood and suave tempo even as they become increasingly, and astonishingly, intricate.

Gil was the nonet's leader in spirit, contributing to it not only with his own arrangements but through his encouragement, guidance, and assistance. By the end of the summer of 1948, however, with the completion of the writing, Gil's direct involvement came to an end. As the Royal Roost date drew closer, it was now time for Miles Davis to take charge.

‡   ‡   ‡

The nonet's debut was announced by a sign outside the Royal Roost: THE MILES DAVIS NONET—then below that, at Miles's insistence: ARRANGEMENTS BY GERRY MULLIGAN, GIL EVANS, AND JOHN LEWIS. This was the first time the role of an arranger was acknowledged publicly by a jazz band, and it was the first time Gil Evans's name had been seen in public since his appearances at Balboa Beach in 1937.

Gerry Mulligan described playing in the nonet as a challenge, not only because of the music's demands but also because of Miles's inexperience in directing a band. "There got to be problems playing this stuff every night—about interpretations." Establishing the interpretations—for example, shifting the tempo or mood of a tune in response to different audiences' reactions—was the responsibility of the leader. "John Lewis and I both used to tell Miles, 'Look, you are not only the leader now, it's not only a working band. You have to assume some responsibility—you're also the lead *player,* and you've got to tell the guys what the interpretations should be. It's *not* every man for himself.' But he wouldn't do it, so in some ways it started to get kind of tense. Also, the guys that were playing at the Roost hadn't been at the rehearsals, so they had missed out a lot of the stuff that we had worked out."

The nonet had second billing to Count Basie, who, Miles wrote in his autobiography, listened to many of their sets and liked what he heard, describing the music as "slow and strange, but good, real good." One of the many musicians Gil brought down to hear the group was Benny Goodman. In particular he liked Gerry Mulligan's writing. "Gil told me afterward, Benny asked me to write for his band, he asked Gil to ask me," said Mulligan. "Every time there was a chart that he asked who wrote it, it was my chart. So that obviously appealed to Benny." (Mulligan agreed to write for Goodman, but he also urged Benny to hire him as a player. Those familiar with the young Mulligan's quick temper, let alone Goodman's, will not be surprised to hear that the relationship did not survive beyond two weeks of rehearsals.)

The nonet's live performances came and went with little fanfare. The band played just once, a two-week engagement at the Royal Roost. On two of those nights (September 8 and September 18, 1948), the band was featured on live broadcasts from the club. The CD release from these broadcasts includes an introduction by jazz disc jockey Symphony Sid: "Right now, ladies and gentlemen, we bring you something new in modern music. We bring you 'impressions in modern music' with the great Miles Davis and his wonderful new organization . . . ." With all its emphasis on "new" and "modern," the buildup sounds cautionary, almost apologetic, as if it were imploring listeners to give the band a chance before tuning out. In the club itself, the audience response is at best polite; as the set progresses, it is not the applause level that rises but the crowd noise. As the music gets softer or slower, the audience seems to get less and less interested.

Not long after the Royal Roost date, Gil suddenly abandoned his 55th Street apartment, never to return. George Russell was at the apartment when the era of Gil's jazz salon came to its unceremonious end. He was visiting with the last of Gil's stay-over guests, singer Dave Lambert and his wife and child, when the police arrived to evict them. It may have been that Gil simply fell behind in his rent and couldn't afford to come back, but in Russell's view, Gil finally got fed up with the constant traffic and, especially, the emotional demands. "It got to a point where every Tom, Dick, and Harry was hanging out in the apartment, and Gil was being drained by the people who leaned on him. He hadn't learned how to say no to anyone, and too many people took advantage of him." I asked Russell if perhaps Gil's abrupt departure might have been sparked by the nonet's lukewarm reception. After so much work had gone into this music, could Gil have been disillusioned by the experience? Russell's response was immediate and almost scornful: "There's a huge gap between a flop as defined by the music business and a flop artistically. And that was *never* an artistic flop, you know? Gil would never break down over some disappointing sales in something that he knew was art. He believed in himself much more than that."

✦   ✦   ✦

It is to Miles's credit (and to Capitol Records producer Pete Rugolo's) that the nonet's music was preserved at all, for in 1949 it was clearly ahead of its time. Given its lack of public acceptance, it was also obvious that the band would be difficult, if not impossible, to sustain as a working organization. And as Gerry Mulligan explained, that had never been their intention anyway:

> I THINK ALL OF US were impressed with ourselves and what we had done. And we expected the kind of reaction from the musicians—the musicians were very impressed with what we had done. It was only the *business* end—I mean, who cared about *that?* I don't think any of us at that point, Miles included, was equipped to be able to put it together, organize it. Putting a band together is not just rehearsing a bunch of music and getting it polished. A working band is a *business,* and somebody's got to take *care* of business. Somebody has got to organize it, somebody's got to book it— who's going to do all that? And where are you going to work with an odd-size band like that? The concert market didn't exist yet. We weren't trying to be a dance band, which all the functioning bands were. And it was too big for clubs. So, although there *were* clubs around the country that may well have taken it, still, 'around the country?'—right away you're into *business:* you've got to arrange transportation, you've got to do this, do that . . . . What happened with the records, sales and that, is what I expected. I don't think anybody expected anything different. But that it was going to be a big hit? I don't think that really occurred to anybody.

After the Royal Roost engagement, the nonet recorded a total of twelve songs—four tunes in each of three sessions—the first two in January and April 1949, and the last, almost a full year later, in March 1950. Recording this music posed a whole new set of challenges, said Mulligan.

> WHAT WE DID WAS JUST assemble the six horns three on each side around the microphone, so we were all facing each other. It sounded good in the studio, but we weren't really able to get the recorded sound quite right. Remember, they didn't have sophisticated multitrack recording then, to be able to control that sort of thing—and we were doing something that

was different from what the engineers were used to. Pete Rugolo took me aside on the break and said, "Gerry, we're going out of our *minds* in there, because we don't know what kind of sound you guys are looking for." I said we were just trying to get a musical balance between the six horns, as even a balance as we can, that each horn should balance with the others. Obviously, from the recording, they had a hard time. It got the sound of the ensemble, but you couldn't hear individual lines moving, so there wasn't a clarity in the recording.

Gil, on the other hand, did not seem to think the musicians had any trouble at all with this music. In the last recording session, which included "Moon Dreams," his most difficult arrangement, he told Ben Sidran: "I wasn't even there. I had to go home to see my mother in California, so I wrote that arrangement and gave it to Miles. But we were all so in tune with each other that I didn't have any worries at all. They just played it, and when I heard it, it was as though I had been there." Unbeknownst to Gil, however, the recording of "Moon Dreams" was so daunting that it was almost canceled. Gunther Schuller recalled, with no small sense of pride, that if not for his classical training and conducting experience, the band might not have recorded "Moon Dreams," one of the nonet's most striking pieces and arguably Gil Evans's strongest piece of writing to date. "I ended up saving 'Moon Dreams' from the trash can," he told me, "by somehow keeping the band together."

IN THE MIDDLE OF THE PIECE, the time goes out. There's no drums, and it just goes into all kinds of strange—well, I grew up on Schoenberg and Stravinsky and Bartók, so this wasn't strange to me, but in a jazz context these were very unusual things he was doing. And I remember at the record date, we kept falling apart. Once Max Roach stopped playing time in the middle of the piece, we could never get to the end, because it was too complicated rhythmically, and there wasn't enough time to rehearse it. So I ended up conducting, actually, while playing the French horn. And the trick there is, since you're supposed to use your right hand in the bell of the horn, how do you also conduct, you know, with a third hand? Well, I managed somehow to lead that. It's still a pretty rough performance; it isn't really absolutely as good as it might have been.

Beginning in early 1949, Capitol began releasing the nonet's tunes on 78 rpm discs (one song per side) and continued to do so over the next three years. These issues had an immediate influence among musicians—effectively launching what became the cool jazz movement—but the band itself did not gain recognition of any real consequence until the music came out later on long-play (LP) albums. The first of these was issued in 1954, when eight of the tunes were released as part of Capitol's *Classics in Jazz* series. In 1957, a new issue was released featuring all eleven instrumental tunes plus a new album title, *Birth of the Cool*. A third version of the album, which included the nonet's twelfth piece, the vocal tune "Darn That Dream," was released in 1971. In 1998, Blue Note Records released *The Complete Birth of the Cool*, which included remastered versions of the original studio dates as well as transcriptions from the radio broadcasts.

Among its other historical distinctions, the nonet project represents the first Miles Davis–Gil Evans collaboration. Yet despite the fruitfulness of their relationship and their close personal friendship, their partnership came to an abrupt halt. Miles was busy with many projects and had less time for the nonet than anyone else in the group. He was still appearing regularly with Bird when the nonet first performed, and as soon as he left that band, in December, he began to juggle a variety of other playing and recording dates. The fact is, however, that Miles was entering into a very dark and unproductive period of his own. The primary reason he didn't see Gil, or many other friends, during this time was that he had acquired a full-blown heroin habit. Virtually everything he did was dictated by the need for money. The people he remained closest with were his suppliers, not musicians—unless they, too, were junkies. After the final nonet sessions in 1950, Gil would not work with Miles again for another six years.

One can only speculate on what might have happened with the nonet, and with the Davis-Evans partnership, had Miles stayed clean. Would they have devoted more time to this band? Would Miles have gotten the nonet to do more writing, more recording? With the nonet's quick departure from the scene, Gil also disappeared from sight. In truth, it's doubtful that many even noticed his absence. After all, no one but jazz musicians knew of his existence, let alone his stature. Later, with the rediscovery of the nonet recordings, people started asking, "What ever happened to Gil Evans? Where has he been?" "Why hasn't he been doing anything in jazz?" "Well, for one thing," Gil told Nat Hentoff in 1957, "nobody asked me." In one of Gil's last interviews, in 1986, Ben Sidran asked him what he'd been doing all that time. "After what seemed like forever," Sidran told me, "Gil leaned over and sighed. 'I was waiting for Miles.'"

BEHIND THE SCENES

LILLIAN GRACE ANSWERED her telephone late one night in early 1949. On the line was Gil Evans, whom she'd met through her ex-husband, a saxophone player in Claude Thornhill's band. Gil was calling from the Times Square Hotel, where he'd been staying. He was broke, and he asked if she could lend him some money. Lillian took him in and helped him "get his health back." Within a year, Lillian became Gil's wife—not Mrs. Evans, of course, for Gil still hadn't gotten around to settling that little matter of properly registering his name—and thus she became Mrs. Lillian Green.

So began Gil's first marriage—and also the "lost years" of Gil's career. From 1950 to 1956, Gil was virtually a nonentity in jazz. Among his activities there would be a smattering of jazz projects, in addition to ill-fated ventures into the world of commercial writing—radio, pop recordings, and even television orchestras. To a much greater extent, however, Gil's time was devoted to studying. There was much he wanted to learn, both as a writer and as a musician.

I spoke to Lillian Green in early 1992. She would not agree to a formal interview, nor would she offer any details on her own background, but she did speak briefly about her life with Gil over the course of their eleven-year marriage. (I called her again just a few weeks later to see if she might reconsider doing an interview. At the very least, I hoped to find out if she had, in fact, supported Gil in those first years they were together. Had she worked? Did she have her own business? A family inheritance? When I called back, however, I was informed that she had just suffered a stroke and was in the hospital. Later, I heard that she has lived since then in a nursing home. The details of her first account, however thin, provide a number of unique and rare insights that I could not have found otherwise.)

Lillian said that when she saw Gil that night, after he called her from the Times Square Hotel, he looked terrible, like he'd been on a long binge. She suspected his problem was hard drugs ("like with Charlie Parker and those others he hung out with"). Gil always maintained that he never did anything stronger than marijuana. He once said that he did drink heavily in his younger years, but once he discovered pot (after moving to New York), he cut down his drinking and eventually gave up alcohol altogether.

Lillian told me emphatically that her memories of the good times with Gil far outweighed the bad. She and Gil were together in what she called "a time of quality," when people's interests were intellectual and philosophical, when they weren't "money mad." Their parting had been less than amicable, but throughout their marriage, and indeed to that very day, she always considered Gil above all else to be a man of quality and great style. She also thought he had great "star potential." With his handsome features, his worldly outlook, and that cool demeanor, she thought he was "every publicist's dream." When I asked if she ever imagined that Gil might soon hit the big time with his music, she told me they never discussed that notion or even thought about it. The big time wasn't about arriving somewhere; it was about the work itself. And in that sense, she told me, even in their earliest years together, "we *were* in the big time."

The period of the early 1950s was an unsettled one for Gil—with his studies, his practicing, his half-hearted attempts at commercial writing—but it was by no means an unhappy time. Gil and Lillian sustained a modest but comfortable lifestyle. They lived at the Whitby Apartments, a fashionable midtown apartment building which, compared to Gil's former residence on 55th Street, was downright luxurious. Gil was steeped in his music throughout those years, Lillian told me. "He'd practically write whole books to himself, some plan to create another kind of style." By the end of the decade, Gil's music would do just that.

In the meantime, however, Gil's commercial work during this period, such as it was, provided both a source of income and, as he told Nat Hentoff in 1957, another new learning experience: "Since 1948 I've been having a lot of additional experiences in music—act music, vaudeville, nightclubs. I learned to cross voices so that an arrangement that was good in Erie, Pennsylvania, for five voices could be used for twenty musicians on TV. I learned about the pacing of singers' songs. My pacing up until then had been orchestral, not vocal." Gil described this work in more detail in his 1986 interview with Ben Sidran: "A singer would want an arrangement that would sound OK with five men or fifteen men, so I would write some stock arrangement type things for singers. Not the greatest work by any means, but . . . . There was a vocal coach named Sid Shaw, and he had me and a piano player named Jimmy Lyons, and we would go around to these different people's houses, and Sid would pick out the songs that he felt they should sing in their act, and we would write the music for them. I did quite a bit of that."

Jimmie Maxwell, now well established in the New York recording and broadcasting scene, offered to help Gil find some work, but with little success.

> HE HAD A GREAT MANY opportunities, and he was certainly well known enough to all the conductors that they were very anxious to have him. But he did what he'd always had trouble with—he can't get arrangements done in time. And when you tell somebody you want to have a show on such and such a night and the rehearsal would be that afternoon, you can't come in and say, "Well I don't have the arrangement ready yet," which is what he did a couple of times. Like with Patti Page. They were really excited with the idea of getting Gil—and of course that happened. He was supposed to have arrangements for Tommy Dorsey, when he was doing his show, and he'd be fretting in his apartment—"I'm *never* going to have this arrangement in time."

Gil continued to expand his knowledge of jazz and much other music, but he produced almost no music of his own. He did a couple of jazz projects in 1950—one arrangement for a recording by trumpeter Billy Butterfield and four for singer Pearl Bailey—but then he did not write another jazz chart until 1953, when he wrote three arrangements for Charlie Parker. Gil had long been an admirer and personal friend of Parker's, and they'd often talked about working together, but by the time it finally happened, Bird was no longer the same person. His music had become far less adventurous, and in many cases his recordings (including this one, which featured Bird playing with a vocal group) were highly commercialized in their approach. Gil's contributions are virtually indistinguishable from those of any of the other arrangers on this recording.

Gil's next jazz projects did not come for another three years. During this time, Gil was also concentrating on his playing, and he welcomed almost any job in which he could hone his piano skills. He played occasionally in jazz clubs in Greenwich Village, but most of the work was not so high-toned. "I went out and played weddings and beer parties," he told Ben Sidran, "and I played a year downtown at a place that had been there since the speakeasy days, called The Nut Club. I worked there for a year, just to get the practice of playing. And we had drums and tenor, so I would play the bass part. It was a good experience for me."

According to Jimmie Maxwell, Gil had actually been quite a good piano player years before, back in the 1930s. "I liked his playing. It was sort of a cross between Earl Hines and Arthur Shutt, if you can imagine that—he played Earl Hines solos and things like Arthur Shutt, on the Red Nichols records—and he played very well. Apparently he always thought of himself as a piano player also, because even when he was in New York, he would go down to the library and bring home piles of music, classical music, and practice it. Just for the pleasure of playing it."

Part of Gil's challenge was to get past a style of playing that musicians refer to, often condescendingly, as "arranger piano," in which the keyboard serves more as a writing device than a musical instrument. Gerry Mulligan:

GIL ALWAYS WANTED to *play* piano, too, but he was a frustrated piano player, because he could never make the connection between what he could hear and what he could play. You hear that kind of propulsion in Bud Powell's playing. And Gil didn't know how to do that—he simply could not make things come out of the piano with a dynamic rhythm to them. So that was always very hard for him to cope with, because he wanted to be able to do that.

Gil was attracted most strongly to the great improvisers, from Louis Armstrong through to Charlie Parker. In his best writing, he was able to capture in his arrangements and his composition what he could hear in their solos. Gil might never *play* with the virtuosity of a Bud Powell or an Art Tatum, but with his eye for detail and his incredible ear, he could grasp the musicality of something in a way that few instrumentalists could rival. In his own playing, this evolved into a style that was sparse, but not shallow—simple but never simplistic.

Composer and clarinetist John LaPorta came to appreciate the subtlety of Gil's playing during the time Gil spent with one of his rehearsal bands in the early 1950s:

> WHEN HE CAME TO REHEARSE with me, I was running through an original piece of music. We got through the first piece and I noticed he wasn't playing very much. Then the second piece, I started rehearsing that, and I noticed he wasn't playing much on *that*. So I went over to him and I said, "Gil, is there anything wrong with the music?" And he said, "No, I'm just listening." So, as we continued rehearsing in the following weeks, what he did was, through listening, he got to absorb what I was doing in terms of the writing, and then he constructed piano parts that fit the arrangements. And when he left six months later, I was in real trouble, because piano players would just come in and start playing—and they'd just play the chords without thinking much about what's going on—and everything sounded *wrong* to me. Because really, he had, in effect, written piano parts to fit—he didn't write them, but he *conceived* them—to fit what I was doing. He was a fine musician; he made musical sense of whatever he was involved with.

✠   ✠   ✠

It did not take long before Gil turned his apartment at the Whitby into another gathering place. One frequent visitor was Dan Morgenstern, who had befriended Gil when he was a young jazz fan but not yet a writer. Morgenstern went on to become an editor of *Down Beat,* then the director of the Rutgers Institute of Jazz Studies; he is now one of America's foremost jazz historians and authors.

> I MET HIM FOR THE FIRST time in a place called Charlie's Tavern. We'd go to his apartment, which at that time wasn't too far from there. Charlie's Tavern was one of the midtown, Times Square hangouts for musicians. There was Junior's, there was Beefsteak Charlie's, and there was Charlie's Tavern. All these places were not too far from 52nd Street, and the studios were around there at the time, and that was a bar where musicians hung out. When Gil was there, there would always be a lot of

people sitting around, and the conversation would roam far and wide. He was exceptionally knowledgeable about music, and it wasn't in any sense restricted to any particular styles or periods.

One of the things that constantly amazed me about Gil was how much he knew about the history of the music. Of course, he was of a generation that came up during the '20s, and as we all know, he taught himself by taking things off records. But he had a terrific recall for all this stuff, and people who think of him as someone who's identified only with *modern* jazz would be making a big mistake. He was amazing. He knew so much about things like Red Nichols's Five Pennies, Jack Teagarden. And he would tell me about interesting things on records, way off the beaten path—he knew *tons* of stuff.

Gil was a quiet person but he was very social. I don't want to get metaphysical about it, but there was a very special aura that he had. He was a genuinely kind person—he *cared* about other people. When he asked you how you were feeling, you knew that it wasn't just a conventional comment—he really wanted to *know*. I know that if I had ever had a serious problem of any sort, whether it be personal or professional or whatever, Gil is one of the people I would've instinctively reached out for. He was somebody that you had the feeling you could go to with anything. Say you had committed a horrible crime or something—Gil was somebody you could go to and tell him about it. I think he had absolutely no prejudice. He was free of that. He was a free spirit.

Gil's friendships—primarily but not exclusively with musicians and music people—were of the utmost importance to him. Most of the people I talked to felt as strongly about Gil's friendship as he did about theirs. One of these was drummer Elvin Jones, who met Gil in 1954, long before they actually worked together.

PHILLY JOE JONES introduced me to him. We were pretty close friends, Joe and I, and he said, "There's somebody I want you to meet." He didn't tell me who it was—he said, "This guy, this is *something,* this is an experience you'll never forget"—and it was Gil Evans.

The first thing I noticed was, he had canaries. All over. Flying around in the room. And it was just—something like *that,* in the middle of New York *City,* to have that kind of tranquillity, it's very exceptional. And here's this tall guy, very polite and nice, and we sat and we chatted for a long time. It was mainly Joe's conversation because I didn't really know him. But he knew about me, and he was very well informed about everybody around, as far as music was concerned.

There was nothing pretentious about Gil—ever. From that moment until the last time I saw him, he was the same person that I had met years before, with the canaries flying around.

✢   ✢   ✢

After Gil's recording sessions with Charlie Parker in 1953, Gil did not do another jazz recording date until 1956, but now his fortunes finally took a turn for the better. Indeed, 1956 turned out to be a very busy year. In January, he wrote an arrangement for vibraphonist Teddy Charles and another one for Gerry Mulligan. In March, he wrote three arrangements for the debut recording of singer Johnny Mathis. In April, he wrote and arranged two compositions ("Jambangle" and "Blues for Pablo") for a recording by alto saxophonist Hal McKusick. In June, he worked on an album for vocalist Helen Merrill. In September, he did an arrangement for another Gerry Mulligan recording. And in December, he wrote a new chart for Billy Butterfield and three for singer Marcy Lutes.

From a career standpoint, the most important of these assignments were those for Johnny Mathis and Helen Merrill. His writing for Mathis brought him into contact with Columbia producer George Avakian, who would soon figure prominently in Gil's future. And Gil's work for Helen Merrill represents the first engagement for which he was hired to arrange an entire album.

George Avakian had met Gil previously during a session with the Claude Thornhill Orchestra. His decision to hire him for the Mathis recording was based on Gil's versatility—his ability to assemble, and work with, a variety of orchestral settings. "That whole first album was based on demonstrating what a great variety of things that Johnny could do," Avakian told me. "The budget was next to nothing—I think the biggest group that we used might have been maybe twelve pieces—but it did what we set out to do, to show the industry, the distributors and the dealers, that Mathis was a singer of enormous variety. That's how Gil fit, in that respect, in presenting Johnny Mathis for the first time in a variety of contexts." The career of Gil Evans was well served by this project as well, in that it bolstered Avakian's confidence in him. The record demonstrated

Gil's ability to produce, through his arrangements, an effective musical showcase.

On the other hand, the executives at Helen Merrill's record company did not share Avakian's enthusiasm toward Gil. "The record producers were petrified of him," Helen Merrill laughed. "If he wanted to do something, he did it—not having any sense of *time* in the studio, you know? When I chose Gil for the album, the only thought I had was artistic, because in those days we didn't make any money—it was just kind of artsy-craftsy stuff—and the record company absolutely refused, totally refused." Merrill persisted until the producers finally agreed to hire him.

> GIL WAS ONE OF THOSE people that I wanted to work with. I was born in New York, and I was always around all the great musicians of that era. I'd learned in my teens to listen to all these wonderful people, and I was very very lucky. And the one name that always came up was Gil Evans, as far as music was concerned, as far as arranging was concerned, and all the musicians respected him. Gil was like a god.

There was great mutual respect and a deep sense of community between Gil and his ever-widening circle of musicians. Like most people, Gil preferred to work with friends, people whose company he enjoyed. Among those he called for the Helen Merrill date, for example, were Jimmie Maxwell, John LaPorta, and another Claude Thornhill veteran, guitarist Barry Galbraith. One of the tunes he selected for the Merrill album, "Where Flamingos Fly," also came from that circle. Its cowriter, John Benson Brooks, was one of Gil's cohorts during the 55th Street years.

Despite the album's artistic merits, *Dream of You* did little to further the career of either Helen Merrill or Gil Evans. Helen attributes this not only to Gil's noncommercial orientation but her own. In any case, she told me, commercial success had never been a factor:

> MONEY HAD NOTHING to do with it. If you think in those terms about Gil, then you're on the wrong track, totally. The fact that Gil *wanted* to record with me was far more important than whether or not we ever sold one record. That wasn't the point; music was the point.
>
> There were many musicians like that, not just Gil at that time. There wasn't very much money, so it was the *art* that was important. But he was

sort of the daddy of all of it. Gil personified what everybody went through, what we all did. And we had a lot of fun doing it, by the way—a lot of fun—so I wouldn't trade that for money any time, nor would Gil. No way. It was a lot of fun, and we had a lot of help and camaraderie. It was wonderful.

Initial record sales didn't cover costs, which, as the executives had feared, went well over budget. Helen Merrill, already disenchanted with the American jazz scene, moved to Europe shortly after the album's release, and she lived and worked abroad for several years. Back home, the album had added further, in some circles, to Gil's reputation as a slow and therefore expensive arranger. Fortunately, not everyone in music or on the business side of music took that point of view. There were also people who were willing to look past the balance sheet and who could recognize and appreciate the qualitative differences that time, effort, talent—and, yes, more money—could provide. One of those was producer George Avakian. Another was Avakian's most recent addition to the Columbia jazz roster, that young trumpeter Miles Davis.

Gil was hired by Davis and Avakian to do one other arrangement in 1956, although Gil was not credited publicly for this work until many years later. This arrangement, for Thelonious Monk's "Round Midnight," became the title track for the recording debut of Miles Davis on Columbia Records. Thus began the reunion, however clandestine, of Miles Davis and Gil Evans, and the beginning of one of the most exciting and momentous chapters in the history of recorded jazz.

PART TWO

1957–1964

I have had a mad egocentric attitude toward all music. Every-thing I hear, I hear in terms of my own music.

—GIL EVANS,
INTERVIEW WITH MARC CRAWFORD,
DOWN BEAT, JUNE 1961

MILES AHEAD

SOME TWENTY-FIVE YEARS after embarking on a professional career in music, forty-five-year-old Gil Evans was about to create the greatest music of his life. He would finally win the respect of musicians and jazz aficionados beyond the New York scene. Nineteen fifty-seven was his breakout year not only in America but worldwide, just as it was for his friend and colleague, Miles Davis.

For Miles and Gil as a collaborative team, the roll began in February, when Capitol released the studio recordings of the Miles Davis nonet for the first time as a complete set—now on a long-playing album with a catchy new title, *Birth of the Cool*. The LP's newfound popularity followed the resurgence of Miles's career and, interestingly, the highly successful recordings of West Coast cool jazz, including, most notably, those by several Gerry Mulligan bands. In September, Columbia Records released its new Miles Davis project, the album *Miles Ahead*, arranged and conducted by Gil Evans. A month later, largely as a result of the success of *Miles Ahead*, Gil recorded a Prestige album called *Gil Evans Plus Ten*—his first album as a leader and his first appearance on record as a pianist. Over the next eight years, from 1957 to 1964, Gil and Miles produced a remarkable body of work, both on their own and together. Among these, three of their collaborations—*Miles Ahead, Porgy and Bess,* and *Sketches of Spain*—are unqualified masterpieces.

With the great artistic and commercial success of Miles Davis's debut album on Columbia, *Round Midnight*, Miles's star was rising fast. For Miles's second album, Columbia producer George Avakian had even bigger plans:

I WANTED TO PRESENT Miles in a different setting, and it was important to make it a good one, that would make it memorable and would sell records, because that's the bottom line, after all. We didn't just want to be artistic successes—I wanted to see Miles become a *financial* success, because he was really scraping along at that time. He needed support, and that's one reason he came to me to ask if I would sign him up. He was also finishing up his Prestige contract with the quintet, so there was a lot of quintet material coming out on the market rather quickly. Therefore, obviously, we had to go into a different direction, and what should it be? Well, I loved the sound of the nine-piece band, but then I thought, why not make it *bigger* than that? I've got the budget to do it, and that would make a more spectacular splash for Miles.

In addition to the nine-piece band's music, there was one other precedent for this project—a little-known recording made earlier that year, also produced by George Avakian, by the Brass Ensemble of the Jazz and Classical Music Society. Cofounded by John Lewis and Gunther Schuller, who conducted the ensemble, the Society was among the first organizations to actively pursue the fusion of jazz and classical music. Schuller, in fact, coined the phrase "third stream," by which this approach to music would become known. Miles played on two tunes: "Three Little Feelings," written and arranged by John Lewis, and "Jazz Suite for Brass," written and arranged by trombonist J.J. Johnson (yet another nonet contributor). "Miles was very impressed with the opportunity, which had never come his way before, to play with a large ensemble," Avakian recalled. "After that, I got the idea that—hey, wait a minute, *this* can be the second album, but it has to be a little different."

Miles was also enthusiastic about doing a big band record, and the more he and Avakian talked about how to make sure the album would truly make a "spectacular splash," the clearer it became that Gil Evans should be hired. Miles had marshaled Gil's talents quite effectively for the nonet experiment—in that case, with the object of capturing the sound of the Thornhill orchestra using the fewest possible instruments. Now he would challenge Gil to work his magic on the *grandest* scale.

‡   ‡   ‡

The concept for *Miles Ahead,* sketched out by Miles, Gil, and George Avakian in the fall of 1956 on the proverbial napkin over lunch, was to showcase

Miles fronting a nineteen-piece orchestra conducted by Gil. "The idea," said Avakian, "was not to present a group of people with Miles as leader. It was to present Miles period—in front—and then the setting was all Gil."

Taking that idea to its logical conclusion, Gil proposed to arrange each tune on the album in the form of a concerto: Miles would be the only solo voice. Furthermore, Gil would write transitions between the tunes—brief orchestral segues that were later spliced in to link the tunes together, thus forming a virtually uninterrupted suite. This in itself gave the album a novel structure and a beautiful continuous flow. Even more striking is the cohesiveness Gil achieved through his arrangements, despite the remarkable diversity of his selections. He drew from the classical repertoire ("Maids of Cadiz," by the nineteenth-century French composer Léo Delibes) and theater music (Kurt Weill's "My Ship"). His jazz selections were themselves eclectic, ranging from the hard-swinging (John Carisi's "Springsville") to the dark and introspective (Bobby Troup's "Meaning of the Blues" and J.J. Johnson's "Lament"). In the tune "Miles Ahead," Gil returned to the cool, relaxed sound of the nonet. His own composition "Blues for Pablo" came by way of themes originating in Spain (Manuel de Falla) and Mexico (Carlos Chávez). In his orchestral interludes, he added yet more new colors—shades of Ravel and Debussy, Stravinsky and Schoenberg—to an already expansive palette.

Next came the art of the arranger as musical architect. In the nonet experiment, whose recorded works listed numerous composers and arrangers, each tune belonged unmistakably to that ensemble alone. Similarly, in *Miles Ahead,* Gil demonstrated how the arranger can bring the same sense of unity and cohesion not only to different tunes but also to widely differing musical genres. *Miles Ahead* offered the best example yet of Gil's genius for "recomposing"—transforming other people's music into something all his own. This was evident throughout his earlier work, but *Miles Ahead* was clearly a watershed in his artistic development. In this instance, Gil re-composed each tune, including his own arrangements—for "Blues for Pablo" (done a year earlier for an album by Hal McKusick) and Miles Davis's "Miles Ahead" (for which Gil was later credited as cowriter). He went a step further by organizing the tunes and linking them together to form a jazz suite. Finally, he conceived a band-soloist framework in which his orchestra provided both the setting for and a counterpoint to the voice of Miles Davis. Miles's playing sometimes drove the band and sometimes followed it, sometimes calling out to the orchestra and at other times responding to its lead. And at all times Miles remained front and center—exactly according to plan.

It was Miles Davis's sound that attracted Gil, just as Miles was drawn to Gil's sound. Together, they created a new sound greater than the sum of its parts. The balance and blending of Gil's orchestral voice with Miles's solo voice was the crowning touch for *Miles Ahead* and would become the hallmark of the Davis-Evans partnership.

Not only was Miles's sound beautiful, Gil maintained, but it was the first new entirely original trumpet sound in jazz since Louis Armstrong. "He was a sound innovator," Gil told Ben Sidran:

> EVERYBODY UP UNTIL that time came out of Louis Armstrong. Maybe out of somebody else—like Roy Eldridge came out of Louis Armstrong, and then Dizzy came out of Roy—but it was all basically like that. Miles loved the trumpet, but he didn't like "trumpet" trumpet, you know? And so he had to just start with no tone, no sound whatsoever at first. That first record he made, "Now's the Time," it's just a skeleton tone that he uses. He gradually filled it in with flesh and blood, from hearing other people that he liked—like Clark Terry, Harry James . . . Freddie Webster especially—and it all went into that funnel and came out his sound.
>
> He didn't even *realize* it. One night, he was playing at the Village Vanguard, and we were sitting around during intermission and I said, "Miles, it just occurred to me. I don't know if you ever thought of it or not, but you're the first person to change the tone of the trumpet since Louis Armstrong." Which he was.

As much as he loved the tone, the waveform itself, Gil also marveled at Miles's ability to mold that sound within a given interpretation, something that not all soloists could do. In another interview (quoted by Jack Chambers in his Miles Davis biography), Gil said:

> FINALLY, MILES HAD HIS OWN basic sound, which any player must develop. But many players keep this sound more or less constant. Any variation in their work comes in the actual selection of notes, their harmonic patterns, and their rhythmic usages. Miles, however, is aware of his complete surroundings and takes advantage of the wide range of sound possibilities

that exist even in one's own basic sound. He can, in other words, create a particular sound for the existing context. The quality of a certain chord— its tension or lack of tension—can cause him to create a sound appropriate to it. He can put his own substance, his own flesh, on a note—and then put that note exactly where it belongs.

The contrast between them could hardly be greater: Gil, the writer, toiled endlessly over each and every note, whereas the genius of Miles, the performer, lay in his spontaneous choices and interpretation of those notes. As Miles told Marc Crawford in a 1961 *Down Beat* interview, "When Gil is writing, he might spend three days on ten bars of music. He'll lock himself up, put a 'do not disturb' sign on the door, and not even his wife Lillian can come in. It's torture for her when he's writing. It's like he's out to lunch. Sometimes he'll get in there and play the piano for twelve hours."

Together, each man brought the other something neither had on his own. "Miles has the melodic gift that Gil probably admired most," Gerry Mulligan offered. "If melody was his gift, the way Miles did it would have been his choice. And so it was a perfect voice for him to write for. He became the focus for a whole period of Gil's writing, which is probably some of the most effective and widely known writing that he did, because he *understood* Miles's playing so well." One of the key elements of their success, George Russell added, was Gil's use of space. "Gil had a particular talent for expressing beautiful harmonies and beautiful sounds but also using space as part of the music. Miles always needed space. His whole thing was to underplay things, not to overemphasize them. Gil understood the understatement, he *always* understood it, he was a master of it, and that's what Miles needed."

In Gil Evans, Miles told Marc Crawford, he found the writer he could never be:

I USED TO WRITE and send Gil my scores for evaluation. Gil used to say they were good but cluttered up with too many notes. I used to think you had to use a lot of notes and stuff to be writing. Now I've learned enough about writing *not* to write. I just let Gil write. I give him an outline of what I want and he finishes it. I can even call him up on the phone and tell him what I got in mind, and when I see the score, it is exactly what I wanted. Nobody but Gil could think for me that way.

Gil's remaining contribution to *Miles Ahead*—as the orchestra's conductor—was as crucial as his writing was to the album's success. He proved to be just as fastidious about choosing the players and working with them in the studio as he was about every other detail. "My arrangements don't sound right unless they're played by a certain group of players, and unless I've rehearsed them," Gil told Nat Hentoff. "They're very personal, and they're not so highly stylized that it's easy to catch on to what I have in mind right away."

Miles Ahead was recorded in four sessions—more studio time than most jazz albums would normally be allocated, but still much less than this music really needed. "They were tough, no doubt about it," said trumpeter Louis Mucci. "His music was not easy to play. In the first place, all these sessions were sight-read. We didn't go out and play any concerts to develop these things. At that time, I thought nothing about that, because that's the way it was." Projects like *Miles Ahead* were even more challenging in that the music existed solely in a studio setting rather than a working band's repertoire, and recording budgets rarely included rehearsal time. Musicians earned a fixed rate per session, typically three hours. "They'd call you to do a date," Mucci explained, "and you never knew what it was going to be, what kind of music it was—and it was sight-read. I think that's phenomenal. Now that I look back, I think it's *really* phenomenal."

One of the things that made Gil's music unique was the unusual demands he made of his players. A brass or reed part would be written in a high register, for example, yet played very softly, and often for excruciatingly long durations. This approach (which one musician described to me as "hernia music") had been used to great effect in devising the sound of the nonet. In the *Miles Ahead* sessions, Gil often insisted on doing take after take, even when everyone else thought it unnecessary. "I remember the brass men, especially, got worried," George Avakian recalled. "Toward the end of at least one session, maybe more, they would pull me aside and say, 'Tell Gil, for God's sake, don't go over things again and again. We *know* what to do, but the lips are going and we can't keep *playing*.'" This helps to explain the final album's mistakes—a split note here, a flat note there—but it also shows how effective these efforts could be, flaws and all.

Another challenge was Gil's conducting style—his direction or, as some would put it, his lack of it. Most conductors are very explicit about what they're going for—and Gil was, too, for that matter—but he also wanted the musicians to interpret the music *themselves* rather than be guided through it. In his efforts to elicit such performances from his players, Gil succeeded far more often than he failed.

And of course, Miles Davis rose to the occasion. As the album's only soloist, playing highly sophisticated music, fronting a nineteen-piece orchestra, he responded to the challenge of Gil's music with one outstanding performance after another. Another hero, largely unsung, was George Avakian. Without his stewardship over the recording and, in particular, the editing of this music, some of Gil's best writing, the orchestra's best playing, and Miles's best solos would surely have been lost.

At the time *Miles Ahead* was recorded, the only way to edit music was to cut the master tape with a razor blade, eliminate the unwanted portion or replace it with an alternate take, then splice the pieces back together. Another device was overdubbing. With the advent of multitrack recording, it became possible to record the master on one track and save the second track for the overdub. A true pioneer in audio "post-production," George Avakian used his skills courageously on *Miles Ahead* and to great advantage. Four of the album's tunes contain solos that were dubbed in by Miles several months after the band sessions. More remarkably, the original master is said to contain over two hundred splices. It is a patchwork of material gleaned not only from the alternate takes but also the rehearsals, which Avakian had also started recording. As he explained in a 1998 interview with Paul Conley for National Public Radio's *Jazz Profiles*, "It got to the point where Gil was *never* ready to make a take, and whenever I felt they were ready, I started to tell the engineer, 'Run the tape but don't say anything.' And Gil didn't catch on at first, but if I hadn't done it we wouldn't have gotten as much material as we did."

Soon enough, though, both Miles and Gil became willing and eager accomplices. "Gil would often record only a little bit of an arrangement at a time," Avakian told me. "He would try to keep track of what he felt was good, but I didn't depend just on that—I made sure that I knew what was good and what wasn't. Gil didn't worry too much about things like that, because he knew that *I* worried about it, and he trusted me. I'm not a musician, but I get into it pretty deeply. I know what's going on and what has to come out, so if I'm sure—'Gil, look, we've got it'—he'd accept that. The technology was pretty primitive, but we managed it."

Miles Ahead was an immediate success on every level—artistic, commercial, financial, aesthetic, and critical. It bolstered Columbia's image in the jazz market. It enhanced George Avakian's reputation not only as a hit-maker but also as a producer of jazz as art music. It solidified the emergence of Miles Davis as the foremost jazz voice of his time. And it brought Gil Evans into the limelight for the first time in his career. *Miles Ahead* was his biggest assignment ever, as an arranger and certainly as a conductor, and only his second project in a recording studio. After years of obscurity and relative inactivity, his return to the jazz scene was an artistic triumph and also the sweetest of personal victories. "It was a big breakthrough for the both of them," said Avakian. "It put Gil on the map, and it put Miles in a completely new context that changed his career and opened it up commercially as well as artistically."

GIL EVANS PLUS TEN

MILES DAVIS'S CAREER was rising at a rate unprecedented in jazz. His move to Columbia resulted in much greater exposure and publicity—indeed, Miles was not only becoming a musical star but also a bona fide celebrity. Gil was on a roll, too. Amid the excitement of his work with Miles, Prestige Records signed Gil to record an album of his own. ("Get Gil! Get Gil!" Miles told Prestige's Bob Weinstock.) This project would be nowhere near the size of the *Miles Ahead* production, yet Gil would treat it with as much enthusiasm and dedication. This, after all, would be the very first recording he made under his own name—complete with his repertoire, his choice of players, and (another first) the opportunity to play.

Gil Evans Plus Ten (also released as *Big Stuff*), was recorded in the fall of 1957 at Rudy van Gelder's famous "studio" (actually his parents' living room) in Hackensack, New Jersey. Along with a collection of seven meticulously prepared charts, Gil brought with him a group of ten musicians, all chosen just as carefully. Among them were old and not-so-old friends and colleagues: two veteran jazz players, drummer Jo Jones and trumpeter Jake Koven, and from the Thornhill Orchestra days, alto saxophonist Lee Konitz and trumpeters John Carisi and Louis Mucci. Gil called in Miles's bassist Paul Chambers, and on two of the three recording sessions, he used another drummer, Nick Stabulas. For further orchestral color, he added bassoon (played by Dave Kurtzer), bass trombone (Bart Vasalona), and French horn (Willie Ruff). Finally, the charts called for three main solo voices: trombone

93

(Jimmy Cleveland), soprano saxophone (Steve Lacy), and piano—Gil himself in his recording debut.

Compared to the brand new *Miles Ahead,* the music on this album is relatively low-key and much less eclectic, but it is no less ambitious. One of the distinctions of this collection is its great subtlety. In the ballads, such as Irving Berlin's "Remember," the melody is stated cleanly and simply, as are the solos on piano and soprano saxophone. Behind the melodies, however, are several layers of texture, each emerging so softly and blending in so effortlessly that one can easily overlook its incredible intricacy. In "Ella's Speed," a tune by blues legend Leadbelly, Gil's piano establishes the tune as a swinging, lighthearted romp, to which straight-ahead solos by soprano saxophone and trombone are added; then the full ensemble is brought in for a round of powerful, elaborate choruses played in unison. Once again, the listener is charmed by the energetic swing of the music, not its complexity.

For Steve Lacy, then just twenty-three years old, meeting Gil and working with him on these sessions was a life-altering experience. "He opened the skies to me," Lacy told me. "My whole thing is unthinkable without him. And he came along at a stage—not at the very beginning, but when I was ready. I had never done *anything.* Like all the things he asked me to do, I had never *done* before. What could be more stimulating and challenging than that?"

But these songs don't *sound* as complex as those, say, on *Miles Ahead.* How difficult was this music? Lacy gasped incredulously.

BOY, THAT STUFF WAS very very difficult to read. I was one of the slowest readers in the band—really, these guys were *experts.* I was the clumsy one, and yet I was playing *lead,* so it really forced me to come to terms with paper. That was one thing, but there were a hundred things like that, that made me learn. How to blend. How to be a color. How to disappear. How to get *lost.* How to be *beautifully* lost. Gil put me in situations where I would be lost and he would be *finding* me. And I would be lost and he would be *featuring* that. It was a very exciting experience to be part of these artistic inventions. You couldn't explain it, man. He was a magician.

Lacy's relationship with Gil began in a most unorthodox fashion: "He sought me out. He heard me with my amateur Dixieland band on Arthur Godfrey's talent show in '52. And in '57, when he was about to make his first record for Prestige, he found me for that record and he called me up out of the blue. Well, that says a lot about Gil. It means he's really a hound for a sound, you know? Once he hears something, he locks on it—even for five years he can hold onto it—and then use it when he needs it."

Lacy became friends with Gil during the course of preparing for the album. "It involved several sessions at my house, looking over material and trying out various things, and sort of jamming a bit. Gil loved to jam. He could jam all the time, and he always thought he needed to play like that to improve his abilities. So it involved playing over some of the stuff and discussing it, and then he showed me what he was going to do. It was very exciting for me, a very challenging experience."

NEW BOTTLE,
OLD WINE

IN THE SPRING OF 1958, Gil returned to the recording studio to begin work on his second album as a leader. This project reunited him with producer George Avakian, who had recently left Columbia Records to join World Pacific Records. The result was *New Bottle, Old Wine,* subtitled *The Great Jazz Composers Interpreted by Gil Evans and His Orchestra.* In the repertoire for this recording, Gil traversed jazz's half-century of history. Four tunes are from the swing era and earlier (written by W. C. Handy, Lillian Hardin Armstrong, Jelly Roll Morton, and Fats Waller) and four are from the post–swing era of the 1940s (by Lester Young, Thelonious Monk, Dizzy Gillespie, and Charlie Parker). In "interpreting" this music, Gil paid his respects to these writers and demonstrated his mastery of their respective idioms. This recording made it clear that the authenticity of his writing for these tunes was the result of years of study and firsthand experience. On the other hand, the album was an object lesson in arranging as re-composing. While retaining the fundamental character of the originals, Gil gave each of them a completely new personality—old wine, new bottle. He achieved this through unique and often unorthodox orchestrations, choice of musicians, and most importantly, writing, through which he not only brought together all of the aforementioned elements but also added his own interpretation of the music. Jazz musicians do this every time they solo, and the ability of a soloist to create tunes within tunes—quoting and paraphrasing as many different songs as the moment inspires—is one of the basic measures of great improvisation. Like the greatest composers, Gil achieved the same effect on paper. His written interpolations flowed with the same apparent ease and spontaneity of the most gifted improvisers.

One of the most fascinating aspects of this recording is Gil's juxtaposition not only of melodies but also of different idioms. His "King Porter Stomp" owes as much to Charlie Parker as it does to Fletcher Henderson. In Parker's "Bird Feathers," he moves with equal agility from small ensemble sections to big band unison choruses—with more than a passing nod to his own bebop charts for Claude Thornhill. One of the most exciting examples of Gil's jazz-within-jazz combinations is his arrangement of Dizzy Gillespie's "Manteca." The tune begins with the bass line from a different song altogether ("I'll Never Go Back to Georgia"), over which he introduces a slow, delicate treatment of the "Manteca" bridge section. When he does finally state the Afro-Cuban theme, the music is suddenly bold and brassy, just as Dizzy's big band might have played it. On returning to the bridge, the flutes and reeds again play soft and low, but now Gil has given it a swing-band tempo—sustaining its energy while taking the tune in yet another completely new direction.

Another highlight of *New Bottle, Old Wine* is the spectacular performance of its principal soloist, alto saxophonist Julian "Cannonball" Adderley, one of the most versatile and exciting improvisers of the day. With his grasp of each of the forms Gil was exploring—especially blues and bebop—Adderley was the perfect choice. "Cannonball played great on that album," Gil told Ben Sidran in 1986. "Just the very opening he plays on "St. Louis Blues," it *still* gives me the chills."

Adderley had joined Miles Davis's band only a few months earlier and was still relatively new on the New York jazz scene. In fact, he was in the studio in March, just finishing his first record with Miles, when Gil was about to begin the *New Bottle, Old Wine* sessions. It was that Davis album, *Milestones,* that solidified Adderley's reputation and established Miles's sextet as one of the most influential and successful jazz ensembles. Yet even as *Milestones* was being hailed by critics and audiences, and the sextet was packing jazz clubs across the country, Miles had already set the wheels in motion for his next project—a new collaboration with Gil Evans and their follow-up to *Miles Ahead.*

PORGY AND BESS

GEORGE GERSHWIN WAS INFLUENCED greatly by the jazz, blues, and gospel music of African-American culture, both in his popular tunes and in his "serious" works. With the premiere of *Rhapsody in Blue* in 1924, Gershwin was lauded for introducing jazz to the concert hall. ("Mr. Gershwin will bear watching," said one reviewer. "He may yet bring jazz out of the kitchen.") A decade later, Gershwin boldly announced that in his forthcoming work, he would bring black American folk music to the opera house. The "folk opera" *Porgy and Bess* was inspired by a best-selling novel, *Porgy,* written in 1925 by DuBose Heyward. *Porgy* is a tragic love story set in "Catfish Row," a poor black shantytown modeled after a real-life district in Heyward's hometown of Charleston, South Carolina. (In 1927, Heyward and his wife, Dorothy, adapted the story for the theater, and the play, too, was a big hit, running more than a year in New York.)

Gershwin read the novel in 1926 and wrote to Heyward to express his interest in putting the story to music. The two met shortly thereafter and agreed to collaborate on a new work. There were no further discussions until 1932, however, and work did not begin in earnest until more than a year later. In early 1934, Gershwin paid two visits to Heyward in Charleston, and he returned to spend the summer to work exclusively on *Porgy.* This extended stay brought him into close daily contact with the local black community. Heyward described the visit as an invaluable experience, providing them "a laboratory in which to test our theories, as well as an inexhaustible source of folk material." For Gershwin, Heyward said in 1934, the visit was "more like a homecoming than an exploration. . . . The quality in him which had produced *Rhapsody in Blue* in the most sophisticated city in America found its counterpart in the impulse behind the music and bodily rhythms of the simple Negro peasant of the South."

Porgy and Bess opened in Boston in November 1935 to lukewarm reviews. In New York, it ran from October to March and closed after just 124 performances. Ticket sales barely covered production costs, and the show's backers, including George Gershwin and his brother Ira, lost their entire investment. The critics were unimpressed by the very notion of "folk opera," calling the production "a hybrid, fluctuating constantly between music-drama, musical comedy, and operetta." Even the show's better tunes were criticized for standing out rather too much: "Perhaps it is needlessly Draconian to begrudge Mr. Gershwin the song hits which he has scattered through the score and which will doubtless enhance his fame and popularity. Yet they mar it. They are cardinal weaknesses. They are the blemishes upon its musical integrity."

The opera was also criticized by the black community for its stereotypical portrayal of black life. The same argument had been made against both the novel and the play; now, Gershwin, like Heyward before him, was accused of bigotry. No less a figure than Duke Ellington lambasted Gershwin's "lampblack Negro-isms."

Despite harsh critical reception and poor box office results, two of the tunes, "It Ain't Necessarily So" and "I Got Plenty o' Nuttin'," were immediate hits, while a third song, "Summertime," went on to become one of the best-known songs of the entire Gershwin catalog. *Porgy*'s orchestral score, quite apart from the hit tunes, also achieved an afterlife on the concert stage. In 1936, Gershwin himself wrote *Catfish Row,* a five-movement suite based on the original score, which he conducted and played during concert appearances. In 1941, the composer Robert Russell Bennett wrote *A Symphonic Picture,* which became the definitive orchestral version of the opera score.

Meanwhile, not long after the dismal first run of *Porgy and Bess,* new productions began to resurface. Its first revival was in 1938, a year after Gershwin's death, when it was performed in Los Angeles, Pasadena, and San Francisco. In 1941, producer Cheryl Crawford mounted a new version that was faster paced (forty-five minutes shorter than the original), less expensive (reduced cast and orchestra), and somewhat simplified. The new version was well received by the public and critics alike ("A smoother and more melodious production," wrote the *New York Evening Mail.*). The production enjoyed an extended run in Maplewood, New Jersey, and then in New York, followed by a successful national tour. Over the next three decades, the opera was performed throughout the world. In 1959, a movie version was released, starring Sidney Poitier as Porgy and Dorothy Dandridge as Bess (with vocals overdubbed by Robert McFerrin and Adele Addison) and also featuring Sammy Davis Jr. Despite an all-star cast and the continuing popularity of several of its tunes, the movie was not successful and fell quickly into obscurity.

Had George Gershwin lived long enough, he would have been proud to see all that became of *Porgy and Bess.* The music, if not the opera itself, not only survived its initial commercial and critical failure but went on to become a perennial favorite in concert halls across the world. Alongside *Rhapsody in Blue, Concerto in F,* and as part of an unending stream of Gershwin variations and interpretations, *Porgy* has been performed and recorded by symphony orchestras, chamber ensembles, and the world's greatest solo virtuosi. He might have been just as proud, and perhaps even more excited, by *Porgy*'s emergence in 1958 as a jazz masterpiece.

‡   ‡   ‡

In early 1958, a new production of the opera was playing at New York's City Center. Among the cast was a young dancer named Frances Taylor, who was the girlfriend (later the wife) of Miles Davis. Miles said that it was the performances he attended that inspired him to make *Porgy and Bess* his next project with Gil Evans. Although this incident might have provided the impetus for Miles, at least one of the opera's tunes had already been under consideration as early as 1957, when *Miles Ahead* was being recorded. As George Avakian explained,

> THE NEXT ALBUM that we were going to do with Miles and Gil was going to be an album of exotic music from around the world, and Gil and I worked out quite a bit of repertoire. Having been the head of the international department for so many years, all kinds of records would come to me from the Columbia affiliates, so I had records from Java, from India, Africa, even China and Japan. But in the course of doing this, we also had

American music in mind—and "Summertime" was a piece that Gil liked and wanted to do.

In fact, Gil's knowledge of this music went back further still. In a 1965 *Down Beat* article on Gil's early years, George Hoefer referred to a 1941 article in *Music and Rhythm,* in which the writer mentions listening in on the Skinnay Ennis band in Chicago. They were rehearsing a Gil Evans arrangement of a *Porgy and Bess* medley.

☩   ☩   ☩

Jazz musicians had played Gershwin tunes for decades, but until the Miles Davis–Gil Evans collaboration, the music of *Porgy and Bess* had never been treated as a jazz suite. Like *Miles Ahead* before it, the *Porgy and Bess* album would feature Miles as principal soloist with a large orchestra led by Gil. This combination in itself would have delighted Gershwin. As an accomplished instrumentalist and improviser, he would have relished Miles's melodic gift and his superb playing. As a composer, but never a strong orchestrator, he would have been impressed, if not astounded, by Gil's arrangements. Better still, Gershwin might even have acknowledged that the Davis-Evans collaboration, more than any performance before it, was the most successful realization of his own vision of this music as a synthesis of African-American "folk" and Western European "serious" forms. This achievement, among many others, was immediately apparent to Gunther Schuller: "I knew the music very well, and I remember how impressed I was, and I still am, how on one hand, Gil projected a tremendous loyalty to the music—not completely changing it around but retaining that Gershwin quality, particularly in the harmonies—and at the same time giving it his own special touch. That's a balancing act which very few people could do."

Beyond his analysis of the writing, Schuller got a closer look at *Porgy and Bess* when he was hired to play French horn on all four of the album's recording dates. "To be involved with this was a great honor and a great thrill," Schuller said. "There were some surprises and revelations. The way he would bring some of the groups of instruments together—he'd mix saxophones or flugelhorns, or flutes, with French horns—all kinds of unusual ways of combining instruments, which were not traditional. This had all been done before; it just hadn't been done in jazz." In some respects, Schuller noted, the project might have been too ambitious: "Right away it became clear that this music was not only magnificent but damn difficult. There were intonation problems, because these were very sophisticated, advanced harmonies—bitonal, polytonal things—and not all the musicians knew right away how to do that." Other technical problems were encountered. Recording the music in stereo, a brand-new technology, proved to be a daunting task, with which neither the musicians nor the production team had much experience. To achieve clean separation and balance between the left and right channels, the instruments had to be physically isolated. "We were all separated into these little puddles of musicians," Schuller recalled, "rather than sitting close together, being able to hear each other—the result of which was that some balances are still not right on that recording to this day."

There were again problems resulting from Gil's conducting. "The difficulty of the music, and his inability to conduct it—or confirm in clear and quick terms what something should be—that combination created problems," Schuller remembered. "I'm sure it was clear in his mind how he wanted it to sound, but he couldn't express it verbally, the way a conductor or leader of a group really has to. Gil just wasn't geared that way."

Unlike George Avakian, producer Cal Lampley did not record the studio rehearsals, and as a result, many of the takes had to be used, flaws and all. (Schuller commended Teo Macero for performing some masterful editing on the album.) But for Schuller, the greatest disappointment was not with anything they recorded but rather with the music that Gil eliminated.

NOBODY KNOWS THIS—I don't think Miles or Gil ever talked about this to anybody—but very often, under the pressure of time, realizing that this could not be worked out in a certain passage, he would just cut things out. There were things that were cut, things that Gil had written that never got recorded—eighteen bars, sixteen bars—just cut out. There were sections of *instruments* that were cut out, because we just couldn't get it together in time, so the quick solution was, "Okay, trombones, why don't you just lay out here"—and the flutes and the French horns would play it or something. So what I'm trying to say is that what he so masterfully wrote, I would say that only about eighty percent of that got onto those records.

✛   ✛   ✛

Painful as such cuts must have been, it could not have taken long for the wounds to heal, for the losses were inconsequential compared to the recording's achievements. *Porgy and Bess* was another instant hit for the Davis-Evans partnership. According to Miles Davis biographer Jack Chambers, *Porgy and Bess* remained Miles's best-selling album until 1971.

Gil's arrangements delivered an accurate interpretation of Gershwin's music while he also broke considerable new ground of his own. He juxtaposed numerous themes and variations to form intricate, beautiful combinations; three tunes from the score come together as "Fisherman, Strawberry, and Devil Crab." As he introduced the melody line in "Bess You Is My Woman Now," he wove in Charlie Parker's "Anthropology" as its graceful, subtle counterpoint. He wrote a mournful, majestic arrangement of the spiritual "Gone, Gone, Gone," then transformed the same theme into "Gone"—the fastest, hardest-driving piece in the entire suite. (Although the original album listed him as only the arranger of "Gone," he was later credited as its composer as well.) Gil also turned again to the modal form, which Miles was beginning to favor. In his arrangement for "I Loves You Porgy," Gil scored long passages using just two sustained chords for the orchestra and, for Miles, a single scale. "He only wrote a scale for me to play. No chords," Miles told Nat Hentoff. "And in 'Summertime' there is a long space where we don't change the chord at all. It just doesn't have to be cluttered up."

The modal form is one of many vital elements Gil used to showcase the melodic genius of both the composer and the suite's principal soloist. Miles completed the picture—his sound, his performances, shining brighter than ever. Once again, the Davis-Evans partnership triumphed.

GREAT JAZZ
STANDARDS

IN FEBRUARY 1959, Gil returned to the studio to record *Great Jazz Standards,* the second album of his two-record deal with World Pacific. This album began as an extension of the concept of *New Bottle, Old Wine*—Gil's interpretations of more of the jazz classics—but it also bore several notable distinctions. On *New Bottle, Old Wine,* Gil focused almost the entire album on one soloist. On *Great Jazz Standards,* he spread the solos across almost the entire band—piano (Gil Evans), trumpet (Johnny Coles), soprano saxophone (Steve Lacy), tenor saxophone and clarinet (Budd Johnson), trombone (Dick Lieb, Jimmy Cleveland, Curtis Fuller), guitar (Ray Crawford), and drums (Elvin Jones). The repertoire was as eclectic as *New Bottle's,* but the music was more forward looking than retrospective. For example, Gil again revisited the swing era ("Davenport Blues," "Ballad of the Sad Young Men," and "Chant of the Weed"), but in this case, his evocations of the swing orchestral style and sound—which dominated the *New Bottle* album—all but disappeared. *New Bottle* was also strongly bebop-oriented, both in its repertoire and in the style of several of the arrangements. On *Standards,* Gil's only direct reference to bebop was the inclusion of "Straight, No Chaser"—and his treatment of the song was not so much a tribute to Thelonious Monk's roots as it was to his transcendence of bebop conventions. It was in this tune, in fact, that Gil stepped out front and center to declare his own point of departure.

Gil opens the album with a sparse, low-key arrangement of "Davenport Blues." Similarly, Gil's "Chaser" also begins as a respectful, relatively straightforward reading—and in fact he initially puts more emphasis on the solos than the arrangement itself; of the four solos (trumpet, soprano, trombone, and piano), three are accompanied only by the rhythm section. But then, two-thirds into the song, Gil shifts direction dramatically. Over a series of five choruses, he introduces slight variations on the melody line, embellishing each chorus with new layers of sound—some of them scored, some improvised. As the density builds with each successive chorus, the melody line is intensified and increasingly abstracted—on one hand, becoming obscured within the total sound of ensemble playing, while remaining distinctly evident in each one of its individual parts. The lines between the written and improvised, the planned and the unexpected, are blurred.

He uses a similar technique to even greater effect on the album's closing tune, his own composition, "La Nevada." Behind a solid tenor saxophone solo by veteran Budd Johnson, Gil again builds momentum by layering new textures—in this case, primarily with one- and two-note phrases extracted from the original theme line. "La Nevada" also heralds another shift in Gil's approach to composing. Only the theme itself was actually written, leaving everything else in the tune to be improvised. This is standard fare in most jazz settings but a major departure in the modus operandi of Gil Evans. From this point forward, his arrangements would start to leave more and more space for improvisation, not only for the soloists but for the ensemble players as well, and the further anyone strayed from the written notes, the better Gil liked it. Gil was deeply influenced not only by great writers but also by great improvisers. He had been fascinated by the great melodic lines improvised by Bird and Dizzy, as Max Roach said of Gil's music in the mid-1940s, and which, as many other musicians pointed out, was prevalent in so much of Gil's later work.

This in itself made Gil unique among arrangers in that, increasingly, his music, whether re-composed or original, would be determined collectively—and, better yet, spontaneously. He would rely not only on the unique sound of each of the players but also on their contributions as improvisers and interpreters. Again, the technique was Ellington's, but Gil's use of it was all his own. For even more variation in the sound of the band, Gil would then bring together musicians with vastly different *playing* styles. Steve Lacy explained: "He believed in mixing people. He would take an old trombone player and mix it with a young clarinet player and come up with a certain flavor that was unique. Then he would write a certain thing and he would tell you to *moan* when you played it. And the combination of this little instruction and what he had on paper—and the player that he *wrote* it for—was magic. It was like a personalization."

One other ingredient in the formula was the musicians' enthusiasm toward the music and toward Gil himself. Elvin Jones:

> HE WAS SUCH A GREAT leader that he could speak individually to people and give them the sense that *what they did* was the most important thing that was going on there—their part. I mean, the second alto player or the third trumpet player—he'd say, "That note that you play is essential." And from that point of view, I think he brought out of musicians the best that they had to offer, that they had to give. And it wasn't like he was playing favorites with anybody—the whole *band* was like that. You know, *poised,* waiting for Gil to give them their instruction, their cue.

Thus inspired, it was not unusual for musicians to find themselves playing better than ever—not in spite of his demands but because of them. On the other hand, it becomes obvious why it was also so important to Gil to find exactly the right people—and so fortunate when he did.

Gil's ability to inspire Miles Davis, and vice versa, was one of the great strengths of their partnership, infusing not only the style of their music but also its form and substance. In his arrangements, Gil would establish the perfect setting for Miles's voice, then Miles's playing would complete the puzzle, the crowning touch, of Gil's magnificent constructs. There was no better showcase for both of them than the jazz concerto format—no other solo voice but Miles's playing Gil Evans arrangements together with a Gil Evans orchestra. They had proven this in both of their previous Columbia projects, and now they would do it again. And just as *Porgy and Bess* had been so completely different from *Miles Ahead,* so, too, their third album would be distinctive in nearly every respect.

SKETCHES OF SPAIN

Our music must be based on the natural music of our people. It has occasionally been asserted that we have no traditions. We have, it is true, no written traditions, but in our dance and our rhythms we possess the strongest tradition than none can obliterate.

A STATEMENT SUCH AS the quote above could have been proclaimed by any African-American composer of the past century, extolling the virtue and oral history of jazz or blues. In fact, these comments were made early in the twentieth century by Spain's greatest contemporary composer, Manuel de Falla. Like numerous others before him, de Falla drew freely from the "natural" music of his homeland, and he was a champion of the hybridization of musical forms, from within Spain and beyond. He had studied at the turn of the century in Paris and was strongly influenced by Maurice Ravel and Claude Debussy (both of whom had a great affinity with Spanish music). Consequently, much of de Falla's work was a synthesis of French impressionism and traditional Spanish folk music—in particular, the gypsy flamenco music from the northern region of Andalusia.

In the music of modern America, folk themes and popular music had been successfully adopted by composers such as Aaron Copland and George Gershwin. In jazz, almost since its inception, there have been many artists with strong ties to classical music, not the least of whom was Gil Evans. His sound and writing style were influenced by both the French and Spanish impressionists and by other twentieth-century modernists. At the same time, he was deeply rooted in the world of jazz, blues, and popular music—all of which, he would insist, was *pop* music, and all of it among the truest and greatest of America's "natural music." It is ironic, then, that of all the music written and recorded by Gil Evans, the best-known, best-selling, and arguably the most accomplished of his musical hybrid projects owes less to American jazz than to Spanish flamenco.

Miles Davis traces the beginnings of the *Sketches of Spain* project to a visit in early 1959 in Los Angeles with a musician friend, Joe Montdragon, who sat him down and played a recording of Joaquín Rodrigo's *Concierto de Aranjuez.* "So I'm sitting there listening and looking at Joe," Miles wrote, "and I'm saying to myself, Goddamn, these melody lines are strong. I knew right there that I had to record it, because they just stayed in my head. When I got back to New York, I called up Gil and discussed it with him and gave him a copy of the record to see what he thought could be done with it. He liked it, too, but said we had to get some more pieces to fill out an album."

Gil was already well acquainted with Spanish music, and he approached Miles's concept with enthusiasm. His research for the project was both exhaustive and comprehensive. The result was a collection that encompassed both traditional and contemporary themes and that drew not only from Spanish music but also from Latin American music: "The Pan Piper," written by Gil, is based on a Peruvian Indian tune; "Song of Our Country," recorded for *Sketches of Spain* but not included on the album, is based on a melody by the modern Brazilian composer, Heitor Villa-Lobos. ("Song of Our Country" was added to the 1981 Miles Davis album *Directions* and, in 1997, to *Miles Evans–Gil Evans: The Complete Columbia Sessions*). Two other pieces, "Saeta" and "Solea," were written by Gil using traditional Andalusian song forms.

Rodrigo's *Concierto* is a relatively contemporary piece of music—it was completed in 1939 and premiered in Barcelona in 1940—and yet it is, by design, a highly traditional work. As Rodrigo put it, it was written with the intention of "restoring traditional values after their disappearance in Spanish music immediately after the [Spanish Civil] war." In the book *Joaquín Rodrigo and the Concierto de Aranjuez*, author Graham Wade described the music as "conservative and even provincial, rooted in Spanish themes, textures, and idioms." On the other hand, Wade pointed out, the *Concierto* also has strong links with twentieth-century music: "Its musical style, influenced above all by Manuel de Falla's example, is, in retrospect, a characteristic piece of neo-classical impressionism."

One further connection, of particular interest in the context of a jazz adaptation of this music, can be drawn: the influence of Africa on Spanish flamenco, which parallels Africa's influence on American jazz and blues. As Miles wrote, "The black Moors were over there in Spain, because Africans had conquered Spain a long time ago. In the Andalusian area you have a lot of African influence in the music, architecture, and in the whole culture, and a lot of African blood in the people. So you had a black African thing up in the feeling of the music, in the bagpipes and trumpets and drums."

The title *Concierto de Aranjuez* refers to the Royal Palace of Aranjuez, located just south of Madrid. It was built in the Middle Ages as a castle by the Knights of the Order of St. James and later became royal property under Ferdinand and Isabella. "It was my intention," wrote Rodrigo, "to evoke a certain period in the life of Aranjuez—the end of the eighteenth and beginning of the nineteenth century at the courts of Charles IV and Ferdinand VII . . . during the reign of the Bourbons—at a time when Spain was in the throes of a new enlightenment and an upsurge of national feeling."

One can easily conjure romantic images of this era—particularly in the first and third movements, which are bright, colorful, and lighthearted in spirit. "The *Aranjuez Concierto* is meant to sound like the hidden breeze that stirs the treetops in the parks," Rodrigo wrote, "and it should be only as strong as a butterfly, and as dainty as a veronica." In both the first and third movements, Rodrigo employs rhythms and folk melodies of southern Spain. However, in the middle movement, the famous Adagio (slow movement), he turns to the Andalusian gypsies' saeta form. The music is every bit as majestic, but in sharp contrast with the levity of the first movement, it becomes a sorrowful elegy. In truth, Rodrigo was in a state of mourning at the time he wrote the *Concierto.* His wife had at this time suffered a near-fatal miscarriage. In the documentary film *Joaquín Rodrigo at Ninety,* the Adagio is depicted as the composer's farewell to the child who was not to be. It was the Adagio's heartrending, powerful melody that both Miles and Gil found irresistible.

☩ ☩ ☩

The idea of developing a jazz interpretation of the Adagio was a stroke of genius. *Sketches of Spain* opens with one of the most beautiful melodies in all of Spanish music—and one that was almost completely unknown in America, even to classical audiences. The *Concierto* had been heralded since its premiere as one of Spain's great treasures, yet at the time of *Sketches of Spain* there existed just one recording of the music—the Narciso Yepes album (recorded in 1956), which Miles's friend had played for him.

To sustain the grandeur and emotional intensity of the *Concierto,* Gil balanced out the album with a richly varied repertoire, from de Falla's modernistic "Will of the Wisp" to the original tunes he wrote using traditional folk themes. Gil had admired Manuel de Falla's music since at least the 1940s. Gil's "Blues for Pablo," which he first recorded in 1956, was based on a theme from de Falla's 1915 masterpiece, the ballet *El Amor Brujo (Love, the Magician)*. Gil returned to this same score when he began working on *Sketches of Spain.* Whereas "Blues for Pablo" used just a single melodic phrase—from "Danza ritual del fuego" ("Ritual fire dance"), Gil's arrangement of "Will of the Wisp" was based more fully on de Falla's original song, "Canción del fuego fatuo" ("Song of the Will-o'-the-wisp").

The saeta is "the flamenco-like arrow of song," wrote Joaquín Rodrigo, "which bursts from the people spontaneously during the religious procession in Holy Week . . . piercing the celebrational clamor with its plaintive lament." In the *Concierto,* the saeta form is used to create a "mournful dialogue between the guitar and instrumental soloists," as Rodrigo wrote. In Gil's hand, the saeta became the perfect form for a dialogue between the trumpet of Miles Davis and the orchestra of Gil Evans. Gil used this form for virtually the entire repertoire of *Sketches.* Like the blues, the saeta offers virtually unlimited possibilities for melodic improvisation—an ideal vehicle for the leading jazz soloist of his time—and Miles responded with some of his most inventive and expressive solos on record. Gil elicited the full impact of the form in his tune "Saeta," establishing the street procession—his counterpoint to Miles's voice—with little more than a snare drum and other percussion instruments and a brass fanfare. As always, Gil's orchestral settings were matched superbly to the soloist; on *Sketches,* his writing runs from the spectacular and ornate to the very sparsest of embellishments.

Along with its passionate lyricism, flamenco music is characterized by its dramatic rhythms. One need only hear the clicking heels of a dancer—or as Gil would demonstrate in the album's opening bars, the sound of castanets—to be instantly transported. Gil went to great lengths in his research to develop the rhythmical elements of the project, calling upon his friend Elvin Jones for just that purpose. "Leading up to that recording, we were together nearly a year," Elvin recalled. "He was showing me all the music that he wanted to do, and he wanted me to write part of a section. It was like a march, a street beat, so he wanted me to orchestrate that for him. And we talked about using timpani, we talked about using gongs, castanets, and band cymbals, marching band cymbals. He had studios that he'd rent, and I'd arrange to use timpani and things like that, and we'd fool around for three or four hours, just kicking ideas around." Elvin was then enlisted as principal percussionist for the recording sessions, where he would play alongside Miles's drummer Jimmy Cobb.

The official credits for *Sketches of Spain* indicate just three recording dates, but in fact the project was much longer and more involved. Album producer Teo Macero told me there were at least six sessions for the *Concierto* alone—and these were just with the orchestra: "The whole band was there for six sessions without Miles. It was like a giant rehearsal—three-hour, four-hour sessions, just going over the music. And finally Miles came in, and it all came together. With Gil, he was such a stickler for corrections, it took forever sometimes. And in those days, when you went past three sessions to do an album it was almost unheard of."

It is obvious, perhaps, why Columbia management did not want to publicize the full extent of the production; if *Sketches of Spain* was seen as the new precedent for jazz albums, how many bandleaders would try to expand their own sessions? On the other hand, in a 1987 interview in *Musician* magazine, Macero gave full credit to Columbia's president for supporting *Sketches* wholeheartedly. "It was a budget problem, but the president of Columbia at the time, Goddard Lieberson, a musician himself, asked, 'Is it going to be a good album?' I said, 'When it's finished it's going to be a fantastic album.' So he said, 'So stay with it, even if it takes you twenty sessions.'" In the end, Macero said in that interview, it took fifteen sessions. These "excesses" were primarily the result of Gil's relentless attention to every detail of the music, something that Elvin Jones remembered with great admiration: "Some days, all he wanted was for the orchestra to play maybe two or three different chords, to correct the voicings—and he worked his way through the entire composition like that. He was that meticulous. And it was perfect. If you listen to it now, you can see how that kind of attention to detail makes sense. He was a great artist; it's as simple as that. And he took the time to do things properly."

Many of Gil's charts were designed to provide an open, expansive backdrop for Miles's solos. While these backgrounds are often sparse, they are never simplistic and certainly not easy to play. Typically, the score would call for one of his famous ensemble effects—endlessly sustained notes or, at the other extreme, a sequence of elaborate phrases played at breakneck speed.

As Miles pointed out in his autobiography, Gil as usual showed no mercy for the musicians:

> GIL HAD LIKE MICRO-BEATS in the score. It was so tight that one of the trumpet players—a favorite white trumpet player of mine named Bernie Glow—turned all red while he was trying to play this Mexican melody. He told me later that was the hardest passage that he ever had to play. I told Gil to write another arrangement, but he didn't feel that anything was wrong with this one and couldn't understand why Bernie was finding it so hard to play this arrangement.

Most of the players Gil hired, including Glow, would eventually become accustomed to being asked to deliver the impossible. That was both the challenge and the reward of working with Gil, and they knew that more often than not they would be delighted, if not astounded, by the results. Said Elvin, "Sometimes there were 25 or 30 musicians in the orchestra, with strings and harp and a percussion section, and they were very enthusiastic about responding to Gil's requests—because they had so much respect for him. I know *I* did. I had tremendous respect for him, always." Not everyone shared Elvin's admiration of Gil's unique way of doing things, nor were all musicians as successful with his music. New York session players are among the most accomplished in the business ("Most of these guys could be half asleep and play Stravinsky's *Rite of Spring*," Elvin laughed), but the issue here was not the notes on the page, but rather how Gil wanted them played. Once again, part of the difficulty was Gil's conducting style. "Either you know him," said Elvin, "and you know what he means when he gestures, or you don't." The solution, wrote Miles, was to make sure you got the right players:

> IN THE BEGINNING, we had the wrong trumpet players because we had those who were classically trained. But that was a problem. We had to tell them *not* to play exactly like it was on the score. They started looking at us—at Gil, mostly—like we were crazy. They couldn't improvise their way out of a paper bag. So they were looking at Gil like, "What the fuck is he talking about? This is a concerto, right?" So they know we must be crazy talking about "Play what *isn't* there."

Miles, of course, had challenges of his own. As in their previous projects, he left most of the planning and preparations to Gil and kept his involvement to a minimum until they actually began recording. It was only then, in the studio, that he came face to face with the difficulty of these new arrangements. "I always manage to try something I can't do," he joked to Nat Hentoff. "What I found I had to do in *Sketches of Spain*," Miles wrote later, "was to read the score a couple of times, listen to it a couple of times more, then play it. For me, it was just about knowing what it is, and then I could play it."

In the case of the *Concierto,* Miles had the luxury of being able to listen to several complete takes that had been recorded with the orchestra. Lead trumpeter Louis Mucci recalled that Miles also played through the piece with the orchestra before recording it. "Miles hadn't played these pieces with an orchestra; he'd just talked about them with Gil, so while we were rehearsing the pieces, he kept playing. One of the trumpet players said, 'Hey Miles, how about when we do the master? You're not going to have any *chops* left, you should cool it.' He said, 'Well, I haven't played them with anybody. I've got to get used to my entrances, get used to playing with the orchestra.'" Taking full advantage of Miles's prestige and status at Columbia, and the consistent profitability of his records, Gil and Miles used all the studio time they needed in order to perfect the music before them—something that Gil on his own, and few if any other jazz artists, could never have done. Elvin Jones:

THAT'S PROBABLY ONE of the greatest albums Miles ever made. At one point during the recording, he had everybody in the whole studio—including the engineers, the janitors, and everyone else—they were just awed. And it was because he rose above himself, in the solo parts that he played. It was one of his greatest performances, I think, and it was the way Gil had cushioned the arrangement *around his sound* that made that possible. I thought it was magnificent.

✦   ✦   ✦

One of the great achievements of *Sketches of Spain,* and to a lesser extent *Miles Ahead* and *Porgy and Bess,* is its blending of jazz and classical music. Gil and Miles were not the first to combine different idioms within a jazz setting, classical or otherwise, but *Sketches* is among the most effective musical hybrids and by far the most popular. *Sketches of Spain* became another huge and instant hit—the third in a row for Miles and Gil. It won them a 1960 Grammy award ("Best Jazz Composition of More Than Five Minutes"), the first award either of them received. *Sketches of Spain* remained one of Miles's top-selling records, second only to *Porgy and Bess,* for nearly ten years.

"Well, the melody in *Concierto de Aranjuez* is beautiful," Gil told *Coda* magazine in 1985. "I think the main thing about that album is that beautiful song. The other songs are interesting, and I think the music filled some kind of an emptiness in the popular repertoire, you know? . . . Everybody needed that tune apparently in their library." On the other hand, there were many disapproving purists, both in jazz and in classical camps, who saw *Sketches of Spain* not so much as a musical hybrid as a mongrel. Gil was told, in fact, that Joaquín Rodrigo himself was "very angry" at him for his arrangement. "Teo Macero told me that [Rodrigo's lawyer] wrote to him and lodged a complaint, wrote to Columbia from Madrid. So Columbia, being what they are, a conglomerate and arrogant and all that, they didn't even answer his letter. They sent him a check, his first royalty check for $40,000 and they never heard from that lawyer again."

Classical music had been used in jazz, and vice versa, as early as the 1920s, but in the 1950s there was renewed interest in the form among jazz musicians. Much of this music, its critics argued, was too intellectual, too formalized for "real" jazz. On the other hand, many advances came as a result of these jazz-classical music experiments, both from within and apart from the formalized "third-stream" movement spearheaded by Gunther Schuller. "All those experimentations were a very important part of the whole development and the increased sophistication of jazz," Schuller maintained. "It was almost the new form of music that everyone was pursuing. Dave Brubeck's quartet—a lot of what they were playing is unthinkable without the influence of classical music. Gerry Mulligan, when he took away the piano and the drums, and it was all counterpoint and polyphony—that came out of a study of Bach's music. All the fugues that John Lewis wrote, and the Modern Jazz Quartet played—I mean, there was so *much* like that going on."

By Schuller's definition, third stream is an equal balancing of classical and jazz ("You didn't lean toward one side or the other, in your work or your attitude"). Gil Evans was never associated with the third-stream concept, even though much of his work, especially with Miles on the Columbia projects, offered a picture-perfect example of third stream's elusive "symbiosis" of the two forms.

> I NEVER TALKED TO GIL about that specific subject, but I think because he grew up in jazz and continued to work as a jazz musician, he thought of himself more on *that* side. I think he drew from both realms. In terms of color and timbre, certainly the *major* influence was Duke Ellington. But Gil's *sound* world is a very special one. There are certain soft, velvety, satiny sounds which he preferred. That was his sound palette, just like certain painters paint with only certain colors. He loved that quiet, darker color—and he would take those colors from wherever he found them. He could find them in jazz, in some cases, and he could find them in classical music. In that sense, I think he *was* a third-stream sensibility, because he took from both areas, I would say almost in an equal amount.

Despite the enormous success of *Sketches of Spain,* neither Gil nor Miles showed any interest in returning to the classical idiom. Working together and separately, Gil and Miles would continue to pursue the synthesis of diverse musical forms—indeed this would be a defining element for both of them—but classical music would no longer figure in their plans.

OUT OF THE COOL

IN THE FIRST YEAR of the new decade, Gil turned another corner with his music. He had started 1960 in very fine style indeed, with the completion of *Sketches of Spain.* Now he would end the year with a new record of his own—one in which he redefined his concept of what a jazz album could be. After finishing *Sketches* in March, Gil and Miles went their separate ways. Only half-jokingly, Miles wrote that he needed a break from Gil. "After we finished working on *Sketches of Spain,* I didn't have nothing inside me. I was drained of all emotion and I didn't want to hear that music after I got through playing all that hard shit. Gil said, 'Let's go listen to the tapes.' I said, '*You* go listen to the tapes, because I don't want to hear it.'" Gil wanted a change, too, though, and when it came, it was for him the high point of the year.

It was a club date, at the Jazz Gallery in Greenwich Village. For six nights a week over six consecutive weeks, he got to play piano, perform his own music, and lead his own group in front of a live audience. It was his first engagement as a bandleader since his Rendezvous Ballroom days in Balboa Beach, California, back in 1937, more than twenty years earlier. The gig put Gil exactly where he wanted to be—performing music, not just writing, and improvising, not just following charts. Better still, it took place just before he was to begin recording his new album in November for Impulse Records. That meant that for the first time, he was be able to "workshop" his music—developing the tunes, playing them with the same group—before going into the studio.

The resulting cohesiveness of the music is apparent in the opening bars of the new record. In a new arrangement of his modal opus "La Nevada," Gil starts out with a piano introduction, then he is joined by the other players, one by one. Once everyone has settled in, some two and a half minutes later, the theme is stated by the full ensemble in several repeating choruses. This is followed by no less than five extended solos (trumpet, bass trombone, tenor, bass, and guitar). Behind each solo, Gil sustains the backgrounds using fragments of the theme, as he had in his previous version of the tune, but here they are played by various and ever-changing combinations of instruments. Remarkably, "La Nevada" was recorded in a single take.

"La Nevada," and, later on the album, Horace Silver's tune "Sister Sadie" (included in the 1996 re-issue) are among the hardest-driving jazz arrangements and performances Gil recorded, yet these are sharply contrasted by each one of the remaining selections. "La Nevada" is followed by an almost static "Where Flamingos Fly," featuring a beautiful, haunting melody and the most elegant of any Gil Evans arrangements on record. In "Bilbao Song," Gil's arrangement transforms the comic irony of the Kurt Weill melody into a melancholy ballad—tense and sullen—and then gradually it softens, with a superb Ron Carter bass solo leading into a sultry, gently swinging conclusion by the ensemble, all of it played with great sensitivity. He approaches "Stratusphunk" with great respect for George Russell's blues motif but also his sense of humor. In "Sunken Treasure," another original composition, the mood again turns dark and somber; the arrangement is the most understated, yet most powerful, in an album filled to the brim with dramatic tension.

In the voicings for this album's music, Gil created an orchestral sound unlike anything he had written before. In the high-register ensemble parts, for example, he often emphasized reeds and woodwinds instead of trumpets. He then voiced the brass instruments much more prominently in the low register, using two trombones and bass trombone alongside the tuba, which added further depth and richness. He extended his color range using piccolo, bassoon, and a variety of percussion instruments—including maracas, tambourine, and timpani.

+   +   +

Out of the Cool frames a decade of innovative Gil Evans music. Like *Birth of the Cool,* this album signaled the emergence of a new direction. Once again, the changes came not through an outright rejection of things past but rather through their evolution and their integration with new ideas. Likewise, the new work was a blend of improvisation and composition, but where *Birth of the Cool* focused on the role of writers and arrangers in jazz, Gil now turned his attention to the music's interpreters.

In conceptual terms, *Out of the Cool* is another jazz suite—closer to *Miles Ahead,* for example, than to *New Bottle, Old Wine.* This time, however, the spotlight is not on Miles Davis, or any other soloist, but on the music as a single, unified entity. The result is an album that bears the unmistakable Gil Evans imprint but is different from his previous work in virtually every respect. Each of these tunes is brilliantly arranged and orchestrated, yet on every one of them, his charts provide maximum leeway for the improvisers. Gil, in fact, joins in with them at every opportunity. Even though he does not play any solos at all, his piano sets the tone and atmosphere of every piece. And for all its spontaneity, the album feels more like a theatrical revue than a jazz set—great playing, to be sure, but also great comedy, tragedy, suspense, mystery, romance, and nonstop action. *Out of the Cool* did not signal a new approach to music—he had always drawn from a diverse range of sources—so much as it reaffirmed his commitment to change and growth, exploration and experimentation. After all, this was a new decade, and there were new sounds on the horizon. Welcome, said Gil Evans, in his inimitable way: Welcome to the 1960s.

✦   ✦   ✦

Changing times indeed. Exhilarating as they were in some circles (mostly small and esoteric ones), on the broader scene the new developments in jazz were not very positive. With the continuing growth of rock and roll, it was getting tougher than ever to make a living in jazz. At the same time, jazz was becoming intense, technically complex—and for many, altogether too serious. In the late 1950s and early 1960s, the avant garde music of Ornette Coleman, Cecil Taylor, Albert Ayler, and other radical young artists created new audiences with its wild intensity and abstract forms, but these same qualities alienated others and frightened them away. Known variously as New Wave, Free Jazz, or simply the New Thing, it reinvigorated jazz as a creative force, but it also sparked considerable animosity among musicians.

For radio programmers who tended to prefer jazz that was at least recognizable as such, the multiple personalities of modern jazz were disconcerting, if not intolerable. As program formats generally became more conservatively defined, and as airtime for jazz shows was reduced, audience interest waned and record sales sagged further. Increased promotion might have stimulated sales, but that brought the risk of even lower profits. And so the downward spiral continued. Fewer jazz records would be made, and less money would be spent to promote them. Popular working bands were able to sustain their audiences through club and concert appearances, but many outlets were also reducing their jazz bookings. The biggest stars found themselves playing in smaller venues. For growing numbers of musicians, the brightest ray of hope came from Europe, where jazz was thriving both as popular entertainment and as a much respected art form.

Gunther Schuller, an early exponent of avant garde, attributed its negative effects primarily to lesser talents who mistook free improvisation for mere anarchy. "This almost destroyed jazz, because it was an avant gardism which said, 'Well, anything goes—no more harmony, no more melody, no more rhythm—you know, just whatever comes into your head. If you want to screech, you screech; if you want to fart, you fart,' or whatever. And that was not *Ornette's* lesson at all. I mean, Ornette, with all of his modernity and fragmented playing, at heart he's an old *blues* musician."

With rock and roll's domination of the music industry on one hand and the disruptive effects of avant garde on the other, there were also fewer prospects for other jazz forms—particularly for iconoclasts such as Gil Evans. "Between those two things," said Schuller, "the exciting and new things that were happening in jazz just didn't make it. And Gil got caught in that. There just was no commercial interest, nor were there large enough supportive audiences for it to be able to continue in the fullness that one could have expected." Like many other writers and arrangers, Gil did not have a regular working band. Given the number and the caliber of musicians required for his music, the costs of operating such an ensemble were simply prohibitive. Gil's records were made by small labels that lacked the resources to promote or distribute them widely. His music, while not wildly experimental, was nevertheless hard to categorize; thus it got limited radio exposure.

Another financial disadvantage was Gil's predisposition toward working with other people's music rather than his own compositions. Composers earn royalties for their music based on record sales and airplay. Arrangers, on the other hand, work for a fixed fee, usually on a flat per-session or per-arrangement basis. They do not earn any royalties for their work, even if their arrangement turned an otherwise mediocre tune into a commercial hit. Gil's compositions were often the highlight of his recordings, but he was even slower at composing than he was at arranging, and his output remained limited. Moreover, try as he might, Gil seemed incapable of resisting the challenge of a great new song. This was, after all, his first love—how he started in music, how he learned his craft. Arranging other people's music continued to inspire much of his best work. In one of the few sensible moves that Gil made, financially speaking, he started a publishing company, Gillian Music, which was co-owned, and presumably co-operated, with his wife Lillian. Music royalties are paid both to composers and to their publishers; thus self-published artists have the potential to double their earnings. (Gil may have been encouraged to start Gillian Music by Miles Davis, who had published his own work for several years.) Between 1957 and 1960, the company had accumulated only a short list of tunes under its banner—"Blues for Pablo," "Jambangle," "Theme" ("La Nevada"), and his three original titles from *Sketches of Spain*: "Solea," "Saeta," and "The Pan Piper"—but ownership of these publishing rights would later prove to have substantial and far-reaching value.

Finally, there is the matter of artist earnings derived from record sales. In a typical recording contract, the artist—not the record company—is responsible for the cost of recording and production. Normally, artists are paid an advance upon signing, but do not receive any further payments until production costs have been recovered. Gil rarely made any money beyond his advances. (When I met him in 1973, for example, he told me that for some of his work dating back to the 1950s, he was still getting invoices, not checks.)

In the early 1960s, most jazz musicians and writers, and virtually all jazz arrangers, were struggling with the same financial problems. Yet surely, one might expect that Gil Evans would have fared better than most. He worked with Miles Davis, after all—the most famous jazz artist in the world. He had just made three consecutive best-selling albums with Miles, including a recent Grammy award winner. What might it have taken to put this visibility to advantage, perhaps to assemble an exciting band and mount a successful tour? The right manager? Publicist? Booking agent? Gil had none of these. Nor did he have the ambition or desire to get out and hustle. Instead, he went in the opposite direction—withdrawing from the marketplace instead of pursuing it. Rather than look for more work, he chose to do less. "I only work for Miles and myself," he told *Down Beat*'s Marc Crawford.

In the midst of this, Gil's personal life was also in turmoil. In 1961, his eleven-year marriage came to an end. Neither Gil nor Lillian spoke publicly about their divorce, but from Lillian's standpoint, it seems obvious that their marital problems must have been aggravated, if not caused, by Gil's financial woes. Contrary to what many people assumed, Gil did not earn much money at all—not even when he and Miles were at the height of their popularity and were producing very successful records. "Well," Gil would say with a shrug, "I'm a living example of the fact that fame and fortune are not synonymous." Gil may have been resigned to the harsh realities of the arranger's life ("a chump's life," as he put it), but the lack of reward was harder for Lillian to accept, especially considering the effort that Gil put into his work. John La-Porta recalled an incident some years earlier, at a party at the Evans's apartment, that illustrated Lillian's frustration. "She just *wasted* him," said LaPorta. "She said, 'You know, you get *paean's* wages for your writing.' Of course, it didn't stop him. He was a free soul that way—he just laughed it off—but it was true. He spent hours writing maybe two measures of music, and for the amount of time he'd put in, he'd be getting very little money for it."

As part of his divorce settlement, Gil signed over his share of Gillian Music, the publishing company that he and Lillian had formed together. None of the tunes registered by Gillian had yet earned much of a profit, but Gillian Music also owned the publishing rights for the tunes Gil had written for, or cowritten with, Miles Davis. At the time of the divorce, these tunes had already started earning royalty income, and they would continue to do so for decades to come. Whatever money Lillian might have spent during the time she supported Gil would be repaid many times over. In *Milestones,* Jack Chambers wrote that in 1983 Gil told writer Richard Cook that to that point, Lillian had received almost a quarter million dollars from the *Sketches of Spain* royalties alone. Technically speaking, Gillian Music should have kept only the publisher's share of these earnings and should have paid an equal amount, the artist's share, to Gil. However, Gil never pursued the matter with Lillian, and it was not rectified until several years after Gil's death, when his total body of work was amalgamated by the Evans family under a new publishing company, Bopper Spock Suns.

LIVE AT
CARNEGIE HALL

GIL'S OUTPUT IN 1961 consisted of a single concert appearance with Miles (albeit a major one), and then, finally, he started production on a new record. If Gil had been excited about his club appearance a year earlier, he must have been ecstatic about his concert debut. Here he was, leading a twenty-one-piece orchestra, accompanying Miles Davis, his favorite soloist and musical partner, and performing before a sold-out audience at New York's fabled Carnegie Hall. It was Miles's first concert here, too, and the first time the great Davis-Evans collaborations were performed before a live audience.

The concert, on May 19, 1961, showed Miles in top form, playing with tremendous force and authority, both with Gil's orchestra and with his own quintet. Gil's contributions included an orchestrated introduction to Miles's "So What," which opened the concert, and one new arrangement, the ballad "Spring Is Here." Following these tunes, Miles played two tunes with his quintet, after which Gil returned to the stage to close the set with the full orchestra. They performed excerpts from the *Miles Ahead* suite ("The Meaning of the Blues," "Lament," and "New Rhumba"). After the intermission, Miles played four tunes with the quintet, then Gil and the orchestra rejoined him for the concert's grand finale—a full reading of the Adagio from the *Concierto de Aranjuez*. The initial 1962 album, *Miles Davis at Carnegie Hall*, did not include the *Concierto*; this track was released, along with the remaining three quintet tunes, on a 1987 album, *More Music from the Legendary Carnegie Hall Concert*. In 1998, a remastered two-CD set presented the entire concert in its actual sequence. This full-length concert edition casts a much more favorable light on Gil's orchestra than the first releases, both in its performances and also its contributions in elevating the event to great proportions. In opening the concert, Gil set the tone for Miles's spectacular entrance; he closed the first half of the concert with a blazing hot "New Rhumba"—then he returned to close the evening with the great opus that everyone had surely hoped they would hear. The concert and the recordings are also historic in that they represent their first—and last—live performance of these works by Miles and Gil together.

INTO THE HOT

GIL'S NEXT PROJECT, his second Impulse album, was not quite so triumphant. *Into the Hot* is in fact a remarkable album, filled with excellent writing, arrangements, and performances, but it is a "Gil Evans" album in name only. To fulfill his contract with Impulse, Gil invited two writers into the studio to record under Gil's "aegis" (as Nat Hentoff's liner notes put it). One of these was John Carisi, and the other was the controversial avant garde pianist, Cecil Taylor.

Doing the Impulse record seemed to Gil like a step backward—nothing more than a contractual obligation, which he could not get excited about. Gil had recorded *Out of the Cool* with producer Creed Taylor, but Taylor left Impulse shortly afterward to join Verve Records. Gil wanted to continue their relationship, as did Taylor, and Verve had already signed Gil to a multi-album contract. It is likely, therefore, that Gil just wanted to get it over with. According to John Carisi, Impulse had already done the artwork and photography for the new album's cover, and Gil somehow managed to convince the Impulse team that they could release an album featuring Gil as its A&R (artist and repertoire) director, rather than as an arranger. John Carisi explained:

> HE WAS LIKE AN ENTREPRENEUR. He got hold of Cecil Taylor and me—
> and to this day I have never met Cecil Taylor, we didn't go to each other's
> sessions—and he got up his own group, I got up my own group, and Gil

acted as an A&R man. He sat there, in the booth, and asked for certain things to be played over again—he directs a little bit from there, and you'd hear his voice a little bit, 'Play that last passage again and we'll splice it in'—that's what he had to do with it. He didn't write one note. If you read the liner notes, you see that everything was done by other people.

Gil had long respected John Carisi's writing and probably welcomed the opportunity to offer him a record date that he might not have gotten otherwise. His choice of Cecil Taylor, however, was something else altogether. As he told Nat Hentoff for Hentoff's liner-notes essay, "All I can say about Cecil as a pianist and composer is that when I hear him I burst out laughing in pleasure, because his work is so full of things. There's so *much* going on and he is such a wizard that whatever he does bristles with all kinds of possibilities." Taylor's group for this recording also bristled with talent, including drummer Sunny Murray, trombonist Roswell Rudd, and another revolutionary-in-waiting, tenor saxophonist Archie Shepp.

Even if Gil did not actually contribute to any of the music on *Into the Hot,* his choice of Cecil Taylor for this album is in itself a powerful statement about this New Thing in jazz that was so upsetting to many others around him. One of the most vocal detractors of this movement, in fact, was Miles Davis, who was critical not only of Taylor and Shepp but also of Eric Dolphy, Ornette Coleman, Don Cherry, and even John Coltrane. "I didn't personally like a lot of the things that were happening," Miles wrote, "not even the things that Trane was doing; I preferred what he had done in my band, maybe during the first two or three years."

While Miles resisted free jazz, however, Gil embraced it. While Miles ridiculed many of the most radical players, Gil sought them out. All this came at a time when both men were at a crossroads in their careers. Miles's most popular band was no longer together—by now, Cannonball Adderley, Bill Evans, and John Coltrane each had their own groups—and Miles still had not found a satisfactory combination of new players. Gil, in the meantime, was steeped in his writing, preparing for his new project at Verve. Free jazz was one of many new elements he was exploring. Despite these differences and divergent interests, however, their friendship was unaffected, and Miles and Gil continued to work as partners and collaborators.

QUIET NIGHTS

TO THE GREAT DELIGHT of Columbia Records, in early 1962 Miles announced that he was ready to return to the studio and, better still, that the
project would be a new collaboration with Gil Evans. The eventual outcome
of this endeavor was the album *Quiet Nights,* which featured jazz-infused traditional and contemporary Brazilian music. Latin jazz, in general, and bossa
nova dance music in particular, had become hugely popular in America. The
biggest bossa nova hit was "Girl from Ipanema," from the 1962 album
Getz/Gilberto, which featured music written by Brazilian composer Antonio
Carlos Jobim and performed by Stan Getz and Jobim's wife, vocalist Astrud
Gilberto. (The album was one of many successful albums made by Verve
Records' hottest new producer, Creed Taylor.)

Columbia's management had every reason to be optimistic about *Quiet
Nights.* Not only would it mark the long-awaited return of the Davis-Evans
combination, but it also held the potential to tap into the pop mainstream
market by way of the trendy Latin jazz sound.

Six tunes were recorded for this album in three sessions, in July, August,
and November. Miles's best performance is on the ballad "Summer Night,"
taken from one of his quintet sessions, but Gil's work stands out on several
of the album's tunes. Two of the tracks—"Song #1" and "Song #2," co-writ-
ten by Miles and Gil—are as grand and colorful as any of Gil's best large-
scale orchestral arrangements. "Once Upon a Summertime," constructed
from two takes held together by a painfully obvious tape splice, nevertheless

salvages some exquisite Gil Evans backgrounds, featuring sustained flute and reed harmonies. On "Wait Till You See Her," Gil extrapolates the opening theme from Béla Bartók's 1943 *Concerto for Orchestra*, the same one he used in his 1956 arrangement of "I'm a Fool to Want You" for Helen Merrill. Here, he brings the Bartók melody into a Latin American context using a simple, highly effective blend of rhythms and percussion instruments.

Neither Gil nor Miles was happy with the results. "I didn't really feel nothing about the music we did on this album," Miles wrote in his autobiography. "I knew I wasn't into what we were doing like I had been in the past. The last thing Gil and I did on *Quiet Nights* in November just wasn't happening. It seemed like we had spent all our energy for nothing and so we just let it go. Columbia brought it out anyway to make some money, but if it had been left up to me and Gil, we would have just let it stay in the tape vaults." Almost a year later, when it was apparent that Miles had lost interest in the project, Columbia released *Quiet Nights*. Another tune ("Summer Night") was taken from a separate recording session Miles had done earlier that year, bringing the total musical content to seven tunes and just twenty-seven minutes.

Instead of adding to the partners' recent string of successes, the new album brought their winning streak to an abrupt and unceremonious end. Although it sold well initially, *Quiet Nights* was poorly received by the critics— and roundly condemned by Miles and Gil themselves. "They should never have released it," Gil told Leonard Feather in *Down Beat*, "It was just half an album. But I guess they had to." Miles's reaction was not so mild. He was so furious with Columbia, and especially with producer Teo Macero, that he refused to work with Macero again for almost four years.

╪   ╪   ╪

At the same time Miles was working on *Quiet Nights,* he also agreed to contribute a tune to a Christmas jazz album. This unusual session brought Miles together for the first time with saxophonist Wayne Shorter. Miles had commissioned jazz vocalist Bob Dorough to write the song and hired Gil to write the arrangement. The result, "Blue Xmas," was recorded just a few days after the second *Quiet Nights* session. In a follow-up session two days later, they also recorded two of Dorough's other songs—"Nothing Like You" and "Devil May Care"—which Gil also arranged. "I heard [Gil's] music before I met him," Shorter told me. "I used to *see* him, sometimes, at Birdland, with Miles, when Miles was down from the bandstand, in the bar area. I used to see this tall, white-haired man once in a while, and he and Miles would go off together, leave the premises, and I had the feeling that they were real buddies."

Wayne soon came to regard Gil as a close friend and an important influence. "Just in general, the light bulb went on when I first met him and first heard him. And I went back to hearing what he did with Claude Thornhill's band and the whole *chandelier* went on. The same thing happened with Miles, because Miles used to say he acquired more and learned more by being with Gil than any other person. And Gil didn't have to be a *player* for Miles to receive that—Gil just had to be born as he was." Wayne remembered many great conversations with Gil—about art, philosophy, life in general—that often stretched long into the evening without touching on music at all.

> WHEN WE GOT INTO the musical area, we talked about writing—writing music—as a very solo-like situation. We talked about being left *alone*, leaving people *alone*, having space and artistic license. And we talked about manipulation, like when you're with record companies—someone trying to put their input or their "producer-ship" into a recording, to make it go the way some kind of historic formula seems to have proven to them how something should go.
>
> After he did *Sketches of Spain* and all those things—*Porgy and Bess, Miles Ahead*—that was the talk of the town, meaning the metropolitan area of whoever was hip. Musicians thought he could write his ticket—to Hollywood, films, the whole thing. The phone would be ringing off the cradle, you know? When *I* met him, he was doing an industrial film.

Gil told Wayne he had done a number of industrial and documentary scores and that he preferred doing these smaller projects over anything that might stir up unpleasant memories:

> GIL DIDN'T WANT THAT. He had experienced that whole political situation when he was one of the writers in the Bob Hope radio show. And I remember him saying, "I'll never do that again." That's how Gil saw it— "I'll never do *that* again." And anything that looked like, smelled like, felt like that kind of situation approaching him, I think he maybe put a feeler out, a little radar out there, and then just made like a quick confirmation—Hey, this is the same handcuffs, the same political thing. The

lunches, the dinners, the "I'll trade you this for that" and all that. I think he kind of stayed away from that, because he knew that the music would not be his own. He would be subject to rinky dinky "Arrange this, Gil"— "Hey Gil, can you do this by five o'clock?" He didn't want that.

Gil continued to work occasionally in film, but only a few of these projects are identified among his records. In 1967, he wrote the score to an independent Danish feature, *The Whistle,* and two other films, *Parachute to Paradise* and *Fragments.* None of these titles was distributed widely, and all have long remained out of print. In the early 1970s, he scored another little-known film, *The Sea in Your Future,* but he was not active in film again until well into the 1980s.

✦   ✦   ✦

One night in February 1963, Gil went to Birdland to see John Coltrane. At the club, a friend introduced him to a young woman named Anita Cooper. "Actually he had a date with a French girl, a French jazz writer," Anita told me. "I can't remember the details, but somehow he ended up with me." At that time, Anita had just earned her master's degree and was preparing for a career in social work. She was not involved in music professionally, but she was a passionate and dedicated jazz lover:

> I WAS A FAN. I heard Thelonious Monk and Bud Powell when I was eleven or twelve, and it blew me away. I used to go while I was still in high school. I would come over from Staten Island, where I grew up, and go to Birdland and all the clubs, so I kind of knew the musicians. They treated me as this little girl who came around to listen, and they were absolutely heaven. I knew Miles, really, before I knew Gil, just from going to hear the music.

Gil and Anita spent that first evening together at the club ("We stayed right to the very end of Coltrane"). After another encounter shortly afterward, the relationship blossomed. "Miles used to call him the Duke of Windsor. That's the Gil that I fell in love with, really—that guy in those suits and that whole Duke of Windsor look."

Four months after they met, they were living together at Anita's apartment in Greenwich Village. Gil might have *looked* like the Duke of Windsor, but as

Anita soon discovered, the life he led was far from privileged. "He moved in with *me*. I was taking care of *him*. He couldn't pay his rent, so he had to move out of his apartment and into my apartment. When he moved in, I was doing post-graduate work. I was into doctoral studies then, and I had a grant. That's how I helped support him, with my post-graduate grant." At first, Anita thought Gil must be one of those absent-minded, mad-genius types who could not be bothered with trivial matters like balancing a checkbook.

I DIDN'T REALLY BELIEVE IT. After all, I had all his records, so anybody whose records could get out to my little burg had to be rich in *addition* to famous. I just thought he was wildly eccentric. I didn't think anybody could be that unconnected from money, you know? But it was such an incredible exchange. I mean, so romantic. I was so into the music. I just lived and breathed jazz, and here was this person whose music I'd had even before I moved to the Village. And being this third-generation, civil-servant kind of a "Do-your-education-and-watch-out-for-your-pension" person, it was *wonderful* for me.

There was no royal palace in this picture, but it was a fairy tale romance nonetheless. For Anita, there were no regrets—and no illusions:

BEFORE WE WERE MARRIED, I remember a call coming from the director of [the film] *The Pawnbroker* [Sidney Lumet]. Gil had some other music in his head that he was working on—not that he was given a dollar to do it, but it was something God gave him to work on, and he was. And he said, "No, I can't take this thing"—an offer for a Hollywood score. He said, "But there's this great young man around town named Quincy Jones—I think you should give *him* a call. I think he's very talented and he'll go far and he'll be great." I don't know if Quincy knows to this day that Gil recommended him for this first thing that made him famous.

That was my first experience of how it was going to be—you know, the first little clue you get. Wow, I couldn't understand how he could turn that down. On an intellectual level, I could always honor it—you know, the cosmic work is so different from what the economic requirements are. Stuff was being sent into his head to work on, and it had nothing to *do* with an assignment—it's like an assignment from God, you know? He was always busy on those.

TIME OF
THE BARRACUDA

ALMOST TWO YEARS AFTER signing with Verve and ten months after recording anything at all, Gil finally went into the studio to start his new album. In September 1963, he recorded two original tunes, "Flute Song" and "El Toreador," in two separate sessions. But Gil had no sooner started his album than he suddenly put the project on hold. Miles called, asking him to join him in California. In Los Angeles, the British actor Laurence Harvey was preparing to star in a play, *Time of the Barracuda*. He invited Miles to develop an original score for the production, and in turn Miles wanted to enlist Gil. Miles booked two suites, each with its own piano, at the Chateau Marmont in West Hollywood.

Anita went with Gil; this was their first trip together. Just weeks before, she had taken Gil in when he could not pay his rent. Now she found herself staying with him at one of the most glamorous hotels in Hollywood. The visit was marred, however, by their first exposure to a community that, unlike Greenwich Village, was less than tolerant of mixed couples. "Yeah, all that stuff they say about the L.A. police is true," said Anita, an African American. "Inevitably, I'd rent a car, look in the rearview mirror, and there'd be a police car tailing us. It was a rich neighborhood, and I guess they had extra police cars or had nothing to do or something. So I guess that's why we never considered moving to California."

Gil told of another incident that happened one night outside the It Club, where Miles was playing. Gil and Anita went with Laurence Harvey and Miles's lawyer, Harold Arlen:

I PARKED THE CAR across the street. When I came out, it was about four in the morning and there had been a dark red stripe along the curb that had been painted there. You couldn't even see it. But a cop gave me a ticket. Well, that ended up with him wanting to search everybody, and he's saying to me, "What do you do?" And I said, "Well, I'm a composer." And he said, "Well I hope you don't write jazz"—something like that. Imagine a cop bothering to say that to me. He's got Harold up against the car and Harold's turned around. It's really fantastic over nothing. It was because we were all mixed up together. It was a mixture like that, and that policeman took it upon himself to be the cultural dictator besides the social director of the city.

This was neither the first nor the last of such encounters for Gil and Anita, even in New York. But racial integration was only one part of the commotion stirred up by their relationship. When Anita met Gil, she was not yet thirty, and he had just turned fifty. "To tell the truth, there was much more about the difference in our *ages* than the difference in our pigmentation. That was the main thing—'Why would you want to marry someone so much *older?*' That was the big question."

Miles and Gil worked on the score over a period of about two weeks, writing to specific events in the script, often working with the play's star and director. They then spent two days at Columbia's Los Angeles studio to record the score. The orchestration for the recording sessions included three flutes (with two of them doubling on alto flute and saxophone, and one doubling on tenor saxophone and oboe), together with three French horns, bassoon, bass trombone, and harp. The rhythm section was from Miles's newly formed band: bassist Ron Carter, drummer Tony Williams, and pianist Herbie Hancock.

Herbie Hancock had met Gil earlier that year, when he was auditioning at Miles's house, but this was the first time he had worked with Gil. Like Wayne Shorter before him, Herbie was part of a new generation of musicians who had been inspired, and strongly influenced, by Gil's legendary recordings, especially his work with Miles. "*Miles Ahead,* that's the first time I ever heard Gil Evans's music, his arrangements," Herbie told me.

THAT IS ONE OF MY FAVORITE records of all time. As a matter of fact, the two pieces of music that are really my favorite—one is a composition, *Le Sacre du Printemps, The Rite of Spring,* of Stravinsky's, and the other one is the *Miles Ahead* album. When I heard that album, I had to find out everything I could about Gil's music. I went back and heard the arrangements from *Birth of the Cool,* and that stuff blew me away. The colors, the orchestrations, just *killed* me. The harmonies—I mean, there were so *many* things that I learned from studying those records.

Herbie had gone into the *Barracuda* session expecting it to be a great learning experience, but he was more than a little intimidated.

To ME, HE WAS THIS incredible *genius,* right? He could have played all kinds of mind games on me and could have manipulated me any way he wanted. I was looking up to him like some god-like kind of *father* figure or something. I looked at Miles in that way, too, and the fact that they had that relationship, that kind of fueled the fire, of this kind of mystique I felt for Miles *and* Gil—which I had carried over from long before I had met either one of them, before I'd even started my professional career. But Gil was just a regular guy. The thing that struck me about Gil was his humility and his sincerity. He was so unassuming. He smiled all the time, he was very encouraging, and he didn't try to appear like he *knew* everything. He really helped to put a very peaceful atmosphere around the recording studio. Miles is—there's so much energy that comes from Miles, his presence is almost *thunderous*—but Gil added a kind of peaceful essence.

I was looking forward to hearing that sound that he has—that use of harmony and all those textures, and of course I wasn't disappointed—but I'd never seen Gil conduct. He's very gentle and easy. You almost can't tell where the *beat* is, the way he conducts—everything is kind of floating—and it was just fascinating to watch him do that. Many times, the conductor will conduct all the way through. Well, when Gil felt that he wasn't really needed, he would just stop conducting, and the band would play. When it was necessary to conduct something, he *would* conduct it—which made all the sense in the world.

The sessions resulted in just under twelve minutes of music—a variety of elements ranging from dramatic fragments of just a few seconds to complete songs. The tape was to have been incorporated into the live performances, but because of a dispute with the musicians' union, the recorded music was never used. In any case, the play's run was soon cut short, apparently due to personality clashes between its star performers. Columbia did not release the music until 1996, as part of the anthology *Miles Davis and Gil Evans: The Complete Columbia Studio Recordings.* Gil later recorded two of the tunes from this project—"Time of the Barracudas" and "Hotel Me." He had brought "Flute Song" with him, which also became part of the *Barracuda* score. Another piece became "Eleven," which was later recorded on separate albums by Miles and Gil.

By its very nature, this music is distinct from any of their previous work together—designed not for an album or concert performance but, rather, as incidental music, keyed to specific emotions and actions of the play. The *Barracuda* sessions are also notable in that they represent the last attempt by Gil and Miles to collaborate on a major studio project. They continued to work together for many more years, but in a far different context. The grand-scale orchestral works were now behind them, never again to be performed, replicated, or even emulated. Both Gil and Miles were more interested in the music before them, not behind them. Miles finally had the kind of band he had been looking for—with Wayne Shorter, Herbie Hancock, Ron Carter, and Tony Williams—and for the first time in at least three years, he was looking forward to making some new music. Gil was excited about Miles's music, too, and in fact he would play a surprisingly important (if unheralded) role in its development. In the meantime, he was in the midst of producing a few masterpieces of his own. His next record, many would argue, was his greatest.

THE INDIVIDUALISM
OF GIL EVANS

"INDIVIDUALISM." ANITA EVANS SMILED. "I remember *that* one. When I *met* Gil he was working on that. We got together and I got pregnant and we got married, I think in that order, and he was working on it, working on it. And the contest was, who's gonna get here first, the record or the baby? And the baby got here first—March 21st, 1964—and the album came out several months later." Anita had become pregnant just weeks after their California trip. She gave birth to a son, Noah. (Fourteen months after Noah was born, there would come a second son, whom they named Miles.) "We lucked out," Anita told me. "Predestination, or cosmic reality. I feel we both had little to do with it. You know, some cosmic forces brought us together—smack—and said, 'These persons will be born, you will be a family, and you're lucky.' That's what happened."

Gil's family was coming together nicely, but finding the music for his new album proved to be a more elusive task. In fact, as of March, Gil still had only the two tunes he had recorded seven months earlier, just before the *Barracuda* sessions. Actually, he had just gone back into the studio that same month, with a quartet, but he regarded the results of that session as no more than "orchestral sketches," which were never intended for the album. In April, the project resumed in earnest. In another single afternoon session at Webster Hall in New York, Gil completed two more masters, "Hotel Me," from the *Barracuda* project, and another original, "Las Vegas Tango."

In his first Verve sessions, Gil's music picked up where he left off with *Out of the Cool,* evolving as smoothly as if the two albums had come just months apart, not years. For *Out of the Cool,* the first tunes Gil had recorded were "Sunken Treasure" and "Where Flamingos Fly"—grand, elegant pieces that were far removed from any of his previous work. Three years later, "Flute Song" and "El Toreador" proved every bit as striking. Abstract in form and virtually static in their rhythmic structure, they set the stage for Gil's conceptual vision of the music as a single interconnected listening experience. And as with *Out of the Cool,* in this album, jazz would be a vital element of the music—but not the only one.

"Flute Song" is a Spanish-flavored melody played by two flutes (Al Block improvises; Eric Dolphy plays from the score), accompanied throughout by harp, guitar, and three basses. The orchestral backgrounds are voiced for one trombone, two saxophones, and two French horns—but no trumpets and, except for one brief passage near the end of the piece, virtually no drums. "El Toreador" features trumpeter Johnny Coles improvising over a bold, sweeping theme played by the ensemble—scored, as in "Flute Song," for three basses, two French horns, and four reeds, plus a second trombone and two more trumpets. The drums are heard only slightly more prominently than in "Flute Song," and they are used more as color rather than as rhythmic elements.

"Hotel Me" was inspired by Muddy Waters (likely his version of the Willie Dixon tune "I Just Want to Make Love to You") and, more specifically, by the distinctive sound of Otis Spann's piano and the harmonica style of Waters's longtime band member Little Walter. At various points throughout "Hotel Me," the harmonica trills are played on virtually every instrument in the ensemble, while the rhythm section (piano, two basses, and a thundering Elvin Jones) maintains a solid foundation—pure blues, set in the caricatured atmosphere of a most decadent striptease club.

"Las Vegas Tango" is the polar opposite of "Hotel Me." Described by Gil in the liner notes as a "plain traditional minor blues" ("You'll find nothing plain about it," countered writer Gene Lees in his liner notes), it is arguably Gil's finest composition. Simple in structure, dazzling in its layering of exotic colors and textures, it is a triumph in musical architecture. "Las Vegas Tango" is the definitive example of Gil's ingenious use of harmonic overtones—the startling dissonant tones created through the combination of two notes that are theoretically incongruous. This third sound, the harmonic "inner voices" of the music, is precisely the same effect that first attracted Miles Davis to Gil's writing in the 1940s—those mystifying "invisible notes" Miles discovered in Gil's arrangement of "Robbin's Nest." Here, the harmonies give "Las Vegas Tango" its tremendous underlying tension, but at the same time, Gil contrasts the intensity by surrounding them with soft, rich textures and melodic themes. Even as the music builds to a fevered pitch, the atmosphere remains serene and utterly spellbinding.

‡   ‡   ‡

The next session, also at Webster Hall, was on May 25, 1964. John Lewis's "Concord" was the first of two pieces done on the session, and the first of the entire project to date that could readily be identified as jazz. Gil's arrangement embellishes Lewis's jazz fugue with elegant unison and counterpoint ensemble lines that weave continuously through the tune. For this piece, Gil invited veteran jazz violinist Harry Lookovsky to play the tenor violin, an obscure instrument for which he scored written and solo parts. The instrument's distinctive tone (lower in range than the viola but higher than the cello) gives "Concord" an authentic baroque flavor, even as it glides along at a brisk jazz tempo.

The second tune of the day was Willie Dixon's "Spoonful." It features extended solos by Kenny Burrell, Gil, Thad Jones, and Phil Woods, but the focal point of the arrangement is this tune's infectious two-note blues vamp ("That spoon, that spoon, that spoon-ful") sustained here in a solid, laid-back, fourteen-minute groove by Paul Chambers, Elvin Jones, and Gil.

‡   ‡   ‡

Three months later, in July, Gil recorded two more songs, this time working at Rudy van Gelder's studio. He came with two arrangements—"Time of the Barracudas" and a Kurt Weill tune, "The Barbara Song"—and he made several changes in the orchestra. In the brass section, he stayed with two French horns and a tuba, but used only one trombone and no trumpets. He added Wayne Shorter as a fifth player to the reed section; Shorter would serve as principal soloist on all of the remaining tunes. He also brought back the harp, which he had used in the first two sessions. Instead of two basses (or three), this time he used just one, played by Gary Peacock. Known at that time primarily as an avant garde player, Peacock had met Gil when he played briefly with Miles, but he had not worked with Gil before this session. "He was very relaxed," Gary recalled. "Very clear about what he wanted, but very soft—not meaning weak, I just mean a gentleness, a softness to him—and yet really firm, very together. And you couldn't help but like the guy on first meeting him."

The charts for "Time of the Barracudas" that Gil brought to this session were essentially unchanged from the arrangement he and Miles recorded in Hollywood in 1963. Following a bass/drums introduction, the theme is played by flutes, accompanied by the brass and reeds (notably, the bassoon). Wayne takes the first solo and is followed by Kenny Burrell and Elvin Jones. Elvin's solo continues into the closing chorus, a softly textured background of flutes and harp. Energetic yet relaxed, driven with power and authority by Elvin and Gary, "Barracudas" is a showcase for soloists and ensemble players alike. Gary Peacock:

> I REMEMBER WALKING in and seeing—not a whole lot of musicians. And then when we started to play, there was this *huge* sound—from so few musicians. It was unbelievable. And the magical aspect of his music was that you rarely had to *say* anything about what was intended. Because once you heard it, you knew what was intended. He didn't have to say, "I want you to play a little quieter," you just heard it, you'd hear the way it's supposed to sound. That's a mark of brilliance, somebody who could do that. It's like the old Count Basie band, you know? You'd hear the horn section come in, and they all come in exactly at the same time—wait, how do they *know* that? He had the spirit of Basie in his arrangements. His compositions had that character.

Obviously, he conceded, Gil's choice of musicians was a key factor. "You got the kind of people he selected for *Porgy and Bess,* or for the one I did—I mean, these guys come in and sight read something the first time and make it happen. So selection was critical. It was really funny, he was telling me he'd asked one of those guys to play just a one-bar solo, a two-bar solo, and he absolutely refused. "Nope. All I do, I read." Their whole *life* was perfecting a particular role. He *selected* them for that." Not so obvious, Peacock emphasized, is the kind of work that goes into the writing of Gil's music:

> WHEN HE'D SIT DOWN and do an arrangement, he didn't say, "Well, I think I'll have the saxophone do this and the trombone do that." No, no,

no. You have to hear what that combination's going to sound like—*inside*. There's no easy way, it's an enormous amount of internal work. And he was working since he was like sixteen, seventeen—I mean, copying stuff off the *radio*. I think it's an important thing to look at, the process of his education. Contrast that with today—if you want to do arranging, you can go to a hundred different schools. Now they've got all his stuff transcribed, you can study his *scores*. When Gil was coming up—you're going to spend eight or nine hours a day because you heard something on the radio and you wanted to get what it was, and there's no books to *tell* you what it was. You have to get the record and listen to the record over and over. You start with the lead line, then figure out what the harmonies are and put those in, try to hear what the saxophones are doing. Then a week goes by and you finally get fifteen minutes of music. That's a week of your *life*—to get fifteen minutes of music that isn't even your *own*. Only someone with an enormous amount of integrity would have done that, somebody who music meant that much to. And that comes through in his music.

"The Barbara Song" is Gil's third arrangement from the Kurt Weill book, after "My Ship" (for *Miles Ahead*) and "Bilbao Song" (for *Out of the Cool*). In Weill's *Three Penny Opera*, "The Barbara Song" is lively and robust, sung in the brash, angular style typical of German expressionist theater. In Gil's arrangement, the atmosphere is solemn, the textures are smooth, and all the colors are dark and mysterious. It opens with a swirling bass flute line that weaves through the opening theme, played by the ensemble but voiced predominantly for the French horns, English horn, and flutes. Ensemble parts dominate the entire performance, yet the backgrounds are played so softly, so low, that every note played over them shines out like a beam of light across a dark sky. Fully halfway into the piece, the tenor saxophone fades slowly into the foreground. Wayne Shorter's extended solo—forceful, contemplative, beautifully executed—revisits the entire piece, section by section, transforming it once again. Surreal and otherworldly as it might be, Wayne reminds us, Gil Evans's "Barbara Song" is a jazz experience after all.

✦   ✦   ✦

For the last Verve date, in October, Gil began the day with "Proclamation," the shorter but more demanding of the two arrangements recorded at this session. An original composition, in which Shorter improvises over a montage of diverse colors and sonic effects, "Proclamation" is essentially Gil's first foray into the netherworld of the avant garde. It has no discernible melodic or harmonic form, no real progression in its theme or structure—yet, unlike most "free jazz," virtually all of "Proclamation" is written except the tenor solo. The music is adventurous but surprisingly low-key. Shorter's solo remains peaceful and subdued throughout. Elvin Jones, playing a shuffling little soft-shoe pattern on brushes, gives the tune a strangely innocent atmosphere—relaxing but also unsettling, in the manner of, say, a David Lynch film.

If not a radical composition—compared to Cecil Taylor's work or Ornette Coleman's—"Proclamation" is fascinating music—and indeed a proclamation. It is a clear endorsement of the new wave in jazz and an unequivocal acknowledgment of its value and significance. Coming from someone of his stature, and at a time when the music had gained very little acceptance, Gil's gesture would have been viewed by many avant garde artists as a much-welcomed show of support. "What people were going out for was still mainstream," said Gary Peacock. "The playing that I did in the early '60s—with Paul Bley, Jimmy Guiffre, Albert Ayler, Don Cherry—I mean, there were no *venues* for that music. You didn't make money playing that stuff. You did anything you could just to be able to play some place. And it usually cost—it used to *cost* musicians just to be able to do their music."

The final tune of the session, "Nothing Like You," is the song that Gil and Wayne recorded with Miles in 1962, when the three of them worked together for the first time. (Miles's version was released in 1967 on the album *Sorcerer*). While similar to the original charts, the tune is scored for fourteen instruments (Miles's session had six), and in this arrangement, the vocals are eliminated. As Wayne delivers one last full-throttle solo, Gil's charts spread out more fireworks across the whole band. Short but sweet, hot but light-hearted, "Nothing Like You" is the perfect conclusion to one of the most ambitious, elaborate, and unusual recording projects in jazz.

‡   ‡   ‡

When the original album was first released in 1965, *The Individualism of Gil Evans* included only five of the twelve tunes Gil recorded, and it contained less than thirty-three minutes of music. Verve later used the unreleased material to put out a second album. However, Gil was not consulted in the selection or editing of the material for this second album, nor was Creed Tay-lor, who by this time had left the company. This second album included two tunes from Gil's 1964 quartet session (much to his displeasure) plus an edited version of "Spoonful." In 1974, Verve compiled all the tunes into a two-record set and released it under the original *Individualism* title. Finally, another re-issue was produced in the mid-1980s, this time with Gil's partic-ipation; the quartet tunes were eliminated, and "Spoonful" was restored to its original length.

The full collection more than doubles the playing time of the original album, and it sheds new light on a remarkable period of Gil's career. On the other hand, it is important to note that the brevity of the original release did nothing to diminish its critical acclaim or its impact on musicians. More im-portantly, in terms of its artistic conception, the original five-song collection conveys a much different listening experience than the latter edition—less diverse but more focused and cohesive. Gil's selections for the original— "The Barbara Song," "Las Vegas Tango," "Flute Song," "Hotel Me," "El Tore-ador"—capture his strongest and freshest new writing; at the same time, each of them is also highlighted by the inspired performances of his impro-visers. From start to finish, the album uses virtually none of the rhythmic, harmonic, or structural conventions associated with jazz. The jazz-oriented pieces from these sessions included some of Gil's most exciting arrange-ments, yet originally, he had chosen not to include any of these on the album.

The Individualism of Gil Evans is Gil's tour de force not only as an arranger but also as a composer, orchestrator, bandleader, and recording artist. There had never been a jazz recording like this, and there would never be another one, not even from Gil Evans. Despite the acclaim, including a 1965 Grammy nomination, after this album, Gil withdrew from the jazz scene once again. He continued to work on other people's projects, but his own music remained far from public view. When he did resurface, some five years later, there would be a brand-new Gil Evans sound. By that time, the Gil Evans Orchestra of the early 1960s would be ancient history.

Gil Evans, 1960.
Photo by Chuck Stewart

Gil Evans, 1959,
at the piano.
Photo by Al Avakian

Gil Evans, 1972,
New York City.
Photo by Ichiru Shimuzu;
Gil Evans Archive,
courtesy of Anita Evans

left
Baby Noah Evans with Anita,
1965. *Photo by Chuck Stewart*

below
Noah and Miles Evans,
1974, Italy.
*Photo by Anita Evans; Gil Evans
archive, courtesy of Anita Evans*

bottom
Noah, Anita, and Miles Evans,
1972, Central Park,
New York City.
*Photo by Gil Evans; Gil Evans
Archive, courtesy of Anita Evans*

Gil Evans Orchestra, 1976, Tokyo.
Personnel (left to right): Keith Loving, guitar; Warren Smith, percussion;
Ryo Kawasaki, guitar; Jeff Berlin, bass; Gil Evans, keyboards; Bob Stewart,
tuba; Susan Evans, drums; Tom Malone, trombone; *(cont. next page)*

NS Orchestra

George Adams, tenor saxophone; John Clark, French horn; Kohsuke Mine, tenor saxophone; Kunitoshi Shinohara, trumpet; Pete Levin, keyboards; Lew Soloff, trumpet.
Photographer unknown; photo courtesy of Pete Levin

Gil Evans, 1986, "Jazz in Vienne," France. *Copyright © Mephisto Photo*

Gil and Anita Evans, 1987, Milan, Italy.
Photo by Dany Gignoux; Gil Evans Archive,
courtesy of Anita Evans

left
Gil Evans and the Monday Night Orchestra,
1987 (probably), New York City.
Personnel (left to right): Gil Evans, keyboards;
Gil Goldstein, keyboards; Chris Hunter, alto
saxophone; Danny Gottlieb, drums; Lou
Marini, tenor saxophone; (not visible) Shunzo
Ono, trumpet; Miles Evans, trumpet; John
Clark, French horn; Mark Egan, bass; Dave
Tucker, trombone; Tom Malone, reeds; Pete
Levin, keyboards; Dave Bargeron, trombone;
Hiram Bullock, guitar.
Photo by John Driscoll; from
Larry Hicock collection

Noah and Anita Evans, at Gil's posthumous induction to Canadian Jazz Hall of Fame, Toronto, 1998.
Photo by Grant Martin,
courtesy of Canadian Music Awards

Miles Evans is still leading the Gil Evans Orchestra today, with Anita Evans as director.
Photo by Steve Joester

Gil Evans, 1985, Toronto.
Photo by Brock May,
Outside Exposure Photography

PART THREE
1965–1979

All my life I'd been sitting in front of that piano trying to figure out another way to voice a minor seventh chord. For thirty years I was sitting there. I sat there for so long, I had calluses on my ass. One on each cheek. I hadn't even realized it until my wife said to me, "You've got calluses on your ass."

I'd been sitting there and I was so tired of it, so bored from doing it for so long. It was such a lonesome thing that I decided that I needed adventure, and the only way to get adventure was to get a band together.

—GIL EVANS, INTERVIEW WITH
JOHN SNYDER, 1981

RE: INVENTION

HISTORY MIGHT WELL DECLARE that the greatest writing by Gil Evans took place in the 1950s, with Miles Davis, and that in terms of his own recordings, he reached his pinnacle in 1964. Yet it is equally true that in the latter stages of his life, Gil continued to explore new music and to break new ground. He also continued to inspire new generations of musicians. To these individuals, the "new" Gil Evans was every bit as gigantic a figure as the "old" Gil Evans had been in the lives of so many others before them. Far more interestingly, whatever "history" was recording for posterity was of little consequence to Gil himself. History was about the past, and while Gil had the greatest love and respect for the jazz tradition, his own music was rooted firmly in the present. History is generally measured in terms of the product of jazz, whereas Gil, increasingly, was interested in the process. There were new forms to explore, new sounds to be discovered—so many wonderful new people. "Living spirit," he had said years earlier, "that's what I look for in music." In the early 1960s, Gil was drawn to the vitality and energy of avant garde jazz. By the middle of that decade, new sounds were also emerging from an increasingly adventurous pop music scene. Technology added still another dimension, with new instruments like electric pianos and electronic synthesizers—great new sounds, new *waveforms*. Gil Evans was intent on exploring all of them.

There was to be another gap in Gil's career—from 1965 to 1969—in which he made no new records of his own and appeared in public as infrequently as ever. Yet as in his past "sabbaticals" (1950–1956, 1961–1963), Gil was both active and productive throughout this period. "That's always a little confusing to me," said Anita Evans. "They say, 'Well, Gil disappeared from so and so.' It wasn't that he wasn't working. He worked *all* the time. His day was a busy day, but they weren't necessarily always *famous* days. When the money came, and when his notoriety was up or down, had nothing whatever to do with it. His head was always on music, he was always doing flatted fifths and A minor 7ths. That was his life."

✝   ✝   ✝

Just weeks after Gil wrapped the last session for *Individualism,* he returned to the studio to work on guitarist Kenny Burrell's album—*Guitar Forms,* also on Verve, and also produced by Creed Taylor. Burrell was one of the most active session players in New York. After playing on record dates with innumerable jazz and popular artists, he was now looking to develop his own music. "I just personally felt I wasn't growing fast enough," Burrell told me. "I also felt, and I still feel, that if I had stayed in the studios, my career really would not have continued very long." As a follow-up to his first album (*Midnight Blue),* Burrell worked with Creed Taylor to develop something different—a concept album, featuring the guitar in a variety of musical settings. Taylor then suggested working with Gil. "Gil Evans was a master painter, a musical painter," said Burrell, "so he could go in various directions and really soar on this thing."

Considering all of the delays on the *Individualism* project, Taylor was understandably concerned about how long the Burrell album might take. Sure enough, the project, at least in the writing stage, did not move quickly. "The problem with [Gil's] being slow happened *before* we went into the studio. Creed was becoming a bit impatient about how long it took for him to get the arrangements done," Burrell recalled. "My position was, I didn't care *how* long it took, because I would see him maybe once a week or every two weeks, and I knew he was working, and I said, 'Hey, when it's done, it's going to be great.' And it *was.*"

Once Gil arrived at the studio, the sessions went as efficiently and effectively as any Burrell had done. Gil's arrangements—five of the album's nine tunes—were recorded in two days. Kenny Burrell:

WE DIDN'T HAVE A PROBLEM. If there was one, I didn't know about it. My feeling, in the studio, was that he was not that concerned about what *I* was going to do. I got the feeling that he had the utmost confidence that I was going to play my part correctly—not to worry. But because his writing is so unorthodox, blending these different kinds of instruments—flutes and French horns—his concern was getting the proper blends in the studio, getting the balances, the textures right. Because it's not like having four trombones and four saxophones and four trumpets—he's got to blend these different instruments that don't normally play together. So I remember him spending a lot of time working with the phrasing, developing the texture through volume control, dynamics, et cetera—and then the mic placement, working with Rudy van Gelder, in and out of the control room. In other words, some of the guys would have to play maybe a little softer than normal, some maybe a little louder than normal. But he knew what he wanted. He was just very meticulous, in terms of trying to get this sound.

The key to the sound Gil was after was in his orchestrations for the reed players—seven instrumentalists, most of whom played at least one other instrument. His scores included parts for alto, soprano, and tenor saxophones, flutes, alto flute, oboe, English horn, bass clarinet, and bassoon. He used reeds and woodwinds to great effect in the two most elaborate arrangements, "Lotus Land" and "Loie," which, not surprisingly, are the strongest tunes on the album. On "Lotus Land," written by the contemporary British composer Cyril Scott, the orchestra provides a subtle, exotic backdrop for acoustic guitar. The texture is rich and colorful, yet delicate— embellishing the guitar without overshadowing it. "Loie," written by Burrell, is the shortest of Gil's arrangements but also the most dramatic. Here, the melody is played in alternating lines by the acoustic guitar and English horn, which Gil likely modeled after Rodrigo's innovative score of the *Concierto de Aranjuez,* in which the Adagio's melody is introduced in an exchange between the English horn and guitar.

Guitar Forms became the turning point Kenny Burrell was striving for, greatly helping to advance his career as a jazz recording artist. The album earned a Grammy nomination, won positive critical reviews throughout the world, and has remained one of his best-selling albums for over three decades. *Guitar Forms* is renowned for its portrayal of the guitar in an eclectic range of styles, from country blues to classical, bossa nova to contemporary jazz. Gil's contributions were central to the success of the album and also, Burrell told me, provided a good measure of inspiration:

I FELT THAT HE WAS ONE who was surviving very much with his art, and he was not that *concerned* about the music business. You couldn't rush him.

If you didn't want his work, then don't call him. He seemed to have the confidence and the love—confidence in himself and the love for what he was doing—that he was going to survive. And he *was* surviving, and he was happy with it, he was grooving with it. And I admired that. I particularly admired it because of the work he had accomplished—the stuff with Miles was wonderful, and Claude Thornhill. These were all stepping-stones. He was a guy who was making a living, maybe a modest living, but he was making it doing what he wanted to do.

✢   ✢   ✢

Miles Evans was born in July 1965, fifteen months after his brother Noah. It was a happy occasion for everyone, although the baby did arrive during a time of serious financial hardship. It had been more than seven months since Gil finished *Guitar Forms,* and he had made virtually no money since then. Anita's college funds were gone, and they were now living on money left to Anita by her grandparents. Yet still, Anita said, Gil could not seem to grasp why there was no money. Apart from the lack of paying jobs, he had apparently overlooked the fact that most of his publishing royalties now went to his first wife and that the records he did after his divorce were still not showing a profit. "He just had that attitude," as Anita put it. "'I'm doing my best, I'm working hard—what is this? Why isn't there a check in the mail for me?' Gil never had a problem with the fame thing, he just wasn't hooked up. He didn't have [jazz promoter] George Wein or any of the other people who make the stars, so he didn't have any access to the money. He wouldn't play the game. He couldn't deal with those rules."

One person Gil did have access to was Creed Taylor. When Gil called him looking for work, Taylor (still at Verve) was just then beginning to plan a new album for another of his artists, the Brazilian vocalist Astrud Gilberto. He offered the arranging assignment to Gil. Gil welcomed the opportunity not only to make some money but also to do another album of Brazilian music. Following the success of *Guitar Forms,* Taylor could see similar potential for Astrud's album—not in changing her sound or style, which was still hugely popular in the wake of the 1962 mega-hit "The Girl from Ipanema"—but rather to enrich the album with Gil's arrangements. Gil had not done an album of vocal arrangements in ten years, but those arrangements, for Helen Merrill, had accomplished that very goal—casting the best possible light on their principal subject.

He achieved the same thing for Astrud, writing seven arrangements for her 1966 album, *Look to the Rainbow*. Clearly Gil worked in a supporting role, but in the process he delivered several moments of brilliant, colorful orchestral writing. On "Birimbau," featuring the Brazilian instrument of that name, his arrangement capitalizes on the distinctive sound of the birimbau itself. Great dynamic tension is created by contrasting the driving rhythms of the tune against Astrud's sultry, low-key vocal style. On "Once Upon a Summertime," based on his *Quiet Nights* arrangement for Miles, Gil's backgrounds (intricate and very delicate brass and flutes) are a perfect complement to Astrud's wistful tone. And once again, as Astrud wrote to me, working with Gil was a sheer delight:

> BESIDES BEING A MUSICAL GENIUS beyond comparison, he had this wonderful way about him. His mere presence transmitted a feeling of peace and calmness that I have seldom seen. He seemed to carry within himself some very unique wisdom, which, combined with his obvious spontaneous love of people, gave him an air of a spiritual guru. He was very humble. When he worked on the arrangements for my album, *Look to the Rainbow*, he welcomed all of my "nosy" suggestions about how I thought the arrangements should be. I went many times to his apartment to work on this project together with him. I would sit next to him at the piano, and he would ask, "See if you like this introduction," or "What do you think of these chords here?" No "big ego" problem with Gil. He was also very paternal. I remember that I had a bad cold during the recording of my vocals, and Gil would bring tea bags, honey, and scotch to the studio, so that I could have some hot tea with a bit of honey and a dash of scotch to "open up" my voice.

Look to the Rainbow turned out to be the last project Gil did with Creed Taylor. Taylor left Verve in 1967 to join A&M Records, where he went on to produce a series of very successful jazz records in the slick, polished style that became his stock in trade. Astrud's album also represents one of Gil's last assignments as a freelance jazz arranger. From this point on, he focused almost entirely on his own music, his own albums, and ultimately, his own band. Despite a steady stream of offers, it would be almost twenty years before Gil worked on anyone else's records—that is, anyone else's records except those of Miles Davis.

MILES DAVIS
AND COMPANY

WHEN WAYNE SHORTER JOINED Miles's band in 1964, alongside Ron Carter, Herbie Hancock, and Tony Williams, the new quintet was complete. This band is widely acknowledged as having been the best jazz group since Miles's earlier combination of star soloists John Coltrane, Bill Evans, and Cannonball Adderley. Miles made a series of recordings with the band—from *E.S.P.* in 1965 to *Filles de Kilimanjaro* in 1968—that documents one of the most remarkable and exciting developments not only in Miles's illustrious career but also in the whole of contemporary jazz. With each successive album, the music became less structured, freer, and more spontaneous. "I loved that band, man," Miles wrote, "because if we played a song for a whole year and you heard it at the beginning of the year, you wouldn't recognize it at the end of the year." The music was not as radical as that of the avant garde players of this period, but neither was it in direct opposition. In fact, even Miles began to acknowledge that there was more to this New Wave music, of which he had previously been so critical. "What was good about Ornette Coleman was that his musical ideas and his melodies were independent of styles, and being independent like that would make you appear to be creating spontaneously."

Miles attributed his change of attitude in large measure to Tony Williams—"listening to what he had to say about what Ornette was doing." Tony Williams, just eighteen years old when he joined Miles in 1963, was the new band's youngest player and the most adventurous, both in his play-ing and in his diverse musical interests. Williams played an increasingly prominent role in the evolution of Miles's music with this band. And on the other end of the age spectrum, there was also the continuing presence, and active participation, of Gil Evans.

Gil's name did not appear in any of the credits for the quintet's albums, and his involvement did not become public knowledge until years later. Given that none of these albums featured an orchestra, it is not surprising that his work would go unnoticed, but in fact Gil participated in virtually all of the recording sessions. "Gil was more or less a consultant," Wayne Shorter told me. "He was always involved with it, and Miles liked to have Gil there." Neither Wayne nor any of the others in the band were aware of any formal agreement regarding Gil's role. "Whatever business arrangement there was, that was between them," he said. "He was there as a friend of the situation, and Miles—and *us.*"

Gil's involvement ranged from "just hanging around" to writing arrangements, composing, and cowriting with Miles. But Gil himself did not seem to consider his contributions to be of much importance. He once described himself as no more than a "midwife" in the recording ses-sions, just there to lend Miles a helping hand. "Miles was used to Gil help-ing him all the time," said Anita, "even on all those records you have no idea Gil did for him—the quintet albums and all that—and if you listen you can hear it. Miles just felt more secure. Gil was like his stabilizer in a way. Gil would write the stuff down for him on a little piece of paper, so that when he went to the studio he would have what he needed."

Teo Macero, who resumed his role as Miles's producer at Columbia in 1966, was often responsible for taking care of Gil's "consulting fees." "He used to come around all the time," Teo said, "whether or not he actually par-ticipated in the sessions. I remember paying him for a number of things. Miles would say 'Pay him for some arrangements,' and I would just arbitrar-ily make up a bill and send it in and get him a couple of thousand dollars or whatever it was at the time that he needed." According to Anita Evans, the financial aspect of Gil's work with Miles pointed out one of the great differ-ences between the two of them:

MILES WOULD GIVE HIM MONEY—walking away with food money kind of thing. Their relationship predated me, really. It was always unbelievable to me, the positions they assumed in terms of the money. But Gil used to say stuff like, "Miles needs a lot of money, I mean he really *needs* it. Money is important to him, so he should have it because it means everything to him." That was Gil's attitude. It was weird—that's a good word for the relationship, on the money level—it was really weird.

✝   ✝   ✝

In early 1966, Gil and Anita went to the Five Spot to see Charles Mingus. One of the players in the band was Howard Johnson, who played tuba, baritone saxophone, trombone, and many other instruments and was a huge admirer of Gil's music. "As I remember him sitting there now," said Howard, "I realize he was just being his usual laconic self, but I thought he was bored. I thought he was unmoved by anything he was hearing. When we took a break, I was going to collar him anyway and try to press myself on him, but when I took my horn in the back and came back out he had already gone. So I thought, well okay, that's that for now, and I didn't have the idea I'd made much of an impression. But I got a call from him some weeks after that."

As it turned out, Anita later told Howard, Gil had not only been impressed with Howard's playing, but in fact it was on that very same night that Gil decided he was going to try to put together a band of his own. "She said that since she had married Gil, he hadn't done anything as a bandleader, and hearing Mingus's band was part of the inspiration for him to get active again."

Right about the same time Gil met Howard, he also bumped—literally—into a young man that would become his next saxophone player. That, said Billy Harper, is exactly how it all began.

I WAS COMING OUT of a little arcade on Broadway, and I turned the corner and there was Gil Evans on the street. I said, "Mr. Evans, hey Gil—this is Gil Evans, right? I'm Billy Harper, I'm from Texas. I've enjoyed your music for years, it's a pleasure seeing you out here." We talked and he went on to mention that he's not doing very much musically—as far as working—but he's doing some writing, and he would certainly call me. And he gave me his number and took mine and said he'd call me. In New York at that time everybody took your number; that didn't mean anything at all. Musicians always do that, and you never hear from them.

After sort of scuffling around New York for some months, at a time that I was really quite distraught, the phone rang—Gil Evans. That meant so much to me, that Gil was calling. He was the first musician to call. Before, I was sitting in, working my way in, and sometimes barging in and playing, and everybody liked it all when I was playing, but no jobs. So Gil called and said, "We're having a rehearsal. Maybe you'd like to come down and play." So I did, and that's how I started in New York. And he hadn't heard me at *all*. That's what's so fantastic about it. He did that often, too. I remember playing with the group, and I would look around, and there was some strange musician I had never seen that Gil invited. Sometimes they were good, sometimes not so good, but they were there. They had a chance to play.

And so it would go. Over the next few months, and on through the years, Gil would bump into various musicians—someone whose sound he liked or, like Billy Harper, someone he had a good feeling about, even before hearing him play—and he'd invite them to join in.

Charles Mingus may have inspired Gil to start putting a new band together, but it was Miles Davis, once again, who brought him back into public view. Miles was committed to perform that spring at the Monterey Jazz Festival, and he helped set up a concert appearance there for Gil. The Monterey organizers also booked Gil for the Pacific Jazz Festival at Costa Mesa, California. This concert was promoted as a reunion of the dance bands that had played back in the days of Balboa Beach. Gil also secured a one-week stint at the popular jazz club Shelly's Manne-hole, in Hollywood, and one more concert at the University of California at Los Angeles. Because of the prohibitive travel costs, it was agreed that for these concerts, Gil would use primarily local musicians, but he did bring Howard Johnson, Billy Harper, Elvin Jones, and bassist Don Moore from New York. Anita came, too, and so did the toddlers, Noah and Miles Evans, on their first road trip.

Not surprisingly, Gil's music proved to be too difficult for the less-experienced players to prepare for on short notice. "It needed time and money," Gil told Leonard Feather for *Down Beat*. "I got an advance, but it wasn't enough. I needed lots of rehearsals and lots of work. At Monterey, we weren't ready. We didn't have time to get everything really ready, so we stretched the ones we did play. Also, I spent a lot of time rehearsing a couple of things that we never got around to playing publicly—like a nice arrangement of John Lewis's "Concorde," which turned out to be a little too hard to play."

Gil was happier with the remaining performances, however, particularly those at Shelly's Manne-Hole. The trip to Costa Mesa, on the other hand, was a strange one. Gil was interested in playing his new arrangements, but for this concert, his band had apparently been expected to play the music of his Rendezvous Ballroom days. It was not to be. As Leonard Feather wrote, "With the exception of 'King Porter Stomp' (which he introduced as a number he had played at the Rendezvous in 1936), the concept was never carried through in the music." Then again, Gil told Feather, "There weren't that many people in the audience that really remembered those days anyway. There were just a few who came around backstage who actually had been there, people I hadn't seen or heard from in thirty years. It was strange; I had forgotten it. Such a long time ago . . . It was like going back to another life." It was even more bizarre for Anita, who had not even been born in 1936, to see the audience's reaction to Gil's new and decidedly modern music: "The women he used to play for in the '30s—by now, all orange-haired ladies—they thought it was kind of wild and crazy. It just wasn't what they had been dancing to in 1933. Some people *were* playing that same kind of music. There were those dance bands—Gil would say the formaldehyde bands—that just preserve themselves, don't develop, don't grow, don't change."

At the time, Gil expected that there would be a new album made from the material that was recorded both at UCLA and Costa Mesa. "I should have one LP, or at least some good tunes for part of one," Gil said. But none of this music was ever released, possibly for reasons of sound quality—and perhaps also because, as the critics apparently pointed out, the tunes were far too long.

WE PLAYED A LONG TIME on some of the tunes. I didn't have control over the soloists—that was a problem, because sitting there at the piano I felt like I was just one of the musicians, and it's very difficult to play the piano and then jump up and direct the band and then go back and play the piano. Don't forget, this was my first time out since 1960. I took advantage of that situation because this was important to my development—I let things go that way, rather than edit too closely, because I never had a chance to play in public. You feel you can't stop. You go ahead and play.

The trip to California marked the beginning of a long working relationship between Gil and Howard Johnson. For Howard, this was the realization of a long-standing dream.

I HAD COME TO NEW YORK in 1963, and Gil was one of the people I had come to New York to meet. When I listened to the *Porgy and Bess* album, I felt it had subliminal messages in it—to me, from Gil—to come to New York and find him. They weren't that subliminal, they were actually the tuba parts. The tuba parts were really calling me personally, I felt. I felt that I had a contribution that I could make, that was already set up for me, and I'd been called by this message, in "The Buzzard Song." And just in case I forgot, there was a little passage in the introduction of the *next* tune, that was saying, "Now don't forget what I said." So I said, "Okay, I'll be there."

Like countless musicians before him and after, Howard was drawn to Gil by what he heard on his records. But what sustained his interest, and his fierce loyalty to Gil, were the challenges posed by his new music and the tremendous personal involvement it required of every player.

THE WAY HE WROTE FOR the tuba showed how he felt about the instrument, which was exactly how I felt about it—or so I thought, because when I actually met him, I realized he had some deeper insights to the instrument than I had. As far as I was concerned, I was stretching it to the limits, because at that time there wasn't anybody quite doing what I was doing on the tuba. For instance, when Mingus would call me—which was every other day, actually—he would call me and play something on the piano and he'd say, "Can you play a figure like this?" And it was always well within the realm of what I could do. When I started playing with Gil, he asked me to do things that no one had ever asked me to do before and that I hadn't thought about myself, just in terms of the touch of the instrument. I could play it bombastically, and I could play it light and melodically, but he had ideas farther on the scale of light and melodic that I really hadn't conceived. I think he got that from having worked with Bill Barber, who was pretty masterful at just that—he could really blend in with trombones in a way that was difficult for me before I got this thing from Gil. And some of it's not easy still. So Gil's approach challenged me the way nobody else's had.

✝   ✝   ✝

Life in New York's Greenwich Village in the 1960s was as rich and vibrant as ever, and it was a wonderful environment for raising a family. New York City is an icon of American arts and culture, yet within it, the Village is a re-markably intimate community—part of the fabric of the great metropolis yet also detached from its frenzied, hectic pace. Among other things, Elvin Jones explained, it was a great place for hanging out with friends and neigh-bors. "He lived on West 15th Street, and I had an apartment on 16th Street, so I would walk around the corner to his house and listen to records, play with the kids. And we would go and take 'em out in the carriage and walk around on the streets of New York." Smiling broadly as he told the story, Elvin suddenly broke out laughing.

I THINK HE HAD A LITTLE frustration about raising his kids when they were babies. He liked peace and quiet, and the babies were screaming and hollering all the time—two rough boys, you know? They had very healthy lungs. So Gil would sometimes come over to my place, and he'd sit around, just to get away. And he'd rent a studio and go up there, you know. He'd do that at night, late at night, when the kids were in bed. 'Cause during the day, he changed diapers and made the formula and all that stuff just as well as Anita did, you know? He took *care* of those kids, he was like a *doctor,* practically.

Anita Evans confirmed Gil's commitment to fatherhood:

HE WAS A VERY MARVELOUS father. Really, the best. That's why I'm still alive and healthy, because he did the hard part, you know? He would stay up all night, marching the kids around. He was at the age where he was to-tally into it. So there would be times when—God, I remember Gil walk-ing around the village carrying both of these guys, these giant kids, one on his back, one on his front. He was totally and completely and thoroughly devoted to the children. Really. Like one of the kids. I mean, *he* was a child.

The financial struggles continued throughout this period, but Anita of-fered strong words of caution about emphasizing the economic hardships of the "struggling artist."

I DON'T HAVE ANY MEMORY of that, so if I read that I'd probably say, "What is he talking about?" I can remember intellectually that we didn't have a lot of money, obviously, but we had all the basic things. We went anywhere we wanted to go, ate anything we wanted to eat, we wore anything we wanted to wear. We didn't have conspicuous consumption, and one shouldn't complain about that. I remember just an awfully gifted life, because of the music and the children, so I wouldn't change anything.

As Anita's family inheritance dwindled and Gil's income continued to come only in trickles, she began to play a more active and prominent role—as promoter, manager, booking agent, and all-around business manager. "He could never get management because they could see immediately they couldn't make money from him. He wasn't going to be a good racehorse. Nobody would have anything to do with him. That's why I had to do it, by default." More to the point, Howard Johnson suggested, is the fact that Gil himself was not up to the task.

THIS IS SOMETHING I'm pretty sure about. What he thought was that everything would work out, that everything kind of *does* work out, and that there's no need to panic, you know? And the fact is, without Anita panicking, things might not have gone as *well* as they did in those times. Because she really had the burden of facing the creditors. I don't think it was so much of an ivory tower thing, as he was just kind of a space cadet, you know? He just really wasn't thinking about that kind of stuff.

FLOWER POWER

IN THE MID-1960S, pop music was getting exciting again for the first time in years. Most of the chart-toppers of the mainstream industry were as formulaic as ever, but innovative new sounds were emerging at every turn. The acoustic folk music of the early '60s protest era galvanized the political unrest and social concerns of the youth-based counterculture. Bob Dylan's poignant songwriting, and his later transition to electric instruments, fueled the folk rock idiom, which was popularized by The Byrds, The Lovin' Spoonful, Simon and Garfunkel, The Mamas and Papas, The Band, and many others. Black American pop once again crossed over to the predominantly white charts. First, in the early '60s, there was the phenomenal success of Detroit-based Motown Records, which introduced the Supremes, Gladys Knight, The Temptations, Little Stevie Wonder, and dozens of other recording stars. This was followed by another wave of R&B—the gospel-rooted soul music of Aretha Franklin, Otis Redding, Marvin Gaye, and James Brown. American pop had also succumbed, in the early '60s, to the British invasion—The Beatles, The Rolling Stones, The Animals, The Kinks, The Who, The Yardbirds—and many of these groups now moved beyond their earlier, simpler pop sound and became increasingly adventurous. The most progressive and experimental rock music emanated from San Francisco's famed Haight Ashbury district, the metaphysical center of the hippie movement and the psychedelic era. This was the spawning ground for such bands as the Grateful Dead, Jefferson Airplane, Moby Grape, Country Joe and the

Fish, and Big Brother and the Holding Company. Then there was the American guitarist Jimi Hendrix, a gifted musician and a central figure of the progressive rock era. His band, the Jimi Hendrix Experience, started out in England but broke out internationally after a show-stopping performance at the fabled Monterey Pop Festival of 1967.

All of these musical forms brought new vitality and energy to the popular music scene. In rock music in particular, there was tremendous cross-fertilization of ideas. Young musicians embraced blues, folk, country, jazz, and many non-Western idioms. Among the more inventive of these young musicians was Robbie Robertson, a guitarist and songwriter—and an early admirer and, eventually, collaborator with Gil Evans—whose music for The Band merged folk, country, and vintage rock and roll into yet another completely original hybrid. Robertson described the period as a necessary revolution in pop music:

> I THINK THAT THIS WAS a particular time when there were rules to be broken—and rules that *needed* breaking. In the beginning of rock and roll, in the mid-fifties, country music, blues, R&B, boogie woogie, all these things were put in a big pot of soup and mixed in all together. This new thing was happening, and the bombs went off for a few years. And right at the beginning of the '60s, something happened and it became very pat. It didn't have the fire that it had a few years earlier. There was a kind of squarishness that had taken over, a pop thing. Then all of a sudden it all just flared up at the same time, and something just kind of *wild* happened. Revolution was in the air—just the whole ambiance in the streets—and people were really mixing it up, doing a lot of experimenting in their lives, and in music. It was a reflection of what was going on in the world. The assassination[s] of John Kennedy and Malcolm X, the war in Vietnam, really brought a lot of people together—or apart. But it did *something*. This was real *fire* in the air.

+   +   +

Gil Evans was enthralled with much of the new music scene, but an early encounter with the new counterculture was less than pleasant. One of the biggest hits of 1967 was "Light My Fire," by another legendary West Coast band, The Doors. Among its other distinctions, this tune bears more than a passing resemblance to one of Gil's songs. As Gil told Helen Armstead Johnston in a 1972 interview, the question of plagiarism arose during a phone call with someone at Columbia Records. "I called him to try to place my album, but he goes through a big thing about—I should sue Electra and the publisher and all that—for 'Light my Fire.' He was convinced that they had stolen it from me, because he was employed at Prestige when I had made this particular album and remembered my number. I didn't even know what he was talking about. So after, I got the record out and played it—and I saw what he meant."

The tune in question on Gil's Prestige album *Gil Evans Plus Ten* is "Jambangle," which has a melody line that is strikingly similar to The Doors's chorus ("Come on baby, light my fire, Come on baby, light my fire, Try to set the night on fire"). Anita felt that Gil should take legal action, but he was not interested in pursuing the case at all. "Gil was insulted that I would suggest such a thing," she said, "but I mean we were a couple of months behind on the rent, no money—so I bothered him until finally he said, 'Okay, you get a lawyer and you take care of it.' I got a lawyer on spec immediately, but Gil wouldn't cooperate, and I think the lawyer thought that was so weird that he dropped out."

"I don't really have any strong feelings." Gil said. "I have no rancor about anything like this." Yet even if he was not prepared to take action, clearly Gil did feel strongly about the mistreatment of artists and their work. He was outspoken, for example, about the discrepancies he saw between Benny Goodman's success and that of Fletcher Henderson. "Willard Alexander, he's Benny Goodman's liaison man—someday I'm going to ask him how come Fletcher Henderson had to die a pauper when Benny Goodman made millions off his arrangements." Gil also cited a more current example involving the 1950s rock and roll pioneer Chuck Berry. At the time of the "Light My Fire" incident, Gil met a copyright lawyer who had apparently just won a significant settlement for Berry from The Beatles and their publisher. "I said, 'Go ahead, keep on going. Go to The Beach Boys and make them give Chuck Berry half—at least half of their royalties—on "Surfin' USA," which was a direct copy from "Sweet Little Sixteen."' Identical, except for the words—the whole thing." Gil's own music had also been copied before. He told Helen Armstead Johnston about meeting a composer who had used one of Gil's records to "inspire" his movie score. "He told me what he did," Gil said. "He took my record and played it all the while they were making a movie, and then he went and wrote his own score based on that sound. So I said, 'Gee, the least you could have done was send me a consultant's fee.'"

Gil's reluctance to pursue cases like the "Light my Fire" incident was due largely to his aversion to confrontation, especially confrontation that involved lawyers or music-business people. On the other hand, he could also see the issue from both sides of the fence. How different, after all, were these copies from the melodies he himself had "borrowed"? Gil had not hesitated, for example, to point to Willie Dixon and Muddy Waters as the root source of "Hotel Me." His "Gone" was a direct descendent of Gershwin's "Gone, Gone, Gone." There is, of course, an important distinction between artistic license and blatant commercial larceny. If Gil had actually made any money, he would surely have been happy to pay a "consulting fee" to Willie Dixon and Muddy Waters and no doubt many others. And he would have been delighted to receive such a fee from the likes of The Doors, of course, but not if it meant hiring a lawyer or even having to talk to one. Gil's preference, as ever, was to avoid the subject altogether.

THESE STORIES ABOUT WHAT GOES on in these music marketplaces are so revolting that it's not really . . . —it's better not to think about it. You do what you can, but once you find out about it there's no use dwelling on it. When it becomes just a thing like a chronic effort at revenge, then you're in trouble. Because revenge, even though it is sweet, is very expensive. Revenge is something that really is too costly. And I have to remind myself, I don't want to ruin my life.

Jazz musicians take great pride in their ability to quote, paraphrase, and juxtapose numerous melodic phrases within their improvisations. Gil applied that same artful practice to writing, as had generations of composers before him. Now, in an era as rich and fresh as the pop scene was at this time, he had no intention of closing his ears. Neither did Miles Davis. He and Gil were among the first jazz musicians to mine the rich new veins of pop, R&B, and rock music. On his own, Miles was taking his quintet in a new direction that led ultimately to the phenomenon of jazz rock, later known as fusion. All through this transition, Miles also worked hand in hand with Gil. In fact, in 1968 (not long after The Doors incident), Miles and Gil were hard at work on the album *Filles de Kilimanjaro*—and listening most intently to the debut album of the Jimi Hendrix Experience, *Are You Experienced?* One of the new tunes Miles recorded was "Mademoiselle Mabry," which was "inspired" by Hendrix's "The Wind Cries Mary." Miles paid no consulting fees either to Hendrix, for his original theme, or to Gil Evans, who cowrote the tune but was never credited for his efforts.

✝ ✝ ✝

Quite apart from his musical interests, Gil's lifestyle and his philosophy were perfectly suited to the 1960s counterculture. Long before anyone of the Flower Power generation was born, he was a nonconformist, an idealist, a left-leaning pacifist, and a nonmaterialist. As Gil told Helen Armstead Johnston,

> IT'S BEEN PROVEN OVER and over again that the human being is really not capable of having too much. People degenerate when they have too much. . . . They start messing things up. So there's really no reason why people should have too much. It's only show-offs, infantile showing off. People get like that, you know. . . . It isn't really necessary. That's what makes me sad about the whole scene. I mean, somebody like Benny Goodman or, well, anybody—Miles Davis, anybody—they are raised and conditioned to play the game the way it's played. So you can't really nail anybody down for that and pick them out and blame them, because their music is beautiful. To blame them for not being hip on that, it's a waste of time, because it's the way they are conditioned.

Gil was also an unapologetic supporter of drugs—soft drugs, that is—as an alternative to what he saw to be the much more harmful effects of alcohol.

> I USED TO DRINK A QUART a day at one time. It didn't seem like much to be drinking, you know, but you can drink a quart a day and not really be— some people think of a quart a day as somebody sprawled in the gutter. There are lots of people who drink a quart a day. A composer just died two weeks ago from doing just that. Hall Overton was his name. He sipped like that while he composed. All his life he had done that, and it ruined his liver. And he got a hemorrhage of the esophagus or something and was taken to the hospital. When I went to see him, he wasn't allowed to have any visitors, and the next thing I knew, he was dead, from that. He'd always lived a respectable, productive life.

Gil's shift from alcohol to pot started shortly after he came to New York in the early 1940s.

I HAD NEVER HAD IT until I came to New York, and gradually I would smoke instead of drink. Pretty soon I was down to two quarts a week. I guess I haven't had anything to drink now for almost five years. But I'm not off it. I taste it. I'm not somebody that takes one drink and has to go off on a binge . . . [but] I'm like that with cigarettes. I quit cigarettes. I can't just smoke one once in a while. I quit for eight years, and one day I smoked a cigarette and I smoked a pack right away, as though I had never quit, and I smoked for a year again and now I stopped again a month ago. If you smoke pot, a little bit, two or three puffs of pot, will take care of you, whereas a whole pack of cigarettes will only take care of you for the whole day maybe.

Gil did smoke "socially," but his use of pot was more for purposes of contemplation rather than recreation. He also experimented with LSD and other hallucinogenics such as peyote and mescaline, but he understood their inherent risks.

IF YOU KNOW YOURSELF well enough, you can take acid. If you don't know yourself too well—and it's surprising the number of people who *don't* know themselves really well—then it's not a good idea to take something like that, because all of a sudden it's revealed to you. The villain in you, for example, is revealed to you. The villain being what's been injected into you by the culture, by the outside institutions. And that's the basis of our schizophrenia, that has been injected into us by the outside world to keep what's inside of us from coming out.

Needless to say, Gil was well versed in the current trends in psychology and psychoanalysis, which were as much a part of the culture as drugs, free love, and rock and roll. In a bizarre and uncharacteristically *long* tangent— at times sounding more like a radical college student than a fifty-year-old jazz musician—Gil shared some of his own experiences and insights with Helen Armstead Johnston regarding psychotherapy and other matters of self-discovery:

I WENT TO A THERAPIST but he didn't analyze *intellectually*. He didn't believe in it. He thought it was a waste of time to analyze dreams and it was a waste of time to find out who and where, when and how you were first brutalized into this condition of so-called civilization. He thought you would get more out of it *physically,* so I would go and we would have breathing sessions. He pressed me all over while I breathed—slow breathing like that, lying on the couch. And he would say, "Breathe a hundred and fifty or two hundred times." By that time, you usually have some kind of breakthrough. You start laughing or crying.

Then there's a thing called the gag reflex, which is something that's really not too well known, but it's a fantastic therapy. It's not easy to do and hardly anyone knows about it, but the gag reflex is an automatic gagging. The word gag is wrong because you don't gag when the gag reflex occurs. It's an involuntary free release from your waist—from your groin right out through your mouth. When you do it is right before you have a meal, so there's nothing in your stomach. So when you exhale, you go . . . ah . . . . And when you do that—especially when you first do it, the first few months when you do it—the anger that you have pinned down there, all of a sudden it roars out of you. It's hard to do, because we live in a culture where you've got people around you and you're afraid—like if you take a breath like that—because you know that when it comes free, you will make a scream. And you think all the neighbors will come and they'll call the police. So you've got all this paranoia, naturally, so it's hard to do, you know. But if you can do that, it helps. So that was part of my therapy—a long answer to the question. That was the therapy I took. Now it's hard for me to do that. Now I can't get it past the gag. It's hard for me to get the thing to go like . . . t-h-a-t . . . and throw that all the way out. Because when that thing goes out, you know you've let something go. You can tell, even though you can't see it. It's the energy in you that's been stuck there, and you know that you've let something out. It's fantastic. All of a sudden this feeling that's been stopping you—like you've been so mad and sulking and wanting to get revenge and going through all that—that's been wasting your time, you know? Oh yes, it's a great thing.

Where the anger comes from is the total misrepresentation that every being has to endure from the time it is born. That's why everybody is angry, basically. It's been brought to light and identified and all that with whatever the circumstances are. And you can turn it on, or you can use it as a vehicle for your anger. You use a certain thing as a vehicle for that anger. So we suffer from misrepresentation—all the way clear through to our congress, I guess. And that's all supported by the individual family which echoes that same thing to their children—because they don't want their neighbors to think that they're different, right? So there's no way, in this particular setup that civilization has now, we can't say that thing should be changed like that, because it would cause havoc. That's the problem. To try to raise a child, let a child raise itself in a natural self-regulatory manner, could lead to havoc. In a neighborhood or household or state or whatever—whatever the situation is, it's based on this other particular anti-life type of situation. The authoritarian family that echoes the state, and does all those things to you and misrepresents to you in an innocent or even a calculated manner, they do it because it has to be done. Parents, for instance, they say, "Well, this has to be done. You must do that." For example, the mother says to the child, "You're a certain age now, you can no longer associate with that person because you have a life to lead now."

It's conditioning. It's a simple thing to understand, too. If you observe your children or anybody to see what conditioning does—how you like this thing because it's familiar, even if it's terrible. It's so simple to understand. People go through such terrible droves of anger and guilt and all kinds of emotions like that, because of their or other people's conditioning. All you can do is figure out what it is and either cope with it or go around it. It isn't always easy to do, but at least you can get around some of it. Even say right out what it is and get that straightened out—or if it looks like an impossible situation, try to be lucky enough to be the artful dodger.

For this artful dodger, the solution to virtually any difficult or unpleasant situation was to become submerged in the world of music. Some would call this approach escapist or delusional; to others it might seem to be a courageous attitude or, at the very least, wonderfully romantic. Clearly Gil had experienced conflict, and he had pursued many different paths to overcome the pain and anger. Whether it was drugs or therapy or a withdrawal from society—each of which was prevalent and widely practiced, certainly within the counterculture of this era—Gil seemed to take the same approach as he did with music: You try a little taste of everything. "It's a question of life and anti-life," he mused. "But life, it's great, sometimes it's terrifying. That's the problem . . . "

GREAT NEW MOVES

IN 1968, THE PACE STARTED picking up for Gil, both in his work with Miles and also on his own music. He organized a twelve-piece band for a concert at New York's Whitney Museum. In April, he appeared with Miles's quintet at the U.C. Jazz Festival at Berkeley, California. Shortly thereafter, he returned to the Columbia studios to record with Miles and a full orchestra. Throughout this period, he continued to work closely (and still anonymously) with Miles on his celebrated new quintet recordings. And by the end of the year, Gil was finally back at work preparing for a new album of his own.

The Whitney Museum concert was Gil's first date since the West Coast tour in 1966, and it was his first New York performance since the 1961 Carnegie Hall concert with Miles. The band included several familiar faces—Billy Harper, Howard Johnson, Johnny Coles, Jimmy Cleveland, Julius Watkins—along with newcomers guitarist Joe Beck, trumpeter Lew Soloff, and bassist Herb Bushler. In what was becoming a familiar habit, Gil hired Bushler for the concert without any rehearsals or preparation. "Nobody told us to start," Herb said. "We just started playing—everybody sort of suddenly sat down and we were playing. Then Gil stood up and said, 'Okay, let's play this chart,' and we went right into it. It was great. The concert itself was like a big party."

The Whitney concert marked the first occasion in which Gil featured electric instruments—an electric harpsichord, which he played, and Herb's Fender electric bass. The technology of music—more sophisticated electric amplifiers and loudspeakers, new electric instruments—was just beginning to emerge. Gil was one of the first jazz artists to try them out and to hire musicians who played them. Herb Bushler, for example, played the Fender before working with Gil. "He never said to bring in the Fender; I just decided to do it. That's the way he was." By way of perspective, it should be noted that many people were shocked even to see an electric bass in a jazz band. "The reason I did that," Herb said, "was because I always felt that you could play bebop or jazz or anything just as good on the Fender as you could on the upright. Of course, there are people who are purists about that, who will say no, but there are enough bass players around, like I was at that time, who were willing to say, 'Sorry but you're wrong.'" Even Miles Davis had yet to add an electric bass to his band; in fact, Miles's first experience with the instrument also came by way of Herb Bushler, who played with Gil's orchestra when they joined Miles later that same year for their concert in Berkeley.

‡   ‡   ‡

The U.C. Jazz Festival concert in May 1968 was the final concert performance of Miles Davis with the Gil Evans Orchestra. Howard Johnson speaks with great pride about this concert, not only because he played that day with Gil but also because without his efforts, the historic event might never have happened. Initially, Gil had declined the invitation, mainly because of the problems he had had on his previous West Coast tour with inexperienced players. Nevertheless, Johnson proceeded to work out all the details in advance with Darlene Chan, the festival organizer:

I WANTED THIS TO HAPPEN—you know, for musical reasons—and I wanted to be out on the coast and all of that. At this point Gil was being obstinate. He said he just absolutely wasn't going to do it. He said, "How can I do it? They don't want to bring a band out from New York, and they mentioned something about using university students—I don't want to have a band with university students." So I said, "Well, I know the woman who runs the festival and she really wants you to be there, and she'll do what needs to be done, you know? So we ought to talk to her."

So I kind of tricked him into talking to her. I had called her up and said, "Look, be at the office and available at these hours." So I started talking about it, and he said, "No, this is not the way I like to do things. It's not the way I want to be handled. I'll send them some music and they can put up a big cardboard statue of me if they want, but I don't need to be there." So I said, "Well I think you would feel differently if you talked to Darlene—let me give her a call." So I didn't let him get away, and I called Darlene. And he got on the phone and immediately he said, "Look, I'm sorry I can't come." And he said, "These are the reasons. In order for me to do that, I would have to have this much money, and I would have to have my wife and my children come out, and we'd have to have our transportation and hotel taken care of, and I would have to have a whole orchestra of competent studio and jazz musicians, and there isn't time to get all of that happening at this point, and I'm very sorry." And she said, "Now, wait a minute—you can *have* all of that. And Howard's already got some people with penciled-in dates for rehearsals and stuff. All we need really from you is for you to say when you want the rehearsals to be." And he just said, "Well, if we're going to play on Saturday night, we better have Thursday and Friday for rehearsal." And that's what happened—and it all came together.

Not only did Gil show up for the concert, but he brought a whole new set of charts—new versions of earlier tunes along with several new ones—all designed for the new, highly unconventional ensemble he wanted for this concert. "It was the most unusual band I ever was in with Gil," said Howard,

BECAUSE IT WAS ABOUT a fourteen-piece band, plus Miles's quintet, and in the band there were no saxophones, no trumpets, and no trombones—a lot of players but no *traditional* sound at all. We played things I was familiar with from his records with Miles—"Gone," "The Duke," and then some new things that he had done with Astrud Gilberto, like "Birimbau"—so it was great playing things I had some familiarity with, but were pretty challenging nonetheless. Like I don't think anyone had ever asked me to play a trill on the tuba before, but there I was, going boi-i-i-i with the valves—a valve trill rather than a lip trill. And it was just like being in another world to me.

The instrumentation for this orchestra included four French horns, two bassoons, bass clarinet, flute, oboe, English horn, mandolin, guitar, pedal steel guitar, and harp. The only players Gil brought with him from New York were

Howard and Herb Bushler, who played steel guitar as well as Fender bass. "The rhythm section per se was with Miles," Bushler recalled. "First Miles went on with his group, then we went out and Miles played some of Gil's arrangements with us. At that time I was forced to play pedal steel guitar, which I had absolutely no idea how to play. I remember he had a great chart—I was very pissed off at him, too, because he *lost* it. Aretha Franklin had "Natural Woman" out as a hit, and he did a chart on that, it was absolutely gorgeous." Just the way Gil wrote out his charts, Bushler recalled, was a revelation in itself:

> I USED TO COPY HIS CHARTS out for him at that time, which is another story. He used to write it out in these little fine, tiny pencil markings—bust your eyeballs to see. And one day I was doing that, busting my eyeballs, trying to copy it, and Anita Evans, his wife, walked by and said, "Well, why don't you use a magnifying glass? That's the way *he* writes it." I said, "What?" And I went in next room and there he was, with this big magnifying glass and this razor sharp pencil, making these tiny little marks on the paper. He didn't see very well, and he wrote everything in just a piano staff—he didn't write it on score paper for all the instruments—he wrote everything like two lines of a piano, right? And next to each note, he'd write the name of the instrument he wanted. And if he wanted it to go up an octave, he'd put a little arrow going up—you know, it's like a different *language* with him. But I learned a lot about orchestration by doing that stuff with him.

✝   ✝   ✝

Wayne Shorter added another perspective on "the different language" of Gil's writing—not what was written on the page but the tacit understanding—something that Shorter had seen in Miles as well as Gil, and also in the chemistry of their partnership. He described an incident that took place when some of the music from the 1968 Berkeley concert was being recorded later that year in New York:

> GIL HAD SOMETHING that the French horns had to play. It was a trill between two notes that are not geared for French horn trilling—the fingering of it and everything, it's very difficult to make it sound like a trill. [Some of them were] New York Philharmonic players, and they were saying it could not be done. They were saying, "Well, it can't be done the way

you wrote it here." Miles was standing on the side, and they kept going back and forth about how "unmusical" it was. Finally Miles just couldn't take it anymore, and he walked up to the podium and took the baton laying there, and he kind of just raised it a little bit and he said, "Just *mash* it." Just mash the keys down and start trilling. I've seen Miles do that on his trumpet. He was expressing an emotion, and emotions are the guidelines to what's musical or *not* musical, you know?

And it worked, Wayne said. Suddenly the music—and the thinking behind it—started making sense.

THEY DID IT. And what they *sounded* like—they sounded like *street* players, they sounded like a person who never studied music, who never studied the French horn. In other words, they did a *don't* instead of all of the *do*'s. And they were chuckling at what they were doing, and it's the kind of chuckle that you exude when you've tricked yourself—you know what I mean? You think that something can't be done—all of a sudden you're doing it. Not only can it be done technically, but they see the light of what Gil was trying to *say*. He was saying, "Okay, take the tuxedos off, unloosen the bow ties, we're going down to Hell's Kitchen for a minute." Not necessarily to Harlem all the time—we're going down to Hell's Kitchen—you know, where maybe their uncle or somebody tried to tell them—like a grandfather tries to tell the grandchild, "Never lose *this*. When you become a grown sophisticated man or woman, don't forget this."

✝   ✝   ✝

Several takes of one tune from this collection, Gil's composition "Falling Waters," were recorded in New York and are included on *Miles Davis–Gil Evans: The Complete Columbia Studio Recordings*.

These sessions for Columbia in 1968 were the last ones in which Miles and Gil recorded with a full orchestra, but Gil continued to participate in Miles's recording sessions throughout that year. Between January and September, Miles recorded enough music to fill three albums—*Directions, Miles in the Sky,* and *Filles de Kilimanjaro.* Each of these show the quintet moving further away from the music they'd made even as recently as a year earlier. Herbie Hancock:

BY THAT TIME, the music had a lot less formal structure than when I first joined Miles's band. It was really different. We were working off of different impressions of things, not even using the chords that came from the melody anymore—just using melodic fragments—and developing music probably in the same general way that classical music is developed. You know, they don't keep the same chords over and over again and just improvise their melodies on top—they develop the musical material that happens when you're *playing* the melody, that kind of thing, organic kind of development. In a way, that's what we were doing.

Gil's contribution during these sessions was in helping to provide the melodic or chord-based points of departure—either in his own original pieces or by writing out the music that he and Miles worked on together. The results were compositions in the sense that they established a predetermined framework for the tunes, but once Miles brought them into the recording studio, they took a form, shape, and direction all their own. This may explain why Gil was reluctant to claim any writing credits. On the other hand, these little handwritten sketches were the genesis of many excellent tunes. Gil's best work for the quintet was on *Filles de Kilimanjaro*, which was the last of the quintet's albums and a precursor to Miles's bolder shift into jazz fusion. It has been suggested that Gil wrote most and possibly all of the music on this album. As Anita Evans would put it, So what else is new?

GIL NEVER GOT ANY producer credits or anything, but you can't blame it all on Columbia. I remember once—and it could be for [Miles's 1967 album] *Sorcerer*—they called and said, "Well, should we give some credit to [you] on this album?" and Gil said no, he didn't want any credit. Except sometimes he'd notice he didn't have any money, and then he'd want [to get paid] but it would be the wrong time. A year later he would say, "Well, wow, I wrote those." But Gil put himself in that position. It was really coming from Gil—being totally non-aggressive about it sometimes, or other times actually being negative about it, saying, "No, I don't want it, this isn't about that stuff." He thought that was crass and commercializing.

Another striking characteristic of the quintet's new sound came from the Fender Rhodes electric piano. This instrument dates back to the 1940s, when Harold Rhodes developed the "Army Corps piano," so named because it was intended for the entertainment of troops during World War II. Rhodes later developed a series of small portable pianos for the education market. In 1959, Rhodes sold his company to Leo Fender's company (makers of the famed electric guitars and bass guitars)—hence the name changed to Fender Rhodes. In 1965, Fender sold his company to CBS, the media entertainment conglomerate. Under CBS, a number of new instruments were developed, and it was the first of the new pianos, the Mark I (introduced in 1965), that found widespread acceptance. This piano had collapsible legs (instead of a heavy cabinet) and a rugged "suitcase" top with built-in speakers and amplifier. Its compact size and design made the instrument easy to transport, but it was the piano's unique sound that made it popular among rock, R&B, and jazz musicians. (CBS sold the company in 1987 to Japanese keyboard-maker Roland. The company has marketed digital pianos under the Rhodes brand, and it has developed digital "patches," software that reproduces the Rhodes sound on Roland electronic keyboards. Since the late 1990s, there has been a resurgence of interest in the unique "retro" sound, but it has been the original vintage-era keyboards, not the digital versions, that most musicians seem to prefer.)

Herbie Hancock had started playing the Fender Rhodes (in December 1967) at Miles's suggestion. "I had been listening to Joe Zawinul playing it in Cannonball Adderley's group," Miles wrote, "and loved the way it sounded; for me, it was the future." The Fender Rhodes was also an ideal complement to the rock-and blues-based rhythms that Miles was also beginning to explore. "The music I was really listening to in 1968 was James Brown, the great guitar player Jimi Hendrix, and . . . Sly and the Family Stone." The Fender Rhodes added considerable strength and volume to the bottom end of the music. Miles, for example, liked the sound of the Fender Rhodes doubling the bass line. The Fender Rhodes also infused the music with its famously distorted electric timbre, which was particularly effective in playing sustained chords, especially those with the kind of angular and often dissonant harmonics favored by the likes of Gil Evans. "See, the Fender Rhodes has one sound and that sound is itself," Miles wrote. "It has no other sound. You always know what it is. I'm crazy about the way Gil Evans voices his music, so I wanted to get me a Gil Evans sound in a small band." Gil felt at least as excited as Miles about the Fender Rhodes. Once he started playing it, Gil rarely performed or recorded without it.

✢   ✢   ✢

"I'm no granddaddy," Gil told Nat Hentoff. "Being an elder statesman may be all right for someone who doesn't want to establish new landmarks. But it's not my groove." These words had appeared in a *Down Beat* article in 1957, co-inciding with the re-issue of the nonet sessions as *Birth of the Cool*. Gil had no problem with being the oldest of his circle, but he disliked the connotations of being associated with the past. "This being mentioned is a disadvantage as well as an advantage," he told Hentoff. "I don't enjoy being called a granddaddy when I'm still active, still learning, still writing, and will always be writing." Fifteen years later, in 1972, Gil had virtually the same message. And despite his monumental accomplishments since that *Down Beat* story was published, Gil was as modest and self-deprecating as ever. "I haven't really done that much yet, you know," he told Helen Armstead Johnston. "I don't feel that I have re-ally had much of a career. It's been very spotty and very occasional, and it's hard for me to assess. That's one of the reasons why I wasn't terribly enthusi-astic about having this kind of an interview, because I didn't really feel that I wanted to be placed by anybody else or myself in a wax museum now, because I still have my future career in mind."

The next shift in Gil's evolution was less about arranging or composing than about playing music with his own band. From this point on, Gil's focus would be almost entirely on his band. The Gil Evans Orchestra would not be a fait accompli but rather a work in progress. Its performances, whether in a studio, concert hall, or jazz club, would be propelled by Gil's sense of ad-venture—"Let's just see what happens"—at least as much as by his writing, and often more so. Nearing his sixtieth year, Gil was approaching his life and his music with something of the zest and energy he saw in Duke Ellington, who at this time was well into his seventies. "Duke has the sense of aban-donment that comes with age. By abandonment, I mean laying off a lot of bullshit that you don't want—you know, the things that you don't want to do—and so you say the hell with it. I realize this—that I have that feeling sometimes."

Ironically, it was a writing fellowship—Gil's first major recognition as a bandleader—that helped finance the development of his new endeavors. The fellowship was awarded in 1968 by the prestigious John Simon Guggenheim Memorial Foundation. The jury's decision was based in part on the three letters of recommendation that accompanied Gil's applica-tion—from Gunther Schuller, John Lewis, and Duke Ellington. "I got nine thousand dollars," Gil told Helen Johnston. "I'd asked for more, but nine was okay. I was glad to get it. It's about the best one you can get, I think. They gave me a letter, you know, saying that I was a Guggenheim Fellow and a "To Whom It May Concern" type of letter. I haven't had occasion to lean on that yet but I'll be glad to when I can. I keep it with me, though, just in case I may need it."

Gil's Guggenheim fellowship of $9,000 was a considerable sum in 1968 dollars, thus it provided welcome financial relief and enabled Gil to devote more time to his new music. (Anita Evans told me that Gil also used part of this grant money to cover the legal expenses required for changing his name. At long last, Ian Green officially became Gil Evans.)

The music that Gil wrote after receiving the Guggenheim award was heard in 1969—on his first record since *Individualism,* recorded almost five years earlier. Originally released as *Gil Evans* and later titled *Blues in Orbit,* the album has all of the hallmarks of Gil's best earlier music, along with some of the many new sounds and ideas he had acquired since then. *Blues in Orbit* is as eclectic in its repertoire as any of Gil's masterworks and even more diverse in its range of new sounds—including electric bass, a more rock-oriented guitar, and Gil's recording debut on electric piano. The album introduces Gil's take on the new rock and funk music (notably, on Billy Harper's "Thoroughbred" and George Russell's "Blues in Orbit"), but it also has equal measures of solid jazz writing ("Love in the Open," by drummer Warren Smith) and pure free-form playing (a new version of "Proclamation," along with "Spaced," which is actually an excerpt from "Proclamation").

Although the writing and the orchestral sound on this record are very different from his previous albums, Gil's musical voice is immediately recognizable. Rather than changing his unique orchestrations wholesale, he added new voices into the mix, and he adjusted that mix according to what he wanted to hear. Howard Johnson:

HE JUST KIND OF EVOLVED THINGS. He never said, "Okay, we're gonna go in this bold new direction." And it was just sort of natural to add elements that were identified as pop, because they were vital elements. They were added not for commercial reasons, because he never got rich off it, but because of their relative vitality. And when things started going that way, it didn't mean we could no longer do the things we had done before. There was always room for everything. And he wanted a fresh approach to anything he might do, even if it was an arrangement from thirty years before.

The strongest of Gil's new tunes is "Variation on the Misery," which features an improvised introduction—Gil on acoustic piano, accompanied by string bass—followed by an intense, disturbing ensemble theme somewhat reminiscent of the pathos of his "Bilbao Song." "General Assembly" (formerly known as "Time of the Barracudas") is another new version of an earlier tune—renamed, perhaps, as a reflection of this new arrangement's much greater emphasis on ensemble playing and group improvisation. "So Long" is a ballad, a tribute to John Coltrane that Gil recorded at the time of Coltrane's death in 1967. "He died just then," Gil told writer Ben Sidran. "He died that week that we made it. And I brought the tape home before I named it. I brought it home and played it and cried bitterly all night long. Because I hadn't really let myself go at the shock of his death. That's how I happened to call it 'So Long.'"

For die-hard fans of the original classics, *Blues in Orbit* might have felt like the beginning of the end, as Gil's musical focus turned increasingly to improvisation and—even worse, to some ears at least—to a decidedly rock-flavored style played on electric instruments. For Gil, however, the album was more like the beginning of the future—the public unveiling of his reincarnated orchestra and the new outlook it embodied.

As Gil explored these new musical territories, so, too, he began to attract a new generation of musicians. One of first of these was percussionist Susan Evans (no relation to Gil), who was the youngest of the new players and also the least experienced:

MY TASTES WERE SO NARROW. I had no idea about any of the big bands' sound at all. When Gil and I met, and I started playing with Gil, that to me was what a big jazz band was supposed to sound like. I didn't know what slick was—and that was the priceless thing that I got from Gil. His band was really just a big small group, but I didn't know that. After that, when I heard other big bands, I thought, "Gee, that sounds so slick, so impersonal."

I used to take drum lessons with Warren Smith, who was at that time in his band, and Gil would come up to [Warren's] loft—not to rehearse the band necessarily, but to just practice. And occasionally I would be up there practicing, and we'd run into each other. We just sort of ended up being at the loft at the same time, and he said, "Why don't we just practice together?" He would fiddle on the piano and I would play on the drums, and we kind of got a little musical rapport going. Then Gil was going to do an album, and at that time Warren was in Europe, on the road with somebody, and he needed a percussionist, so he said, "Why don't you be the percussionist?" And it was my very, I mean my very first record date ever. I hadn't even done any jingles or any film dates or anything before that.

People used to think Gil was my father, from our name, and it's funny, I kind of think of Gil as my *musical* father, because I think he brought out things in me that I didn't know I had. I think he let me develop much in the way a father, a *good* father, lets his child develop. He didn't impose his musical taste on me. We must have been on the same wavelength or it wouldn't have worked, but then at that point he let me alone. He really did. When I played in the band, he very rarely gave me direction—he very rarely gave the *band* direction. It wasn't like he'd say, "Okay, let's play a Charlie Parker tune"—there was none of that. There was no beginning and there was no end. It could have been I was playing when he put the key in the door, practicing some little coordination exercise, and Gil would turn that into a riff and develop a tune on it. Or Gil would be clunking at the piano and I'd go sit down at the drums and Gil would respond to how I was tuning the drums. It was complete stream of consciousness. And that was, to me, a style of playing that I would bring to the gig, in a sense, because his tunes didn't *have* beginnings and ends. . . . The horns would come in and all of a sudden Gil might change the harmony, so it would shift to the tune he wanted to play—all of a sudden we'd be into "Blues in Orbit" or something like that—and then it would kind of peter out, kind of meld into another tune.

‡   ‡   ‡

For all the strengths of *Blues in Orbit,* the album itself was poorly recorded and mixed. This was no doubt the result of insufficient studio time, but greater problems in the production were caused by the difficulty of recording acoustic and electric instruments simultaneously. To this day, achieving a balanced acoustic/electric sound mix remains a daunting challenge for most bands. Current technology and methods have all but eliminated the problem in a studio—most notably, by way of advanced digital multitrack recording, mixing, and editing systems—but mixing or recording a live performance remains a formidable task. In Gil's case, the technical challenges of the day were compounded by the number and diversity of instruments he used—and even more, as Gil told Helen Armstead Johnston, so by the nature of his music:

THE HARMONY GETS THE SOUND. A certain way you harmonize things gives the orchestra a certain sound. Then the choice of instruments to play the music is another thing. It has to be played very carefully. And you depend so much on the balance—the harmonic balance of it—that if it's not played with the right volume, and it isn't balanced and it's distorted, it will sound worse than if you hadn't tried any of that and just played it the plain, same old way. It can sound terrible. Actually, in the old days—and by old days I mean prior to sixteen-track recording and general electronic conditions that prevail now—I always wrote orchestral things so that they balanced themselves. They were written in such a way, and they were arranged how I wanted them, that they were balanced practically automatically.

If an acoustic player is surrounded by electronic instruments, it's very hard for him to put up with it, you know. They have all this energy which they can get with a little turn [of a dial], so physically, he's not capable of competing with it, and psychologically, he's very, very depressed at the idea of somebody being able to get energy like this. And with all the work that goes into learning to play an acoustic instrument, there's something to that. Although a very good player is not going to labor that point or hold that kind of rancor that much—provided he doesn't have to be the unlucky one who's competing for sound, right? And that he doesn't get drowned out by the electronics all the time. And it's a delicate thing in a way, too, because some players don't mind putting pick-ups on instruments, and some do. I don't know, I'll have to speak to some of the players about it. For example, the tuba, as large an instrument as it is, it's a very delicate instrument, and it needs to be amplified when it's played in a low register. I know when it's played up high and it's shouting, you can hear it. But when it's played down low, which you can do very beautifully and agilely and all that, it has to have a microphone. It just cannot be heard over the sum total of the decibels that come from that band—the drums, the guitar, and bass and all of that.

Gil, of course, took such matters in stride, acknowledging the difficulties but leaving it to others—producers and sound engineers as well as the musicians—to solve them on their own terms. Although he was sympathetic to the demands they faced, Gil nevertheless wanted *more* electronics, *more* volume, more of the energy that could only be achieved with these delightful new instruments. As a result, the technical challenges would get harder to overcome, not easier, as Gil continued to welcome every new voice he came upon. Not surprisingly, when the next big advance came along in the early 1970s—the electronic synthesizer—Gil was among the first in line to try one on for size.

The first synthesizer was the Moog, developed by R. A. (Bob) Moog between 1963 and 1968. The instrument made history in 1968 with the release of the hit album *Switched-On Bach,* which featured the music of J. S. Bach sounding as it had never been heard before. Moog's first commercially available model, the Minimoog, was introduced in 1971 and was soon popularized by progressive rock and jazz fusion bands. Gil Evans may not have been the first to feature the synthesizer on a jazz record, but he was certainly among the first to experiment with it. Gil was attracted not only by the new sound of the instrument but also by its versatility. As he explained to Helen Armstead Johnston, first-generation synthesizers (Moog, Arp, Oberheim, and others), crude as they were, were not just another kind of electric piano but rather a whole new class of instruments:

A SYNTHESIZER IS A SERIES of oscillators, which are single basic tones. From that tone, you can stretch it and distort it and do anything you want with it. You can give it any kind of overtones and waveforms. The synthesizer can add any of the overtones that are necessary—the kind of overtones that give the sound of the flute family, or the oboe family, or bassoon family—or you can turn all the oscillators off and just work out some drum sounds. It has all kinds of possibilities. It can be used to imitate what went on in the past, or it can be used to create something you've got in mind that hasn't happened yet. It has a lot of possibilities.

Gil soon had a synthesizer of his own, a Minimoog, but he never played it in the band. Rather, he used it to experiment with its unique sounds and colors. The first synth player to join Gil's band was David Horowitz, who was introduced to Gil in 1971 by his friend, bassist Herb Bushler.

HERB TOOK ME TO MEET GIL and we talked for a while, and without even really auditioning or anything, I was in the band. That's the way Gil did things. And very shortly thereafter, the first gig I played with the band was at a club called Slug's, on the Lower East Side. And that was it, I was in the band. I played synthesizer, and electric piano from time to time.

It was all . . . very loose. Gil gave me the band's book—he had piano reductions of most of the tunes in the book—and I took them home and kind of looked at them. And there really were no written synthesizer parts. I think what he was looking for was to add new colors to the band that weren't easily achievable with acoustic instruments. So I had this set of piano reductions, and I would just show up at the gig and turn my stuff on, and wherever I felt something should be added, I added it. It was really interesting. I learned a lot about arranging that way, too. There were a couple of things where he would say maybe you should double this line or that line, but in terms of what sounds I used, that was entirely up to me.

Unlike the electric piano, these early synthesizers could produce only one note at a time. This could be frustrating, especially if you approached the synth as a traditional keyboard. "They weren't polyphonic," Horowitz explained, "but this made it easier, in the sense that it could be used as a solo instrument, because it was not a chord instrument, it was not an accompaniment instrument. And in the ensembles, because you were limited to one note, you would have to pick the part you wanted to play, find the right sound, and do it." Finding the right sound, as David put it, was no small feat. Each of the oscillators had to be programmed manually in order to produce the desired sounds, and that in itself posed a whole other set of challenges.

ANOTHER INTERESTING ASPECT TO THAT—those things were a bitch to keep in tune. They were very unreliable. You never knew when—in the middle of a solo or playing an ensemble thing—it would drop a half tone or whatever. There was no way to keep it in tune. So there was always a constant battle against that. And unless you were thoroughly, totally familiar with the instrument, you would go to change a patch, and the level would jump like three dB—and you'd suddenly wipe out the whole band. So I was always on tenterhooks, especially playing live. In the studio it was different, because I had a chance to fool around with sounds—but then Gil didn't like to do *overdubs* in the studio. Everything went down live. So that made it kind of a nightmare for engineers.

✝   ✝   ✝

In 1970, the Evans family moved to a wonderful new home just a few blocks from their apartment on West 15th Street. It was Westbeth, an industrial building in the West Village (formerly a Bell Telephone research lab) that had been converted to lofts and apartments to provide subsidized housing for artists. The complex was a closely knit, highly creative community. There were many families with children the same age as Noah (five) and Miles (four), which made it an ideal environment for the whole Evans family. One of its best features was the Westbeth Cabaret, an open space in the basement that was designed to enable tenants to mount exhibits and performances and to host a range of events and social activities. The cabaret was a perfect venue for the workshop-style sessions Gil had in mind for his band. Before long, these informal sessions became a series of weekly concerts.

Two more newcomers to Gil's circle were the percussionist Airto Moriera and his wife, singer Flora Purim. They had met Gil shortly after their arrival from Brazil in 1969. Neither of them were "permanent" members of Gil's new band, but as Flora told me, they both played at every opportunity.

BEFORE I LEFT BRAZIL, me and Airto, we used to spend days and nights listening to all his records, particularly one he did with Miles Davis called *Miles Ahead*. This was like our national *anthem*. We listened to this record day and night—after the gig, before the gig, when we wake up, when we went to sleep. And when we met Gil and he became our friend, it was like . . . [Flora clasps her hands together against her heart] . . . like this. Gil was a very spiritual man, very spiritual. And very simple, very humble in his own ways. And we had a very close relationship. I would say that besides Airto, Gil was my best friend.

My singing was mostly sounds. He wanted me to do just *sounds,* at any time. He would say, "Do it any time, no matter what's happening with the band—if you feel something, come up." He would give me that freedom, and I did experiment a lot, because of it. And the thrill I felt when I sang with Gil was like—I never knew what was going to happen. I was there looking at him, waiting for his conducting, waiting for a sign, and knowing that something was going to happen. The singer in a big band, it's the worst possible thing, because she sings the head, then she sits there, then twelve guys take solos, and half an hour later she goes back and sings the tail and goes out. So I didn't have that kind of role. At all times, I would either play percussion, or if somebody's taking a solo and I felt something, I was free to enhance it—make sounds. And it was a thrill.

Airto felt as close to Gil as Flora did, and he too loved the freedom and energy of Gil's music. "The music, the band of the '70s, was more rhythmical, more aggressive—but the chords that he used were pretty much the same [as his earlier writing]. *Porgy and Bess* and all this other stuff, the earlier stuff, it was more lyrical, more romantic—and more like from the heart, not from the *blood*. This music was so—how can I put it—it was so open and avant garde and beautiful and strong, it was everything. It was *life*. Gil's music was life. And people were not ready . . . Not everybody liked it."

"You mean the *record* companies were not ready," Flora interjected, "because the *people* used to love it. The audiences used to *love* Gil's concerts." "She's got a point there," Airto replied. "Because the record companies, they never look for something new, they look for something *old*."

Gil had never catered to the wishes of record companies, nor did he seem to worry about how his audiences might react. Audiences were welcome to share the experience, but this was a band for players. "Lately, I haven't been working very much," he said to Helen Armstead Johnston. "So whenever I get a chance to work, I don't really care about the audience, because I'm so hungry to play that I'd just as soon let the players all play on every number all they want to. Because it gives me more chances to be active musically, you see. That's what I've been doing. And of course, some people like it and some people think it's just terrible." The sense of freedom in this band extended not just to the soloists but to everyone in the band. Airto:

ONE THING I REMEMBER that he was asking me all the time was to play *louder*. I swear. And actually, the tuba player, Howard Johnson, used to get pissed off, because I was playing right next to him. And, you know, to play in tune and everything, you have to hear yourself really well—and I'm going bla! bla! bla! making all these loud noises, you know? It was strange, because at that time nobody knew about percussion, actually. Percussion was congas and bongos and mirachas, and I had the most strange sounds, and Gil loved it. Gil would look at me and point, "More! More!" And I'm looking at Howard Johnson and he's just looking at me, "No, no!" And I was like in between *fires*, you know? But that's what he always said, "Play whatever you want, and play louder."

✝   ✝   ✝

Freedom of expression such as this was not as common as one might expect in the jazz world, and it was virtually unheard of among big bands. For players that were as hungry as Gil was to push the experience as far as they could, this band was a dream come true. Even more alluring than its great openness and spontaneity was the fact that this was, after all, a *Gil Evans* orchestra. At the end of the day, it was still Gil's writing that was the greatest challenge of playing in this band. And while anarchy had its place in this music, free-form jazz—which is to say, totally unplanned, unstructured improvisational music—was never the end-all and be-all of this band or of Gil's overall musical vision. As he told Helen Armstead Johnston:

> MOST ALL OF EVERYTHING we play is based on a song. It's all a song. We play mostly songs. And to go on and just not play anything but sounds— well, sometimes that happens accidentally. For example, on the Ampex album *[Blues in Orbit]*, they don't seem avant garde to me really. They seem like, well, they're modern. They are not avant garde; they are modern in a sense—like some compositions are unusual melodically, but nevertheless they have a definite tune.

Therein lies the great distinction of Gil's music of the 1970s and later: his balance of order and chaos, form and formlessness, design and spontaneity. Gil's concept was unique and deceptively simple. A tune might begin as little more than a single riff, the merest sound or rhythmic pattern; then one by one the musicians would join in, offering whatever the moment inspired in them. As the music developed, Gil would then begin to shape it, redirect it—with a gesture, the wave of a hand. "You can needle them a little bit," he explained to *Coda*'s Don Lahey. "I can needle them at the piano, or the drums can change sometimes, if the groove is becoming a rut. Sometimes you do it that way. You try to create something that will possibly lead them a different way, a different direction." This kind of basic direction—to shift the tempo or the mood of the music—is something every conductor or bandleader is familiar with, as are most musicians. But beginning in the 1970s, Gil developed a unique style of merging highly spontaneous music with his highly organized written scores. It started with Gil passing his charts out with particular ensemble sections identified by a name or number. When he wanted to hear one of these sections, he would simply call it out. Often, these ensembles were sections taken from his earlier arrangements—the bridge from "Gone" or "Summertime," for example. They might be played as written, or they might contain newly written voicings or playing instructions. Either way, the players had to remain loose—but alert. Airto Moriera:

> LET'S SAY IT WAS A PIECE that was written. In the middle of the piece of music he'd write, "Free—play out," or whatever. So everybody would just go totally crazy. And then while they were doing this, he would choose *another* song, and then put it right there in front of them—a new song, in the middle of that craziness—and then stand up and point his fingers, like— thirty-one or whatever. And then one by one, we would stop playing and put up that page, right? Thirty-one. And get ready. And when everyone was ready, he would go like this with his hands [Airto raises his arms over his head] and start the band, "One, two"—and everybody would start at the same time, the new song. It was an incredible thing.
>
> Some musicians, they didn't really like that, because they wanted to play chops, they were there to show off. I don't say names, but I know this. Some guys, all they wanted to do was jump in front of that band and take a great solo, you see? And that was not what the band was about. The band was about *ensemble*—and we're all the same, and we are playing the music now and that's it. That's why Gil sometimes would stop everything and start something else. And we would go crazy—"Wow, why? This is crazy." But he was not crazy. It was because he was breaking rules. That's what Gil did all his life; he broke musical rules.

It was an intriguing proposition for all concerned: a unique combination of free improvisation blended with some of the most complex orchestral jazz writing ever seen. The band's book included new tunes alongside Gil's earlier arrangements, all of which were subject to change without a moment's notice. Gil's work had always reflected his willingness to experiment with new forms and styles. What was different now were his sources—instead of Ravel and Gershwin, it was John Coltrane and Jimi Hendrix. As he had once incorporated French horns and tuba within traditional big-band orchestrations, now it was electric guitars and synthesizers.

And just as Gil's earlier masterworks were written for the best players of their time, so would his new music rely on the talents of yet another generation of innovators and virtuosi. The concept of this new music had been evolving since as far back as 1966, but it was in the early 1970s that all the

pieces of the puzzle—which is to say, the right people—finally came together. There was rarely enough work to sustain any of these musicians on a
permanent basis, but between 1971 and 1974, Gil managed to attract a nucleus of players that worked on all or most of his projects for the balance of
the decade and, in some cases, even longer. These players would be as crucial to the success of Gil's new music as Miles Davis or Cannonball Adderley
or Elvin Jones or Wayne Shorter before them. In one sense, they faced an
even greater challenge. It was one thing to turn every performance into an
experiment—Gil Evans was far from unique in that respect—but it was
quite another matter to take that leap not just with a trio or a quartet but
with ten, twelve, fifteen musicians, or more. Considerable talent and nerves
of pure steel are required not only of the leader but also of every individual.
Such was the challenge and this band's call to arms. It attracted his core players, countless other jazz artists, and many musicians outside of jazz. It was as
intoxicating as the Pied Piper's magical tune and as irresistible as the
warmth and effusive charm of the maestro himself.

French horn player Pete Levin first met Gil in the mid-1960s. "I think I expected Gil to be about seven feet tall or something," he remembered of his
first meeting with Gil. "Typical Gil—where you'd start talking to him and he
would immediately be asking about *you*. You'd find yourself talking about
yourself to Gil—like that would be typical." He had been introduced to Gil by
Howard Johnson, and it was through Johnson, later on, that Levin joined the
band. "It was a few years later, in the early '70s," Levin told me. "Gil was playing a week at the Village Vanguard, and they needed a horn player in a hurry,
and Howard was in the band, and he said, 'Hey, we know a horn player,' and
I got this panic call, 'Come to the Village Vanguard immediately.' And that was
the start of about a fifteen-, sixteen-year stint with the band. I was the horn
player who came to dinner and never left." Although he started as a French
horn player, Levin shifted to keyboards and eventually became Gil's resident
electronics genius:

> I STARTED TO COLLECT synthesizers in the early '70s, but somewhere I
> asked Gil if I could bring a synth to the gig and make some noises when I
> wasn't playing the horn. And eventually Gil started to write parts for
> what I was doing, and I got so occupied with the synth and the other
> noises I was making that I really didn't have time to get back to the horn
> to get to play the choruses and the stuff Gil was arranging for horn. So he

just got another horn player to cover me so I didn't have to do that. And I played second horn for a while and then finally stopped bringing the horn, and actually completely changed my role in the band, which is pretty unique.

Trombonist Dave Bargeron also met Gil through Howard:

I WAS WITH THE BAND Blood, Sweat, and Tears in 1972, and we were very busy in touring around all over the place, but the band was based in New York. I had been a longtime associate of Howard Johnson, and I guess there was a trombone opening in the band, because he recommended me to Gil. And I came down and played a couple of times, and all of a sudden I was in the band. We played at that time over at Westbeth [Cabaret]. We used to play there every week, on Monday nights. And as my schedule could permit it—because Blood, Sweat, and Tears was right at kind of its apex, so the touring obligations of that band were pretty heavy—but as I could, I'd trundle into New York for a Monday night to play with Gil. That's how it started.

Blood, Sweat, and Tears was one of the most successful jazz/pop fusion bands of its time. Following a string of hits on the pop charts, it played to ca- pacity audiences throughout the world. Thus it was not unusual for Dave Bargeron to play one night to an audience of 50,000 BS&T fans and then play the next night with Gil for maybe a couple of dozen people down at Westbeth. Still, said Dave, being part of this man's band was an incompara- ble musical experience.

AT THAT POINT, of course, Gil was a jazz legend, appreciated to the hilt by all of us, and it was an honor to play with him just on that basis alone. But what got me was, I had not played music that was that adventurous, harmonically—I mean written for bunches and bunches of horns—and an ensemble that was that out.

    Gil exerted no—count 'em—no real leadership from the bandstand that would be counted in any conventional sense as leadership. He just didn't. It was his presence. He had all these people that respected him so much, and respected what he represented so much, that somehow that was the policing agent, or the organizing agent, in an otherwise pretty freewheeling, non-organized, chaotic, sometimes messy situation with this band, you know? "It's just going to happen"—"Whatever happens happens"—that was his thing, you know? Given that atmosphere, there were times when it was terrible. There were times when it reached heights—like, you're asking me the high points? There were concerts in my memory that—minds and communication and the general atmosphere were so electric, and so communicative, and so perfect and so wonderful—it was just the most exciting damn music I've ever played in my life. The best of everything, all coming together, you know? And it's like almost star-crossed. I mean, you gotta play ten *years* with this man, four hundred *gigs,* before you get one like that. Everybody lives for one like that, you know? That's the way it's always been.

Perhaps the busiest of all the players on Gil's list was alto saxophonist David Sanborn. When he joined Gil in 1973, he had been recording and touring with the Paul Butterfield Blues Band, Stevie Wonder, David Bowie, and many other high-profile artists. He, too, got the fateful phone call from his friend (and also neighbor in Woodstock, in upstate New York), Howard Johnson, one of Gil's most dependable recruiters.

HE SAID, "WHY DON'T you come down and play with Gil Evans?" Either there wasn't an alto player in the band, or there was somebody and they weren't doing the gig anymore. Anyway, I remember I went down to the Village Gate and I was scared to death. I drove down from Woodstock and played a rehearsal, and Gil said okay. And I think I came down a couple of days later, or that night, and played. I think it was "Priestess," a Billy Harper tune, Gil's arrangement. Billy played a solo and then Gil said, "Okay now—play." I said, "*What?* I don't know the *tune.*" He said, "Play, just play." I wasn't going to play, I was like completely terrified, you know? Because I hadn't played in a big band for *years*—since I was in college, really. It was terrifying, and he just let me play. Then they had another gig, then there was another gig, and I just kind of became a member of Gil's band. I became the guy that he called.

Trumpeter and multi-instrumentalist Tom Malone joined Gil in 1972 and remained with the band for fifteen years. Like Bargeron, Malone was attracted by the challenge—and the freedom—of Gil's approach.

GIL MADE THIS ACCEPTING framework for all of the people in the band to play what they felt, and it became something that everybody felt at the same time. It seemed like an idea that made sense to me, and a concept that I was ready to jump into. It stimulates all kinds of chemicals in the brain, you know, to actually play whatever is going on in a spontaneous framework, interacting with other musicians. It's something that can be very chaotic and make no sense at all—and it's also something that can make a lot of sense.

One of the key factors that determined if the music would make sense, Pete Levin explained, was not simply the talent but the intuitiveness of the players.

HE WANTED TO PUT his band together and just throw some music at them and see what happens. He was very open about that—"Let me see where this can go." And when he got his own big band together and he had to a certain extent a predictable personnel, eventually the guys playing for him got to understand what it was he had in mind. And we could take the charts way out—I mean just depart from them completely— but we always knew how to get *back* to them. Or sometimes Gil would throw a signal and everybody was just aware that, yeah we should be over here. Sometimes it wasn't even *that* formal. There were always provisions in these charts for ensemble choruses that would either stand on their own, or could be behind soloists, that would just be used when Gil felt that he wanted to hear them. That is, the chart would go to a certain point, and then there would just be this gap which—I think if an entire band were sight-reading the chart they would get hopelessly confused and would grind to a halt, and would need instructions. But we just knew that we should *play,* and that whoever jumped out of his chair first had the solo.

For those less familiar with Gil's signals and gestures, the process could be disorienting, to say the least. Gil's cryptic, Zen-like "directions" could just as easily lead to mass confusion as to artistic enlightenment. One man's anarchy, of course, is another's liberation. To French horn player John Clark, who started played with Gil in 1973, the unplanned elements of this music were its strongest attraction:

THE THING IS, NO OTHER band plays that way, where you play the arrangement and then anything can happen. I don't know any other band that plays like that. In most big bands, everything is structured. You play the chart, and there's a solo, and everyone knows who's going to solo and who's going to solo next and when the background's coming in and how long they're going to play and how many choruses and everything—and after a while, even what they're going to play in their solo. I'm exaggerating a little bit, but this is totally the other end of that. Sometimes with Gil, a tune would go on for an hour, because Gil didn't want to put any restrictions on anybody in any way. Like if Howard Johnson wanted to get up and play a tuba solo, and then sit back down, pick up the baritone and play another solo right away, Gil never wanted to say "Hey, don't do that." He'd hardly *ever* say anything like that. Maybe that was asking a lot from the audience, and maybe from the other musicians, who had to just sit there—but then we could make up a background. If you get tired of listening to a guy play a long solo, you make up a background and start playing. And when you do that, you're *involved*. When you're improvising like that, *you're* the composer, okay? And all fourteen people are involved.

"There wouldn't be a set list with Gil," said trumpeter Lew Soloff.

WE'D KNOW THE OPENING TUNE, we might know something else, but he would do a little tinkling on the piano, and then we would go into our next tune. In other words, it wasn't a show; it was a real creative experience. And it was because that kind of freedom was afforded. But when you afford that kind of freedom, you also have to have the nerve to know that plenty of times it's *not* going to work. Because it's not a show. A show is something that's well rehearsed and works every time. This was well rehearsed, too, but more for the purpose of us learning.

For all concerned, learning and experiencing this music was its sole raison d'être. Tom Malone:

IT WAS ALWAYS A GREAT creative experience. It was never a real money-making thing, but it was something that everybody showed up for. Matter of fact, the first time I played for him, we didn't get paid at all. We all just showed up and played, because Gil felt it was important for the band to play, and people would just show up. He's that strong a person that people were attracted to him creatively. And the job might pay eighteen, twenty dollars [each]—and we *still* showed up. We used to play Monday nights at the Village Vanguard in the early '70s. Whenever the Thad Jones–Mel Lewis band was playing someplace else and was not available for Monday nights, we were sort of the regular fill-in band there for a while, and that only paid eighteen dollars a night. But some great music still happened. It was good times.

✝   ✝   ✝

In 1967, Jimi Hendrix had closed his performance at the Monterey Pop Festival by smashing his amplifier and lighting his guitar on fire, thereby setting off wilder and even stranger-sounding distortion and amplifier feedback than he had been producing all evening. The image of Hendrix, down on his knees, summoning up the flames from his fractured guitar, is a defining moment in the emergence of psychedelic rock. The performance launched his career in the United States and abroad. More than three decades after his death, Hendrix remains one of the most influential guitarists in rock history.

Gil Evans had been intrigued by the music of Jimi Hendrix since at least 1968, as had Miles Davis. Hendrix, at that time, was likewise a great admirer of Miles. Jimi and Miles met in 1969 through a meeting arranged by Jimi's producer, Alan Douglas. Jimi was interested in pursuing a more jazz-oriented direction in his music. He had already played informally with Tony Williams and his jazz-rock band, Lifetime, and with saxophonist Rashaan Roland Kirk, and soon he and Miles were getting together regularly at Miles's house to exchange ideas. Jimi did not read or write music, and he was intimidated by Miles, but he was what Miles called a natural musician, and the two men got along well. "He would pick up things from whoever he was around," Miles wrote in his autobiography, "and he picked up things quick.

> ONCE HE HEARD IT he really had it down. We would be talking, and I would be telling him technical shit like, "Jimi, you know, when you play the diminished chord . . ." I would see this lost look come into his face, and I would say, "Okay, okay, I forgot." I would just play it for him on the piano or on the horn, and he would get it faster than a motherfucker. He had a natural ear for hearing music. So I'd play different shit for him, show

him that way. Or I'd play a record of mine or Trane's and explain to him what we were doing. Then he started incorporating things I told him into his albums. It was great. He influenced me and I influenced him, and that's the way great music is always made.

Two separate deals were proposed with the intent of producing a Jimi Hendrix jazz album. The first was to bring Jimi together with Miles and Tony Williams in a band led by and featuring arrangements of Gil Evans. As Charles Shaar Murray wrote in *Crosstown Traffic,* Jimi was just as excited about playing with a big band as he was interested in exploring the jazz genre:

I WANT A BIG BAND. I don't mean three harps and fourteen violins. I mean a big band full of competent musicians that I can conduct and write for. . . . I think I'm a better guitarist than I was. I've learned a lot. But I've got a lot more to learn about music because there's a lot in this hair of mine that I've got to get out. With the bigger band, I don't want to be playing as much guitar. I want other musicians to play my stuff. I want to be a good writer.

According to Murray, this project was thwarted by Miles's refusal to participate for anything less than $50,000. The second project, proposed by Alan Douglas, was a guitar/orchestra album modeled after *Sketches of Spain.* "Alan Douglas had arranged for us to meet," Gil told Les Tomkins in a 1978 interview for the British magazine, *Crescendo International* (later featured in Raymond Horricks's biography of Gil). "He'd given [Jimi] the *Sketches of Spain* album. And the idea was for him to make a guitar record—not to sing. Because Alan felt, as I felt, too, he wasn't appreciated, even by himself." The concept was to record a live performance—their choice was Carnegie Hall—featuring all new material. Better still, by the time the project had been accepted by all parties involved, Miles had also agreed to join them, presumably for a more reasonable fee. In August 1970, both Miles and Jimi were playing at the Isle of Wight. "Gil Evans called and told me that he and Jimi were going to get together and that he wanted me to come down and participate," Miles wrote in his autobiography. "I told him that I would. We were waiting for Jimi to come when we found out that he had died in London." Jimi Hendrix died on September 18 as a result of an accidental overdose of alcohol and sleeping pills.

Although the collaboration did not come to pass, Gil continued to pursue his interest in Jimi's music. In 1974, he mounted his own concert at Carnegie Hall, a tribute to Jimi Hendrix, and he followed it up with a studio album, *The Gil Evans Orchestra Plays the Music of Jimi Hendrix*. The resulting music represented the first tribute to Jimi's music, the first jazz treatment of his music, and moreover, the first serious acknowledgment of Jimi's talent not only as an instrumentalist and performer but also as a composer and songwriter. In an interview for *GuitarWorld*, published in 1988, Gil told Bill Milkowski, "I'm always going back to Jimi's music and finding new possibilities, and every time I listen to his tunes, I hear something new. That's the mark of a great composer."

Guitarist John Abercrombie worked briefly with Gil's band in the early '70s, and he was one of two guitarists featured in both the Carnegie Hall concert and on Gil's Hendrix album.

I REMEMBER GOING TO [Gil's] house several times. It was kind of like pandemonium—there'd be a tape going and the radio is on, and he's talking, and he's trying to transcribe something, and once in a while he'd walk over to a keyboard and hit a note—but there was *method* in his madness. He was interested in new sounds and new ways to put things together. When he first heard Hendrix, it must have really opened up his ears a lot, because of the *sound* quality of the instrument. I mean it wasn't your traditional bebop guitar playing this sort of dry single tone. There were so many harmonics in Jimi Hendrix's sound, so much sustain and overdrive—and a lot of lyricism and melody. And I think Gil could really relate to that, the passion of it, you know? I think that's what probably drew him into that.

Just as in the 1930s, when Gil had drawn much of his material from Benny Goodman and Fletcher Henderson—the best of the popular music of that era—now he was drawn to Hendrix's playing as well as to his writing. Trumpeter Lew Soloff:

GIL WAS ALWAYS LOOKING for something new, and he was always fascinated with new things. He was hip to Jimi Hendrix and really understood him when he was out there. When Hendrix was out there doing his thing, I dismissed his music. I thought, Oh it was just pop music, right? But Gil and Miles, they were *into* the music then, and for many years into the seventies. When I started to play again with Gil, I started to understand Jimi's music through Gil, and I realized what a genius Jimi was, and what an influence on music he was—and *is*.

Finally, Gil also looked to this music as a way of connecting with a new generation. He wanted to incorporate into his music something of the radical new Jimi Hendrix sound, and in so doing, Gil also saw the prospect of reaching an audience that was no more interested in hearing old jazz tunes than he was. "I'm on your side" was the message that it seemed Gil wanted to convey. Dave Bargeron:

> HE HEARD IN THAT GUITAR-PLAYING the best of anything that you hear anywhere, and yet it was dressed in clothes that made it appeal to hundreds of thousands of people all over the world. That's the way I see it, and that's what I think he did. Gil heard the wail and the scream and the blues and this intense personal expression—which are all, in essence, in the best jazz performances—coming out of a person like Jimi Hendrix. And he *wanted* some of that, he wanted to get closer to that. He said, "Hey, it's that same heart, that same essence, that's the best of jazz, right?" That is now a language that speaks to *this* generation, you know? And he said, "Hey, I'd like to be in that swim. I'd like to be part of that."

‡   ‡   ‡

None of Gil's earlier recordings had sold particularly well, and none of the albums he made in the 1970s would fare much better. Nevertheless Gil was still able to attract sufficient interest from record producers (and in at least a couple of instances, the financial support of good friends) to ensure that the band got recorded. And when it came to performing, Gil was delighting and even thrilling his audiences. He did succeed in attracting a new, younger generation of listeners, albeit in modest numbers, even as many of the fans of his earlier work turned away, disappointed to find that his music was no longer the same as it used to be. Like the musicians themselves, listeners either related with Gil's new blend or they didn't. John Clark:

> I LIKED THAD JONES and Mel Lewis, I liked Count Basie, I liked Ellington—but I liked Elvis Presley and I liked Sly Stone, and I *loved* Jimi Hen-

drix. I mean, to hear a big band playing Jimi Hendrix tunes—for me, it was the perfect place to be. And a lot of the audience felt that, too. But then the jazz audience, the audience that had really liked *Sketches of Spain, Porgy and Bess,* and so on, they came to the club and they just shook their heads and walked out the door.

Gil was unfazed. He had seen all of this before. Talking to Ben Sidran in 1986, he attributed this attitude to "convenience," which he regarded as one of the great afflictions of our time:

WE'RE ALL VICTIMS of the terrible habit of convenience, right? When you're used to hearing a certain type of music, or a certain "sound" of music, and it changes, and you're not with it, or don't follow it any more, you're home and you stop going out to clubs and all that. . . . Like for example, Coleman Hawkins developed his sound starting in 1924, right? And he was *the* jazz saxophone player for ten years. Well, when [Lester Young] came along, people were outraged! Oh, everything you could think of they said about him. You know, "You sound like an alto, why don't you play one." All that kind of thing. Well a new generation comes along and picks up on it, and then the innovator, if he's still alive, and not a disaster, can get some credit, you know? But a lot of times an innovator can come and go and not have a very good life. The same thing happened with Coltrane. People were outraged at that sound. "Why would he want to do that when the sound was so good up until now?" That's convenience, right? The world's most prevalent addiction. We all suffer from an overuse of convenience at the expense of passion.

Ironically, many of the high points of the new band's work, both on record and in concert, were in fact based on Gil's earlier music. The charts were played by a younger generation of musicians, often on new and very different instruments, yet the fundamental Gil Evans sound—the distinctive orchestral colors and textures, the ensembles (written, improvised, or both)—was still there. Indeed, Gil soon proved to be as interested in re-composing his own material as he was in working with that of other people. He relished the opportunity to hear what one of these tunes might sound like with this particular band, with these new soloists and instruments. Although he had never been a prolific composer, he did continue to compose.

His output was even lower than usual—less than a dozen new tunes in the ten years between 1969 and 1979—but he did write some new arrangements as well. Among the best are his Jimi Hendrix arrangements and several tunes by Charles Mingus and Charlie Parker. As always, his music was by no means confined to any single genre. David Sanborn described this as an intrinsic element of Gil's music: "Gil wrote his *life*. Writing was his way of expressing how he felt about the world—what he loved and enjoyed. That was what you heard in his music was his *life*. He *liked* electric guitars. He *liked* loud music. He *liked* chaos. He *liked* density. He *liked* silence. And he liked to *swing*, you know? There's all different kinds of ways to swing— Muddy Waters to Cecil Taylor."

In his new recordings, Gil would explore all these avenues and more. Starting with *Blues in Orbit*, Gil's recordings document his remarkable transformation from master arranger to daring bandleader and experimentalist. Yet the shift did not appear suddenly or abruptly. Just as he acquired all the latest instruments and brought in new players, his new musical choices also evolved—from the people he met and the music he heard around him. Anita Evans:

THERE WAS NO CONSCIOUS thing to do anything radical. It was just about being inclusive on a sound and material level. What is this thing called jazz, or blues, what songs, what things are okay? Gil just put his ear out there to see what enchanted him enough to make him want to do an arrangement of it. He was open to listening to everything. He was always like that—never narrow, always open and available to be turned on by what was real to him. It was just his way as a human being, and our luck as music lovers, to get to experience the result.

THE MUSIC OF NOW

The difference between Gil and somebody who establishes a style and just plays in that style is that Gil was always looking to see what he could do with the sound of today. Loving people like Stevie Wonder. Loving people like John Coltrane. Gil always wanted to have the sound of Now Music, as he would put it. He never looked to the past, he always looked to the present and the future.

—LEW SOLOFF

AFTER *BLUES IN ORBIT*, Gil's next album was *Where Flamingos Fly*—recorded in 1971, but not released until 1981 on Ornette Coleman's independent label, Artists House. "We made it on an album for Capitol," Gil explained to British writer Les Tomkins, "but just as we finished it, a new administration came in and canceled about twenty-five projects—and ours was one of them." Filled with energy, vitality, and spirited performances, *Where Flamingos Fly* features the core of what was becoming Gil's permanent band—Billy Harper, Herb Bushler, Susan Evans, and Howard Johnson—together with guitarist Joe Beck and drummer Lenny White. The album also includes some of the great veteran musicians he had worked with in the 1960s and earlier—trombonist Jimmy Knepper, bassist Richard Davis, violinist Harry Lookovsky, and feature soloist Johnny Coles. Airto Moriera and Flora Purim (on overdubbed tracks) are featured on two tunes. Sitting in for David Horowitz on these sessions is Don Preston, formerly a keyboard player with another innovative California-based band, The Mothers of Invention. Preston, along with Phil Davis, played synthesizers—the first to be heard on a Gil Evans record and possibly the first heard on *any* jazz record. As Gil explained in an interview with producer John Snyder (during the remix of this album in 1981), Preston and Davis came to New York at their own expense—specifically to play with Gil. "Don Preston had this friend who had all this equipment. They lived in Hollywood and he was willing to come—to bring all that equipment and come to New York and go to Europe with me. All I did was pay for room and board. His friend wanted the experience. I think he paid his own plane ticket."

Where Flamingos Fly features three new arrangements ("Nana," by Brazilian composers Moacir Santos, Mario Telles, and Yanna Coti; Billy Harper's "Love Your Love"; and "El Matador," by Kenny Dorham) along with new versions of two earlier arrangements ("Jelly Rolls" and "Where Flamingos Fly"). It also features Gil's newest arrangement of his original tune, "Zee Zee," his first major composition of the new decade. "Zee Zee" has all the grace and style of his earlier writing—an elegant melodic theme, rich harmonic colors, and a somber, powerful atmosphere. And despite the band's new and unwieldy mix—acoustic instruments (including tenor violin) with electric piano, Fender bass, and synthesizers—"Zee Zee" and indeed all of the tunes on the album were superbly recorded.

The title track is the John Benson Brooks tune that Gil recorded in 1956 for Helen Merrill, and again in 1960 for *Out of the Cool*. Another earlier tune, "Hotel Me," reappears as "Jelly Rolls," now credited to Gil alone, rather than to Gil and Miles. As Gil explained to John Snyder, for the reissue's liner notes, this tune was recorded during his collaborations with Miles for *Time of the Barracudas*, but he wrote it himself. "I forget the reason for it, but it was necessary to have a blues. So I sat down at the piano and I played something I learned on a Muddy Waters record when Otis Spann used to accompany Muddy. . . . So I wrote it out for the band, and Miles played a solo on it. The unison that the band plays on this record is based on his solo."

Interestingly, the two older songs are the strongest tunes on the album. On "Jelly Rolls," Gil eliminates the raucous, often-satirical mood of his 1964 arrangement in favor of a pure blues groove. The tune features one acoustic bass and one Fender instead of the earlier version's two acoustic basses; it replaces acoustic piano with electric; and the brass and reeds are augmented with great effectiveness by two synthesizers. Whereas "Hotel Me" had featured trumpet solos (first by Miles and, on Gil's record, by Johnny Coles), in this arrangement, the unison ensemble is the dominant melodic element. On "Where Flamingos Fly," the arrangement is virtually the same as Gil's 1960 recording, but the character of the tune is reshaped by a faster tempo, new orchestrations (notably, bowed acoustic bass, Fender bass, and two synthesizers) and, especially, by a hard-edged tenor solo by Billy Harper.

✝   ✝   ✝

Gil's 1973 album *Svengali* (named after Gerry Mulligan's eight-letter anagram for Gil Evans's name) ranks as one of Gil's finest albums and one of the best jazz recordings of the decade. *Svengali* came about through the efforts not of a jazz impresario but of the renowned contemporary painter Kenneth Noland, who was a personal friend of Gil's. "He was real tight with Kenneth Noland," Anita said. "Ken actually put up the bucks for the *Svengali* album. I think how it was, [Atlantic Records cofounder] Nesuhi Ertegun bought a painting from Ken for thirty-five thousand dollars, and that money went into being the production budget for the album. That kind of stuff was happening a lot in the seventies, with our Soho friends, but that's a big one, because in the world of art they know Kenneth Noland, but I don't know if they know him as a jazz record producer."

By the time *Svengali* was made, Gil had assembled all of the key members of his permanent orchestra, a band now comprised almost entirely of young players. He had a front line of four principal soloists—Billy Harper, David Sanborn, Howard Johnson, and Marvin "Hannibal" Peterson—and an equally impressive group of rhythm and ensemble players. The cohesiveness of this band belied the fact that its concert performances were few and far between. *Svengali,* this band's first appearance on record, is all the more impressive given that every track was recorded in live concerts ("Zee Zee" at Lincoln Center and the remaining tunes at New York City's Trinity Church).

Captured at the height of the jazz fusion era, the music of *Svengali* goes far beyond the typical jazz-rock fare of its day. It blends *several* jazz streams—from swing to bebop to modal to free jazz—with an equally diverse mix of pop, R&B, funk, and rock. Like so many of his earlier recordings, from *Birth of the Cool* to *Sketches of Spain* to *Individualism, Svengali* reaffirms Gil's mastery of the musical hybrid. Although it offers just one new tune (Billy Harper's "Cry of Hunger"), *Svengali* is remarkable in its originality.

On "Thoroughbred" and "Blues in Orbit," the arrangements are identical to those on the Ampex album, but the new versions are invigorated by his new, expanded orchestra (and a much-improved level of sound recording quality). "Summertime" is rescored here for solo guitar played in a relaxed, slow tempo arrangement that recalls the warmth and lyricism of Gil's *Porgy and Bess* charts. "Eleven," not heard since Miles's version (listed as "Petit Machins" on *Filles de Kilimanjaro*), is another showstopper—played much faster than Miles's quintet arrangement and with the added impact of en-sembles played at full throttle by a full-size orchestra. Gil closes the album with a new version of "Zee Zee," his only original composition on this album. Recorded live at Lincoln Center's Philharmonic Hall, during his con-cert at the "Newport at New York" Jazz Festival, the tune features an ex-tended solo by Marvin "Hannibal" Peterson (making his recording debut as a soloist with Gil). This slower, darker treatment of "Zee Zee" is another masterpiece, recalling the drama and grandeur of Gil's writing of the early 1960s.

‡   ‡   ‡

In early 1974, Gil signed a two-album deal with RCA Victor, the first of which would be *Gil Evans Plays the Music of Jimi Hendrix*. The album features arrangements of Hendrix tunes that Gil's band performed earlier that year in a tribute concert at Carnegie Hall. The concert took place on June 8, 1974, nearly four years after Gil's ill-fated attempt to collaborate with Jimi Hendrix. The concert was organized under the auspices of the New York Jazz Repertory Company, which had been established that year by promoter George Wein as a means of facilitating the presentation of big-band jazz. Gil was one of the company's founding directors, along with Sy Oliver, Billy Taylor, and Stanley Cowell.

The Hendrix album was a disappointment in many respects, even though it included some of Gil's most popular arrangements. The record disap-peared soon after its release and remained out of print for more than ten years. "RCA never did promote it," Gil told Les Tomkins in his 1978 inter-view. "The man who is now president of Columbia even wrote them a letter at that time, telling them what a great idea it was. Yet they didn't promote it—even the administration people admitted that." Gil expanded on this point again in 1985, in his interview with Don Lahey for *Coda* magazine. "You know, I get more people that would really like to buy that album, but it's out of print. When a new administration comes into a record company, they don't care about what happened before they got there because they've got their own projects and their own budget, right? And so whatever you did doesn't mean anything; it goes out. They don't even keep it in the catalogue. If they put it out now, they could make some money on it, but it's hard to get someone to do that until you're dead—rich or dead." RCA Victor remixed the album and reissued it following Gil's death in 1988.

Gil Evans Plays the Music of Jimi Hendrix features eight Hendrix tunes; Gil wrote arrangements for three of them. The remaining songs were arranged by band members Tom Malone, Marvin Peterson, Warren Smith, Howard Johnson, and David Horowitz. "Gil was very interested," David Horowitz told me, "in having the guys in the band try their hand at doing arrangements." Although the musicians appreciated the opportunity to write for Gil, Horowitz admitted that the endeavor was not entirely successful. "I think overall, the *Svengali* album was much more successful musically than the Jimi Hendrix one. There was more of a singular vision there."

Tom Malone was one of the first to volunteer his services for the Hendrix project. "I did four arrangements for the concert at Carnegie Hall," he said, "and two of them survived to the album. And that really was a boost in spirit for the band, that we could actually contribute arrangements. And some of the people went to great lengths, I think, especially Howard Johnson, in "Voodoo Chile," to create certain Gil Evans–style voicings in the arrangement. I thought that was great." Except for "Voodoo Chile" and Tom Malone's "Angel," none of the other arrangements appear to have survived beyond this album. On the other hand, Gil's three arrangements—plus a fourth one, "Stone Free," which was not included on the album—would remain in the band's book for years to come. On two of these tunes, "Little Wing" and "Castles Made of Sand," Gil spotlights Hendrix's little-appreciated melodic talents. "Little Wing" was actually recorded a year later and was included in the 1988 reissue. Gil's arrangement of the tune, one of Hendrix's most popular ballads, is highlighted by a soulful David Sanborn solo and a chorus of heavily processed vocals by Marvin Hannibal Peterson. "Castles" features brass and woodwind ensembles, which introduce the melody and then continue to float delicately through Billy Harper's bluesy tenor solo. "Up from the Skies," one of Hendrix's most overtly jazz-inspired compositions, features intricate guitars in the background while the melody itself is again carried by brass and reeds (predominantly the flutes).

As in the case of *Blues in Orbit,* the production flaws of the Jimi Hendrix album often overshadow its strengths. For John Abercrombie, who played on this record, the project was a huge disappointment:

I THOUGHT THE RECORD was very poorly done, and I felt bad for Gil, because we were rushed through this session. And some of the music was
very intricate. There was a thing called "Up From the Skies" that really had
some intricate things in it. I just remember the producer [executive producer Steve Backer] was rushing Gil—"Come on, we gotta get this done!"
I remember being really pissed off that they didn't give him the time. I felt
like the record date was over before it even began, you know? And I'd say,
"This is Gil *Evans*—I mean, he should have *months* to do this project, he
should have anything he wants." I mean, he *is* a legend, he's one of the
most important figures in modern music, and they're giving him, like,
two or three days, whatever it was. I just felt it was very shabby.

There is an overall flatness and lack of definition to the sound, presumably
the result of having too many instruments sharing too few microphones.
Ironically, for a project dedicated to Jimi Hendrix, it is often the guitars,
even in the solos, that lack presence. "The band was recorded with very little separation," Abercrombie explained. "I remember all three guitar players
just sitting in a line." Even after it was remastered in 1988, the inadequacies
of the recording remain painfully clear. "It's a little better," said David
Horowitz. "It's been cleaned up, but I wouldn't want to be the guy sitting
behind the console trying to mix one of those things. Even though they went
to multitrack, you had absolutely no isolation. The band was just spread out
in the room—at RCA, it's a huge, huge studio—and the sound was all over
the place."

"It was a very confused record date," Abercrombie told me. "Nobody was
quite sure what to play. The guitar parts were all kind of—'Well, you play
here and I'll play here, then there'll be a little melody'—and we all played
so differently, nobody really knew how to get *along* with one another. Not
that we didn't like each other, it's just that musically—how do you fit three
guitars into a large band?"

It would be easy to lay the blame entirely on the producer or on RCA's
stingy accounting office, but clearly Gil himself bore at least some of the responsibility for the project's disarray. The technical problems could have
been minimized, if not eliminated, had the sessions been better organized—
but then again, the music would not have been as spontaneous; it would not
have been as "Gil Evans."

+   +   +

No better example exists of both the sweet rewards and dire consequences of Gil's propensity for experimentation than his following album. *There Comes a Time* was recorded a year after the Hendrix project, in the same RCA Victor studio. The album lists Gil as producer, with Steve Backer as executive producer and Teddy Randazzo and Anita Evans as associate producers. The sound quality of this recording is vastly improved, even though the logistics of recording were even more daunting. With twenty-two musicians, many of whom came with three or four instruments, it was at once the most delightful and unwieldy mix of electric and acoustic instruments Gil had yet assembled. Pete Levin:

> THAT SOUNDS VERY MUCH like what he wanted the band to sound like. It was a *huge* band. I can't imagine what the budget must have been for it. There were five synthesizers in the room at the same time, two drummers, horns everywhere. I think he just called everybody he knew—"Look, come do the date." It was recorded at RCA in a big studio, big room—and they ran out of inputs on the mixing board. They said, "Well that's it, no more mics." Even in that room, with a huge board, there weren't enough inputs in the room to mic everything properly.

Despite the problems Gil had had with RCA in this studio a year earlier, he approached this project every bit as casually and spontaneously as the last one. "You'd think, all right, this is going to be a *record*," Pete Levin told me. "The tape is rolling, the tape is only so long, we should try to plan this out a *little* bit—and typically, he would call a chart without assigning soloists. Just like we were doing it live. 'Oh, we'll just play and when it comes to the solo section, somebody will solo. We'll see what happens.' And I still think that's amazing." It is equally amazing that the RCA team could endure Gil's maddeningly chaotic "methods." Nevertheless from Gil's perspective, his approach was less about gambling than about trusting the musicians and giving them the freedom to pursue their own ideas. "It isn't a question so much of pressure," Gil told Don Lahey. "It's a challenge which they're all ready and willing to accept. I can throw them the ball and they love it; I mean, they just go right in and do it with assurance, you know?"

In the case of *There Comes a Time*, the result is an album with some of the freest and most exciting solos on any Gil Evans record to date. Among the standout performances are solos by David Sanborn, Billy Harper, Howard

Johnson, Lew Soloff, and Gil's newest star, tenor saxophonist George Adams. Once again, the whole band rose to the challenge of Gil's ensembles, preplanned or otherwise. In the studio, Gil continued to promote his "anything goes" philosophy, but at the same time, he guided the band through a set of immaculately structured arrangements.

This project comprised four sessions in March and April 1975 and resulted in a total of ten recorded tunes. The original release, limited by the time constraints of vinyl records, contained less than half the material. The reissue, however, which was packaged in 1987 with Gil's participation, featured all but two of the tunes; "Little Wing" (which was later added to the Jimi Hendrix reissue) and "Aftermath: The Fourth Movement—Children of the Fire" were omitted. The 1987 album included two original compositions ("Makes Her Move" and "Anita's Dance"); Gil's arrangement of the title track, written by Tony Williams; and five tunes based on earlier works, including "King Porter Stomp" (from *New Bottle, Old Wine*, which is itself an update of an arrangement Gil played years earlier), "The Meaning of the Blues" (from *Miles Ahead*), "Buzzard Variation" (from *Porgy and Bess*), and "Joy Spring" (from *Great Jazz Standards*).

Gil's older tunes are based on his original arrangements but are rearranged largely, and often dramatically, through new orchestrations and a greatly expanded role for the soloists. "King Porter Stomp" blends Gil's swing-style unison lines with a searing, bebop-charged alto solo (David Sanborn) and a funky rhythm section driven by Fender bass (Herb Bushler); "Buzzard Variation" combines the vintage ensembles of Gil's *Porgy and Bess* score (led by Howard Johnson's tuba) with a sweeping group improvisation featuring flutes, percussion, and synthesizers. On his twenty-minute version of "The Meaning of the Blues," Gil features solos on bass clarinet (Howard Johnson) and tenor saxophone (George Adams), accompanied throughout by elaborate backgrounds (both written and improvised), which are played on an arsenal of rhythm instruments (two drummers and five percussionists), plus two guitars, electric keyboards, and synthesizers, and of course a full roster of brass, reeds, and woodwinds. No matter how far he strayed from the melodies, Gil's sound remained instantly recognizable. As Howard Johnson explained, this is something that Gil's musicians, not to mention his audiences, found astonishing:

HE COULD AND WOULD STILL bring in completely brilliant things that fit the *loose* format but were still solidly Gil Evans, you know? Things like that piece called "There Comes a Time." It's funny—that was an example of something we experienced many times working with him—where we'd get new things and we just could not play them. I mean, it just wouldn't sound good, and we had no clue as to what it was supposed to sound like. It would seem like he'd made some mistakes, you know? And he was just patient, because he knew what he expected, and he would just give us the time to get it happening. "There Comes a Time," that just sounded like something that hadn't really been voiced at *all*, that people had just been given parallel harmonies, like they were all playing the same line in different *keys* or something like that. And then some other parts of it—that sounded like some guy was playing the total wrong thing—*that* turned out to be some independent line snaking its way through there. When that thing came together and started being played, we could not believe it. We could be playing in the middle of the chord, nowhere near *anything* that could be the melody—or even something that was actually in the *key*—but it related to the whole thing in a way that made our playing those notes so special.

There are other people who have said that. It's an observation that Red Rodney made when he was in Claude Thornhill's band. He said he was the third trumpet player, and he was just knocked out to play his part, because of what his individual notes did to the whole thing, you know? And this is something that a lot of arrangers haven't touched *yet*. So that people are given something that playing it means more to them individually than the whole sound together does. It's like, "Oh yeah, *I'm* making this tune happen by playing *these notes.*" It's almost like he had written them for you to play. And of course with the tuba parts, and all the parts that he expected me to play, he *really* wrote them for me, with what he thought *I* could do in mind. And I really did feel that I had a very personal and principal role in the music.

Gil's influence on David Sanborn was as philosophical as it was musical. "To me, Gil's influence was more an attitude toward life, that incorporated music, rather than anything his music gave me as an isolated thing. It was that music is a reflection of your life. It's your way of expressing how you feel about the world." When Sanborn moved to New York City, Gil took him in—both literally (he stayed at Westbeth until he found his own apartment) and figuratively:

GIL TAUGHT ME TO TRUST my instincts a little more. I think I was always wondering whether or not what I was doing was right, and he said, "Why bother? Why think about that? You're *doing* it, just *do* it." Gil just kind of took an interest in me, to help give me some encouragement, and a little confidence. And just being around him you just learned so much about life. Gil just had a perspective on things—he could deflate things without being cruel, you know? He could get right to the heart of the matter. He had a way of *putting* things. I remember he used to call psychiatrists "attitude salesmen."

It was interesting to see really powerful people around Gil. By powerful, I mean in the sense of business: rich, wealthy. Because that shit didn't mean *anything* to Gil. Because he seemed to know that this guy, he's a nice guy—and he also has a lot of money. Or, he's an asshole—and he's got a lot of money—but those two things didn't necessarily have anything to do with each other. For most of us, it's easy to confuse them. It's like the dope addict mentality—"This guy's my best friend, because he gives me dope." I got the feeling that Gil was never confused about stuff like that. He didn't have that doubt about how he felt about someone. And that to me is a tremendously evolved state of being, to have the courage of your feelings. I think that, as a musician, it allows you to tap those feelings in a more direct way, without the doubt. Because what'll kill you as a player is lack of confidence. Because you have to get up there every time like it's the first time and the last time. I mean, that's the goal. It doesn't always happen, but that's the goal. And eliminate all the bullshit in between—like, "I'm going to play this solo because it's going to get me laid," or "I'm going to play this solo because this guy's going to hear me and he's going to make me a star," or "I'm going to play this solo 'cause I'm going to impress this guy over there who thinks he can play." I *never*, in all the time I spent with Gil, ever got the feeling that he ever did anything with those kinds of motives. That, to me, is an admirable human being. And to be that way—to me, that's an ideal to aspire to, that's something to want to be.

WHERE THE WORK IS

THERE WOULD BE NEW ALBUMS, but *There Comes a Time* stands as the last one Gil recorded with his band in a studio. He had been plagued for decades by his reputation for slow, expensive recording sessions. Now there was the further stigma of his predilection for long, unrestricted solos and new, hard-to-record electronics. As a result, producers and record executives were either unwilling or unable to finance a studio production.

Gil had gotten along just fine to this point with little or no business savvy. In fact, it seemed that the less he tried to make things happen, the more people had sought him out. This had been true, albeit sporadically, throughout his career. In the meantime, Anita had honed her organizational and business skills to a fine art—managing the band, booking concerts and tours, and even coordinating a few recording projects as well. "I'm a New Yorker," Anita explained. "I know how to operate. You're supposed to know these things, how to make the environment work for you. So we got by okay." In 1971, Anita organized Gil's first European concert tour and set the wheels in motion for a long and successful run on the international jazz circuit, which became the band's principal source of income, exposure, and creative inspiration.

The timing of the band's overseas ventures could not have been better. Despite the surge of popularity of jazz fusion, there was little demand in America for most jazz music, and almost none for the more extreme, experimental forms that Gil favored. As ever, the costs of touring with a big band were prohibitive, and few of the clubs and concert venues in America were large enough to accommodate—let alone afford—them. Gil's exposure in American markets thus remained very limited. In 1972, he was invited to perform in Washington, D.C., as a founding artist for the opening of the Kennedy Center for the Performing Arts. (According to Anita, the band stayed overnight at the Watergate Hotel—on the very same night of the infamous break-in.) In the fall of 1973, the band mounted another road tour—one week each in Cleveland, Cincinnati, and Ann Arbor, Michigan—but after these dates, they rarely played outside New York City. Outside of New York City, Gil would perform less in America, in fact, than he did in England, Italy, Germany, and even Japan.

The scene in Europe was quite a different matter for jazz musicians of every stripe. Europeans had proven themselves to be more receptive to jazz than any American audiences since the salad days of the swing era. The European club and concert circuits were healthy and profitable, and cultural institutions such as the national radio and television networks were strongly committed to jazz programming. Broadcasters recorded and even commissioned jazz concerts, just as they supported classical music. It was economically viable, therefore, for almost any jazz group to tour Europe—including Gil's. In fact, Gil's band proved to be immensely popular. Touring Europe (and, starting in 1972, Japan) thus became a regular annual activity. By the end of the decade, he had performed throughout both Eastern and Western Europe, traveled twice to Japan (1972 and 1976), and performed in a tour of Southeast Asia (including Hong Kong, Manila, Bangkok, and Singapore). The annual tours involved not only the musicians (at times as many as eighteen players) but also the whole Evans family. Noah and Miles were both on the road before they were ten years old. The summer tours, Noah Evans told me, were just another part of their everyday life. "Miles and I had a whole life that we didn't really realize was special, different, or abnormal in any way. Going on tour in the summer, doing those kinds of things—it was our reality, it was the way life was."

"They always went on tour with us," said Anita. "They were our roadies from an early age, so it really became a family band early on. And they had their responsibilities. That's how they really learned the business—we needed them. It's a good thing they were strong—those four hands meant we didn't have to hire somebody. So they really learned from the ground up."

The summer tours weren't all work. Whenever possible, Gil and Anita would add extra days to the tour for some fun time with the children. Work or play, it was all one great adventure for the kids, and Gil was never far from their sight. "I was very close to my father," Miles told me. "He had a rough childhood; he never knew who his real father was, and it really upset him that his father wasn't there for him, so he vowed that he would be there for his children, and he really was there. He was there all the time, carrying me on his back at Coney Island, and amusement parks in Japan, and all over Europe. It was a great life."

From an adult perspective, life on the road with Gil was less than glamorous and often chaotic. Funds were always limited, which usually meant modest travel and accommodations and, in many cases, a punishing schedule. Gil seemed unfazed by the rigors of travel. Susan Evans:

HE WAS LIKE A LITTLE KID. First of all, he never seemed as *old* as he was; he always traveled well. I remember he would all of a sudden realize he was starving, so he'd run out to a bakeshop and get a big loaf of bread, sit on the bus eating this bread, and say, "Boy, I'm *empty*." I'm empty. Those were his words for hungry. Which, to me, was indicative that he thought of himself as a machine, that got empty and needed to be refueled, and then when he was refueled, he was off and raring to go. There was no such thing as depression, really. He had that kind of innocence that a child has—a *happy* child—that when he's got enough rest and food, would have gone and played. It's only an unhappy child that will, say, mope around the house. When he got the fuel, he'd jump up and say "I'm ready to go"—run out of the bus and prance around the city and just take it in like a sponge.

Touring enabled Gil to experience the world beyond New York and to catch up on some of the things he had sacrificed in order to study music. "Things I wanted to do," he told Helen Johnson, "like travel and study this or that, to see this or that, one by one I had to throw it away. I realize I can never do them. I don't want to throw them *all* away, so I'll shape the rest of my life the way I wish I'd shaped it all, and that is to try to have balance. It's hard to have balance when you're studying something and living to learn something. You've got to get it done and that's that, and balance has to go to hell for the moment."

Touring provided Gil's best and often his only opportunity to play, and this far outweighed any of the pitfalls. John Clark:

WHENEVER WE WENT ON the road, when we'd first land he'd always say to me, "You know, this is a long way to go just to pay the rent." Almost every time we went somewhere he said that. He loved to *play*, and if we had to go to China every Monday, he probably would have done it just to play. But I think it kind of pissed him off that we couldn't work more in this country, that we really never did a tour in this country. Once in a while we'd do a run-out. One time we went all the way to San Francisco just for one gig. And we'd go to New Haven, play at Yale—a gig here, a gig there—but not very often. Mostly just around New York, and never a tour. For several weeks of decent money, we always had to go to Europe or Japan. So, I think, he was not bitter but a little bit unhappy about that. But that's the way it is, for all jazz musicians.

Touring did pay the rent, and it allowed him to keep the band far more active than it would have been in New York. It was also gratifying to perform the music for enthusiastic, receptive audiences. John Clark:

> I MEAN, TO HAVE THE music heard everywhere, and to see that there are people that really care about that music and listen to it. Because if you stay in this country all the time, you get the feeling that no one really cares what you're doing, you really do. And that's the way it is, it's a very small audience. I remember when we played our first night in Tokyo and the audience—Japanese audiences don't go crazy the way, for instance, Italians do. Like every time someone plays a nice solo, they're screaming and whistling and jumping up and down. The Japanese just kind of sit there, but then at the end of the concert there's a little bit of silence and *then* they go crazy, and they come up on the stage with bunches of flowers and stacks of records for you to autograph. I had never seen anything like that before and Gil hadn't either. I think he really did appreciate being appreciated.

Trumpeter Jon Faddis had the same experience when he rejoined the band for a 1976 European tour:

> I REMEMBER POSITIVE REACTION, especially in Eastern Europe. We went to Yugoslavia, Czechoslovakia, Poland. We played a concert in Czechoslovakia, with maybe three or four thousand people in this big theater. After the concert, people were *screaming* for more. And Lew Soloff and I—we were on the way back to the dressing room and the people were still screaming, it's like five or ten minutes after we get all the stuff off, and they're still screaming, more! more!—so we stuck our horns through the curtain and started to play a duet. And the people, *wah-h-h, wah-h-h*—and all of a sudden, two soldiers with these machine guns were right behind us, shaking their fingers, no. That was it . . .

I remember also that we were working so *hard*. We would get into a town, we'd have time to go to a sound check, we'd have time to go eat, we'd finish the concert—and we'd have to drive a long way from the town to the airport, so we'd have to get up real early the next morning and pack and leave. We were all just exhausted. But Gil was always very calm, *very* calm. Nothing really ruffled him. When we were traveling under the most intense stress, having two hours sleep in the hotel, having to leave very early the next morning—very calm, very unruffled.

Gil also found more recording opportunities outside of America than he did at home. From 1975 until the end of the decade, all but one of Gil's new albums were made in Europe, England, or Japan. Most are live performances that were recorded by local broadcast networks or small record companies. Not all of them were distributed in North America, and many were not released at all until many years after they were made. Sound quality, always an unpredictable situation with this band, ranges from spectacular to barely passable.

Gil made two recordings in 1972 during his first trip to Japan—one with a vocalist, Kimiko Kasia, and the second for the pianist and jazz composer Masabumi Kikuchi, who later emigrated to New York where he would work with Gil for many years. Both records, which were released in Japan only, featured an all-Japanese band except for Billy Harper and Hannibal Peterson.

In 1974, Gil's band was recorded at the Montreux Jazz Festival, for an album released in Europe only. Two weeks later, the same band (except for Billy Harper) was recorded at a club date in Malmo, Sweden. This music showed up more than a quarter century later, in 2001, on *Voodoo Chile,* a CD release that offers up some exciting solos and ensemble performances, and several new arrangements—including "Parabola," by trumpeter Alan Shorter, and a blues medley arrangement of John Lewis's "Concorde," Charlie Parker's "Cheryl," and T-Bone Walker's "Stormy Monday." Excerpts from a 1976 concert in Belgrade, in the former Yugoslavia, were included as part of a 1997 release, *Strange Fruit,* which features Gil's 1987 concert in Italy with the British vocalist Sting. The Belgrade recordings include three tunes not recorded before or since—Gil's "Sureal" and two Lew Soloff tunes, "All Over" and "Tribute to M." (each with excellent ensemble parts and fine solos by Bob Stewart on tuba, Pete Levin on clavinet, and an unidentified guitarist).

In 1977, in the midst of all of Gil's activities abroad, the band did one recording in New York—a live concert at St. George Church on May 13

(Gil's sixty-fifth birthday) that was mounted to raise funds for City and Country School, which both Noah and Miles attended. This music eventually became the album *Priestess,* which was not released until 1983. The album features two extended pieces, "Priestess," written by Billy Harper, and "Short Visit," by album producer John Simon, each of which are highlighted by solos by David Sanborn (on one of his final appearances with Gil's band). The album also includes two short pieces: "Lunar Eclipse," by Masabumi Kikuchi, is the most interesting arrangement structurally—and an outstanding example of this band's ability to blend Gil's detailed written ensembles with equally cohesive group improvisations; Charles Mingus's tune "Orange Was the Color of Her Dress Then Silk Blue," here featuring a blistering tenor solo by George Adams, would remain in Gil's repertoire for many years.

In February 1978, the band was recorded in concert at Royal Festival Hall in London for another album distributed only in Europe. In July of that year, Gil toured with an eight-piece group and was recorded in Spain and Italy. In October, he recorded with a nine-piece band in Germany. This music was released (in Europe, and then later in North America) as the album *Little Wing.* The album is highlighted by a twenty-five-minute version of the Jimi Hendrix ballad—poorly recorded, alas, but featuring superb performances by Pete Levin (keyboards), Bob Stewart (tuba), Lew Soloff (trumpet), Gerry Niewood (alto), and Rob Crowder (drums).

And so it went. In America, Gil would work no more than a few weeks or even a few days each year, and after 1975, it also appeared that he was no longer making records. To those Americans who knew of him, this period might well have looked like another one of those extended sabbaticals of his; or they might have thought that this time he really had retired from music. Yet in reality, there he was, playing to appreciative audiences in virtually every corner of the world. There he was, crouched over his electric piano, eyes shut, fronting a band of fiercely dedicated A-list musicians who watched his every move. There he was, building an impressive book of new and newly redesigned arrangements—editing them every single night, shuffling his deck of interchangeable parts. There he was, waiting as his soloists chose their own entries, laughing with gleeful approval as their ideas took new and unexpected directions.

Gil Evans, it seemed, had never been more active or productive. It was a great long wonderful run, with this music and this band of the 1970s. And now Gil was approaching seventy. The twilight years were upon him, and it was time at last to slow down—well, wasn't it?

PART FOUR

1980-1988

Whatever you play, the next thing you do is an experiment. Everything is an experiment, and if it's a success, then it's a masterpiece.

—GIL EVANS,
FROM DON LAHEY INTERVIEW,
CODA MAGAZINE,
AUGUST 1985

CHANGING PARTNERS

RIGHT FROM THE OUTSET, the 1980s opened a markedly different chapter in the life and music of Gil Evans. Since his last recorded concert, in Germany in 1978, there had been a changing of the guard. Among the longtime members who had left were Billy Harper, Herb Bushler, David Horowitz, Susan Evans, and David Sanborn. They were replaced by a succession of new players whose stints ranged from one or two gigs to several years. Most were younger, and many were more radical in their playing. All too often, in the words of several disgruntled musicians (and listeners), they simply played "too damn loud." Some of the veterans left Gil's band to advance in their own careers. Others did not actually quit but simply lost touch as a result of conflicting work schedules. Still others could no longer tolerate the band's increasing loudness and anarchy, nor could they accept Gil's apparent unwillingness to curb such excesses.

Gil's home life had also changed drastically. In 1979, Anita moved to an apartment of her own at Westbeth. She lived two floors up from the family loft, but after sixteen years together, Gil and Anita were now separated. Not long afterward, Gil also rented an apartment up on 76th Street (with some financial assistance from Miles Davis), which he used as a studio. Westbeth was still his official residence, but often when he worked late he would stay overnight at the apartment. Eventually, he stopped coming back to the loft altogether, and Noah and Miles kept it to themselves. "I was sixteen and my brother was seventeen," Miles remembered. "That was definitely early, but it was nice. And even at sixteen, I was a six-foot-three adult that nobody messed with, so it wasn't the kind of thing where he had to worry. But he would come down and check up on us, make sure we were okay."

Remarkably, not only did the Evanses remain close as a family, but Gil and Anita continued to work side by side as partners. "We did the same things we always ever did," Anita said matter of factly. "It's just that we had more space to do them. We had the business; it's how we made our living. It was what we both did, and the children, so it was just normal. And it worked, it really did." Amicable separation? This is an oxymoron in most cases, and obviously there were irreconcilable differences leading to their break-up, yet the fact remains that Gil and Anita continued to function professionally, and effectively, for many years.

And both maintained a close relationship with their sons. Miles was studying trumpet, primarily under the tutelage of Lew Soloff. Noah was also a musician, but he was leaning toward audio engineering and the recording arts. Gil had neither encouraged nor discouraged his sons to pursue a career in music. "He didn't tell us we had to do anything," said Noah, "because he knew that if he didn't just let us discover or decide for ourselves what we wanted to do, that we would be unhappy, or we would rebel against whatever they tried to force us to do." Noah's interest in engineering evolved, obviously enough, from his exposure to the band and all of the fascinating gadgetry associated with playing music and recording it:

I REMEMBER BEING ABOUT SEVEN, eight years old, and Gil gave me a reel-to-reel tape recorder. I remember having this machine on my platform by my bed and having old Jackson Five recordings and Beach Boys and all this stuff. And then of course, when we were a little bit older—about ten—I remember running around in the studio. It just looked like a big playground to us. I didn't even know that there was this guy on the other side of the glass who was working his tail off to get this thing to sound the best that it can possibly be. I didn't even know what an engineer *was* or that one existed. And so I just ended up, as a teenager, in an internship program at a studio and then that turned into a job. So then I had to decide if I was going to go to college or stay in the studio. And so I just decided to stay and that was it, that was the beginning. All of a sudden I was there—eighty-hour weeks—and I was just living, eating, breathing studio.

Unlike many parents, Gil was particularly adamant about not forcing his children to take music lessons. "He was afraid of that," Miles explained, "because he had heard of that in so many situations—parents forcing their kids to play music and then the kids never wanting to do it again. He didn't want to take that risk." Miles's interest in playing came through his early association with the musicians—and especially his friendship with the trumpet players:

THAT HAPPENED WHEN I was about eleven. I was very close with Lew Soloff—I started hanging out with him from age nine. And I was also close with Hannibal—Marvin Peterson, my father's other trumpeter; we did a lot of hanging as well, and he was a really great guy. And I'd hang out with Jon Faddis as well. So I mean, these trumpet players were so nice to me and them being so nice and such great people, I thought, "Wow, if this is the way a trumpet player is, that's what *I* wanna be." And that's how it happened. They influenced me and that's why I started playing. And then later I heard Miles Davis and was totally blown away. Unbelievable! I would listen to him and my father would explain to me, "Yeah, and to top it off, he's a great sound innovator, the next great sound after Louis Armstrong."

And as for Gil Evans, he began the new decade more or less on his own, living in a midtown apartment cluttered with keyboards, score paper, and not much else. A day in the life of Gil Evans in 1980 seemed much the same as it might have looked in 1950, at his 55th Street basement apartment, or in 1960, after he and Lillian had divorced. The recurring image of Gil, unchanging but for the gray hair and increasingly wrinkled complexion, is of him slouched over a piano, hitting a key or two, drifting off with the overtones into space. "He was a very patient, kind of relaxed guy that lived off in the world of tunes," said John Abercrombie. "He lived off in his imagination a lot. I don't think he was always right *there* when you were with him; he might be off somewhere else or dreaming a little bit." Of course this is an image. True or otherwise, it is an impression of the man but not the man himself. The real-life Gil Evans of 1980 was far different than he had been in 1950. He now had a close-knit and loving family. He had his own band. He had a worldwide following that afforded him a modest but respectable living. In his music, as in his life, he was a creative and free-thinking individualist—and it is in this respect alone that Gil was indeed the same man and the same artist.

"He was an artist always in transition, always re-creating himself," George Russell said of Gil's later work. "And I think that's the *consummate* artist, the artist who isn't content to just sit back and rest on his laurels, or her laurels, and is always building a new fire."

✝   ✝   ✝

New fires come from new ideas and new people—new ways of looking at things—but not necessarily from new material. The great French impression-ist master Claude Monet, fascinated by the colors of a haystack as they changed with the movement of the sun, painted more than sixty canvases of virtually the same landscape, each one of them distinctive. Gil Evans now chose to limit the scope of his work to a relatively short list of arrangements: a few of his own earlier compositions and his arrangements of other people's music, pri-marily that of Jimi Hendrix, Charlie Parker, and Charles Mingus. These tunes had been the main subject of his work throughout the 1970s and would remain so—in constantly changing form—for the duration of his career. "It's typical," said Pete Levin, "that he would write a chart and then go on reworking it, changing little things—for years, right? The song, 'Gone,' that's from the *Porgy and Bess* album, and he would just *change* it, a little bit—redo it, recopy it, and here it is again. This went on for years."

If soloists could improvise every time they stand up, then so, too, could Gil, Levin suggested. "The music was kind of floating along, and he wanted to add a certain texture kind of . . . *now*. And he wasn't particularly con-cerned with where we happened to be at that particular moment, or what-ever chart we were playing. I just think he wasn't real concerned. There was something he was *more* interested in—the texture that was being developed by the band at that particular time—and in his cues, he was in effect or-chestrating, he was changing the orchestration." This, too, was a painter's approach, Levin offered. "The rhythm section would be grinding away, or somebody would be soloing, and Gil would be sitting there—with a paint-brush and a palette, just watching the painting—and suddenly gets an idea and wants to go do it, and he would do it." Up would come his signal—a cue card, a hand signal, or a new piano intro—and the band would be expected to respond *now*. Pete laughed as he recalled,

SOMETIMES WE WOULD just kind of look at each other, and we'd say, "Wait a minute, this isn't going to work," and we would hold off for the extra bar or two that was necessary to bring it around to the top of a chorus. Sometimes the band would just kind of stagger in, and guys would make up some notes in the section, and it would kind of collapse half-played. And either way, Gil would have just sat back down at the piano with his eyes closed, gone back to just sit on whatever cloud he was sitting on before he gave the down beat, and we would just wait for the next cue.

The more they played, of course, the better the band became at deciphering and anticipating Gil's inclinations—and the further Gil pushed them. The repertoire reflected the band's modus operandi—a set list of mostly older tunes, played by a group of mostly younger new players. The cohesiveness and the relaxed confidence of the performances were remarkable given the number of new players. These included saxophonist Hamiet Bluiett, trombonist George Lewis, and bassist Tim Landers. Former members Jon Faddis and Arthur Blythe also returned. Only five of the players were his regulars—Pete Levin, Lew Soloff, Hannibal Peterson, Dave Bargeron, and John Clark. The maturity of Gil's approach, and his players' grasp of it, was amply demonstrated on his first recording of the new decade, *Gil Evans Live at the Public Theater,* recorded in New York City in February 1980. Produced by Masabumi Kikuchi (now a member of the band), it was released as two volumes on separate albums, initially in Japan and distributed later in North America as an import. Several European albums were still not readily available in the United States. To most Americans, therefore, this album was Gil's first new offering since *There Comes a Time,* five years earlier.

Volume One of the set includes new versions of three Gil Evans originals—"Jelly Rolls" and "Variation on the Misery," written in the 1960s, and "Anita's Dance," from *There Comes a Time.* "Alyrio" is essentially a vehicle for Brazilian percussionist Alyrio Lima, which in this performance is embellished with improvised saxophone, bass clarinet, drums, and keyboards. The other new tune, "Orgone," is bolder, more intense; it features an energetic trombone solo by George Lewis and concludes with a lengthy ensemble from Gil's *Porgy and Bess* variation, "Gone," led by a featured guest, drummer Billy Cobham.

"Anita's Dance," the longest piece of this set, features extended solos by Pete Levin and Lew Soloff played over a relaxed and pleasantly upbeat groove. This is sharply contrasted by a heart-wrenching version of "Variation on the Misery," the highlight of this album and the definitive version of this composition. Unlike the powerful but all-too-brief original heard on *Blues in Orbit,* this performance features a long, beautifully impassioned alto solo by Arthur Blythe. The solo is framed by an inspired reading of Gil's brilliant orchestral ensemble, a "crying melody" so often heard in his best writing. ("All great music has to have a cry, somewhere," Gil told *Coda* magazine's Don Lahey. "All players and all music, they have to have that.")

Volume Two features two new tunes—Gil's own "Copenhagen Sight" and "Sirhan's Blues," written by John Benson Brooks—along with another Jimi Hendrix tune ("Stone Free") and new versions of Gil's "Zee Zee" (yet another superb rendering, with another stand-out solo by Hannibal Peterson) and Charles Mingus's "Orange Was the Color of Her Dress Then Silk Blue." "Stone Free," which became one of Gil's most popular and frequently recorded Hendrix arrangements, had not been heard on record in America before this performance. Similarly, Mingus's "Orange" had been recorded only once before, in 1977 for the album *Priestess,* which at this point had still not been released. "Copenhagen Sight" was Gil's first great composition of the new decade. It is a brooding, meditative piece in the flowing style of "Zee Zee," punctuated with the dramatic shading of "Variation on the Misery." The tune also has a surprisingly prominent piano feature, one of Gil's strongest performances on record. Here, Gil both solos and leads the band using his latest keyboard, the newly introduced Yamaha electric baby grand (an expensive instrument, which, presumably, Gil would either have borrowed or rented).

✢   ✢   ✢

The Public Theater recordings make it clear that the 1980s version of the Gil Evans Orchestra would continue to evolve as a resourceful and exciting musical institution. But now, for the first time in more than a decade, Gil also began to entertain musical possibilities outside the realm of his beloved band. The first of these was with Lee Konitz, with whom Gil had not played in more than twenty years. Lee came to him with a proposal for something Gil had not done before—a duo performance (alto saxophone and piano).

I HAD A SITUATION COMING up in New York and I thought, well, gee, maybe I can call Gil and we can work something out. It wasn't possible for me to commission him to write a piece for me—I didn't have that kind of wherewithal—so this seemed like the next best thing. He said, "Well, I'm not really a piano player," and he was very reluctant to do it. And I really kept on him for a couple of months. I said, "Look, I'll sit with you as long as you need, to get it together. To me, that represents the closest thing I'll get to playing with your orchestra—you're the orchestra." So we got together, finally, and we sat there five, six hours a day, and he worked out his arrangements. And it was very stimulating to me, and I really felt like playing. We worked at a club for three days—it was all recorded, incidentally—and it was very successful.

Some of the material from the duo recordings was released on two separate albums in the mid-1990s (*Heroes* and *Anti-heroes*), but they have not remained in print. Shortly after the club date, at a New York club called Greene Street, Konitz received another offer.

THE ITALIAN RADIO IN ROME was having a series of composer and soloist programs to give their band some opportunities to perform, and they asked Gil and me for one week—a week of rehearsals, then two concerts with a big band. Then we went out and toured around together, a week of duet concerts. With the radio, it was an orchestra; the tour was a duo. We played a Mingus tune, a Wayne Shorter tune, a couple of standards. I really wanted Gil to call the tunes, so he could do what he was comfortable with.

"It was tough, man, for me," Gil told *Coda* magazine's Don Lahey, "because I'm not a fluent piano player. I went to bed bloody every night, but then I'd wake up feeling great. We played ten concerts in ten nights, and we made $500 apiece every night. I never made that much money. It was great." It was not great enough, however, for him to continue. "We had a week of concerts scheduled for California, at very good money," said Konitz. "He canceled it. He said, 'I can't, it's too hard for me.' So that was the end of that."

Still, it was good while it lasted, Konitz told me, and wonderful to work with Gil again. "If you can imagine an Italian audience sitting and listening to this music. I mean, the tempos would get slower and slower and slower. They say you can't address an audience where they're at—you've got to move them up or down. So we could bring those Italian energies *way* down—and they loved it." It was also fun being on the road together, something they had not done since the days of the Claude Thornhill band.

ONE TIME WE WERE on the coast of Italy, and I stepped out on my balcony, right over where the water was just across the way, along the walkway, and I saw Gil. It was a beautiful day and he had his cut-off jeans on and he looked like a seventy-year-old hippie, kind of sauntering along. A couple of beautiful girls walked by, young girls, and he turned around and looked at their asses and all that. So later, when he came upstairs, I said, "Yeah, man, I saw you digging all the chicks out there, having a good time." He said, "Yeah, you know, I was thinking, seriously, I should meet a seventy-year-old woman and settle down . . ." And that's logical—you know, to meet someone his own age—but it sounded so *ridiculous,* because he seemed like a sixteen-year-old in many respects, spiritually.

Like all good hippies, Gil still loved his pot. "I'd stopped smoking pot," Konitz said, "and he would always take out his pipe and fill the dressing room with pot smoke. And there I was, sitting there, so anybody walking in would try to be noncommittal but they'd think, 'Yeah, two guys getting high.' And I didn't dig that, and I kind of let him *know* I didn't dig it. But one night I said, 'Fuck it, give me the pipe, man.' So I smoked up, too."

Konitz and Gil would soon cross paths again. In the same year of the Italian tour, Konitz was invited by jazz writer Martin Williams to transcribe the music of the Miles Davis nonet for the Smithsonian Institute's jazz division. Two years later, these transcriptions (along with charts by Gerry Mulligan, John Lewis, and John Carisi) would form the basis of a very special concert—the first Gil Evans retrospective.

In the meantime, another reunion was getting under way. After five years of relative seclusion, in which he had not performed, recorded, or even picked up his trumpet, Miles Davis wanted to work again.

✦   ✦   ✦

With the release of *Bitches Brew* in 1969, Miles's already stellar career had exploded once again. His jazz-rock fusion laid the foundation for an entirely new stream of jazz, one that reached hundreds of thousands and was played not in jazz clubs but at huge concert halls, stadiums, and outdoor rock festivals. Miles was condemned by mainstream jazz critics and musicians for "selling out," but undeniably, his new music reinvigorated the jazz scene as a whole. It sparked the interest of a generation of new listeners and musicians. In the fusion jazz movement that followed in the wake of *Bitches Brew*'s international success, virtually all of the key players were Miles Davis graduates—Herbie Hancock, Wayne Shorter, John McLaughlin, Billy Cobham, Chick Corea, Joe Zawinul, Tony Williams, and others.

Bitches Brew was followed by a string of new Miles Davis albums, some just as exciting and innovative, but none as successful commercially. During this period of the early 1970s, Miles's physical and mental health suffered, primarily as a result of drug and alcohol abuse. In 1975, Miles took the first extended absence of his entire career. "I thought I might be gone for maybe six months," Miles wrote in his autobiography, "but the longer I stayed away the more uncertain I was whether I was going to come back at all. And the more I stayed away, the deeper I sank into another dark world, almost as dark as the one I had pulled myself out of when I was a junkie. Once again it was a long, painful road back to sanity and light."

Only a few people even saw Miles during these dark and often-troubled times. Gil Evans was one of them. They had not worked together since 1968, but in all those years Gil and Miles were rarely out of contact for more than a few weeks at a time. "Like brothers," Anita said of their relationship, "brothers who got along—not always *approving* of the other, or the other's choices, but tolerating. I really saw Miles Davis as a sort of brother-in-law. When Miles was a recluse, he was always in touch with Gil. People would be saying this, that, and the other thing, but we always knew what he was up to. Maybe we didn't want to be *bothered* with him, but he was always available."

When Miles resurfaced in 1980—clean, healthy, and ready to play—he wanted a fresh start for his band and his music. "I knew I had to go someplace different from where I had been the last time I had played," he wrote, "but I also knew I couldn't go back to the real old music, either." Once again, he put together a group of young players, including a twenty-two-year-old saxophonist, Bill Evans (no relation to Gil, Susan, or to pianist Bill Evans). "That was the year when I spent a lot of time with Miles," said Bill Evans, "getting to know him and discussing putting a band together and all that kind of stuff. It was the initiation period with Miles." Gil was not involved in these meetings, but he and his music were often a focal point.

I USED TO MESS AROUND at Miles's house with the piano. There were a lot of the old arrangements that Gil had done for Miles. Miles would always want me to hear some of the voicings, so I'd look at some of the voicings and play them. And Miles liked to listen to them, because they were so happening, they were *great*. I mean they were structured so well, the voicings were so perfect, and the way the voicings moved to counterpoint everything that he had going on, it was *serious*.

Gil, in the meantime, was only relatively active during this period. He played just one concert—in February 1981, at New York's Town Hall—and he did another brief but grueling summer tour in Europe ("18 concerts in 21 days," he told *Coda's* Don Lahey). Bill Evans performed with Gil at the Town Hall concert. "He just called me up and said can you come to this rehearsal," Bill said. "And he forgot a lot of the music, so he was writing a lot of it out on the spot, which I thought was pretty amazing." After this concert, Bill's schedule was soon filled up—Miles started touring again—but he continued to play occasionally with Gil's band. "You wanted to be with this kind of person, know what I mean? He never had a bad thing to say about anybody, he was always just kind of floating through. Sometimes I would talk to Gil as just a friend. When he was hanging out with the people in their twenties, you didn't get the feeling he was any older than *you*. As weird as it sounds, it's true."

Gil and Miles began to work more closely toward the end of the year. On Miles's next album—*Star People*, recorded in late 1982 and early 1983—Gil was credited for arranging three of this album's tunes—"Star on Cicely," "It Gets Better," and "Speak"—and he was involved, indirectly at least, over the duration of the project. Bill Evans:

MILES LISTENED TO EVERYTHING Gil said. It was the *law* to Miles. I mean, even little things. Miles would say, "I don't know what I'm going to do," and it was like "Gil? Gil?" Everything was Gil, Gil, Gil. It was just little things—Miles would whisper something into his ear, Gil would whisper something into his ear. It wouldn't dramatically change the band, it was just sort of keeping things on an even keel, you know? Gil never came in and changed the sound of the band, but he did bring in little things. He was kind of the silent partner in the deal.

In late 1982, midway through the recording sessions for *Star People*, Miles hired a new guitarist, John Scofield. John knew Gil as a neighbor (he, too, lived at Westbeth), and he had played with Gil's band a couple of years earlier.

A DIFFERENT ARTIST that lived in Westbeth put on stuff to do a fund-raiser for the building, and Gil's big band played, and I played with them. That was probably in 1980, but maybe a year before, he had come to hear Dave Leibman's band once, and I think that was the first time to my knowledge he ever checked me out. And he was really nice. He said, "Your ideas are coming out when you play, the ideas that you're thinking of are coming through"—which is a really great thing to say to an improviser. What better thing could you say? But also I was completely aware that it was Gil Evans, and was in awe of him.

John played an increasingly prominent role with Miles, on the bandstand, and also in the writing and pre-production sessions at Miles's house:

RIGHT WHEN I JOINED MILES, he and Gil were getting together a lot, and a few times I went to Miles's apartment and Gil was there, and we would play. One time, especially, I remember—Miles had some chord changes, and he had Gil play a bass line. They might have even played two-handed on the electric piano, and then Miles said, "Okay John, you improvise over the progression." And I improvised and Miles taped it. And then we went into the studio a week later or something—this was my first recording session with Miles—and Gil came up to me and showed me this piece of paper and he said, "Look, this is what you improvised over at Miles's house." Miles had asked him to write out part of the choruses. And the song I'm talking about is "It Gets Better," and Gil had rewritten a bass line and transcribed my solo.

For the *Star People* record and the next record we did, *Decoy,* Gil was there all the time—in the studio for all the sessions and talking with Miles about the music. Most of the music was transcribed by Gil from solos. Miles would give him tapes, and Gil told me, "This is something I've been trying to get Miles to do for twenty years—just improvise on his trumpet into a tape recorder and I'll transcribe it and make music out of it." Gil would write out twenty pages of music. It'd just be little ten-, fifteen-bar things that Miles had improvised, some things lasting a whole page. And these [would become] ensemble things that the whole band played, that Miles would then answer. Miles also taped every gig, and he would give those to Gil, too. So Gil was walking around during this period listening to Miles's tapes all the time. And they were really working together.

Neither Gil nor John received full credit for their work—particularly Gil, and especially in the case of *Decoy,* for which Gil was listed as arranger on just one tune and got no writing credits at all. John Scofield:

I REMEMBER ONCE, I asked Gil, "How come Miles does that—takes the tunes and puts his own name to them, when you or I were involved in it?" See, I knew Gil had a history of that happening to him. And Gil said, "Well, it's just fame, Miles wants the fame." And I said, "Well that's funny, because he's so famous already," and Gil said, "Yeah, but he *really* likes that fame." And the way he said it, he wasn't judgmental at all—"Well you know, some people like spinach, some people really like this or that, that's what Miles likes."

As in many of his past efforts with Miles, Gil apparently did not seem to think any of this work deserved a full arranging or writing credit. "I asked Gil once," John told me, "'well, did you change any of the stuff from what we soloed?' And he said, 'Yeah, I polished it up a little bit.'" In truth, these new tunes were brief melodic sketches—nothing at all like the great Davis-Evans collaborations of earlier times—which Gil did not consider "real writing." John felt much the same about his tunes, for which Miles claimed a cowriting credit. "They weren't *songs* that I wrote, in my case, with Miles. He didn't take any stuff that I wrote and put his name to it. He just used my solos, and I realized that, sure, he *should* take credit for that, because it was his idea to *use* that solo." As for Gil's work, John pointed out that Miles was very generous with Gil in other ways. "I think that Gil knew he was getting a lot out of Miles. Miles made a lot of stuff happen for Gil. So I mean, Miles did a lot of great stuff for Gil. And they were collaborators, you know? They both helped each other."

The last recording sessions for *Star People* were completed in February 1983. Gil returned to the studio to work on the *Decoy* album in August and September. In May, between the studio dates for these two Davis albums, Miles's band toured Japan together with Gil's band. The bands played separately, however, and Miles and Gil did not appear together on stage.

☩   ☩   ☩

Two months prior to the Japanese tour with Miles, Gil had been to England to do a series of concerts with an all-British band in Bradford and the surrounding area—the first time he played his music with an orchestra other than his own. The only musician he brought with him on this trip was his son, Miles, who was making his debut as a trumpet player:

I DECIDED TO GO WITH my father. He was doing a tour in England with an all-English band and I just brought my horn to practice. And then I sat in at one of the rehearsals and then I played—and ended up playing the whole tour. And that's when I started playing with my father; that's how it happened.

He made it clear that I had a great opportunity—that a lot of people would really love to be playing in this band and that I should not take it for granted. He did a lot of other things, too—talking about music, you know, just teaching me. Talking about chord voicings and about the way people bend notes in solos and make it beautiful. Just the whole vibe of playing—like the wrong note thing. That you can play a note that's supposedly wrong, but if you play it with intention and you play like you mean it and like you know how it sounds, all of a sudden that wrong note can really work beautifully. Bend it, really feel it, and it's no longer a wrong note . . .

There were a lot of things like that that he taught me. And then the ability to have an open mind—not only know your stuff but have an open enough mind to be able to move forward and see other musicians playing other styles, maybe doing something new. Like the way my father could see Jimi Hendrix. You know, the guy's born in 1912. Most people of his generation would say that stuff sucks and not even think of it, whereas my father was open enough and had his feelers out and was just interested enough and futuristic enough to say, "Wow, he's *playing.* Let's check this out."

The Bradford concert was recorded for an album distributed only in Europe. The record includes Gil's "Hotel Me" (also known as "Jelly Rolls"), Jimi Hendrix's "Little Wing," and two new arrangements—Thelonious Monk's "Friday the 13th" and a new Gil Evans composition, "London." The concert series was organized by a London-based entrepreneur, and the band was assembled by John Surman, a leading British saxophonist and multi-instrumentalist. Long an admirer of Gil's music, Surman had connected with Gil, indirectly, some two years earlier.

I WAS PLAYING AT THE PARIS OPERA—a ballet piece, for one dancer and one musician, me—and at the end of one of the shows, there was a message that said Gil Evans was in tonight to listen, and he really enjoyed the music. I was playing with synths and everything, and he thought that was interesting, I guess. So consequently, about two years after that, Gil was invited to put together a British band, and he asked for me to be in the band—and one other guy, someone else he knew, Don Weller, a tenor player—and we put together a band.

Another of the players who signed on for the tour was a young alto saxophonist, Chris Hunter:

IT WASN'T ANYTHING LIKE I expected it to be. For instance, at the first rehearsal, all the music was written in pencil. That doesn't sound like a big deal, but for us it was kind of strange. We expected these sort of beautifully crafted charts. Everything was very loose, and he really wanted people to contribute in a way that they hadn't been used to doing—you know, with so much freedom. I don't think we quite knew how to handle it.

Even greater changes were in store. Chris agreed to join Gil's band and move to New York. "After I played with him in England, he had a slot for an alto in his own band, for a tour in Japan, and he asked me if I would like to do that. So, obviously I jumped at the chance."

Toward the end of the British tour, Gil was approached by two of the other Londoners in the band, guitarist Ray Russell and bassist Mo Foster. They invited him to perform that summer with their fusion band, RMS, at the Montreux Jazz Festival in Switzerland. The timing, it turned out, was perfect. Gil was already scheduled to perform at Montreux with Billy Cobham, who at that time was living in Switzerland. "Sure," Gil told them. "I'd love to." But first, Gil had some important new business to attend to back in New York.

REINCARNATION

NOT LONG AFTER HIS RETURN from England, Gil met with Horst Liepolt, at that time one of the owners of Sweet Basil, a small jazz club on Seventh Avenue in Greenwich Village, to discuss a possible engagement. Liepolt was a forty-year veteran in the jazz business (as a record producer, concert promoter, booking agent, and club manager). He was also an avid fan, and he hired Gil on the spot:

> I SAID ANYTIME YOU'RE ready, anytime. At first we said, "How long you want to play?" He said, "I don't know, make it four weeks." He only played Mondays, a month of Mondays, and then he just kept on playing. And then there was no more agreement—he just played. Monday night became his home, so it was understood that he was going to play there till he dies, which he did. Without talking about it, that's the way it turned out to be.

As the word began to spread about the legendary arranger's return, Gil's Monday night gigs developed into the club's most popular event. Liepolt recalls, "In the beginning, people said, 'Is that *the* Gil Evans?' Because he hadn't really been around. I mean, ninety-nine percent of the world's population thought he was dead, because he had no profile at all."

Until Sweet Basil, the band had worked almost exclusively on overseas tours, which were usually followed by weeks or months of inactivity. With a regular weekly gig, the band now had a consistent reference point. Even though it was just a single night each week, this proved to be an ideal proposition. Monday is the slowest night for music venues, even in New York, and as a result many jazz clubs do not hire bands. That means that Mondays are the only time musicians are free to get together with other musicians—not only to hang out but also to hear each other and play together. This was the premise behind the Village Vanguard's regular Monday night sessions, which for many years had featured the Thad Jones–Mel Lewis big band. There was little money to be made, but with so few other opportunities to hear a big band, let alone *play* with one, the regular players (and countless surprise visitors) showed up faithfully.

With Gil's band, Sweet Basil began to build a regular Monday night following of its own, far different than the Village Vanguard's both in terms of the fans and the musicians it attracted. Gil's music was looser and more eclectic, and it attracted a broader range of musicians—including fusion, funk, and rock musicians of every age and description. Their participation, in turn, added to the band's diversity and vitality. Regardless of who showed up, of course, the band had its foundation of formidable players—Lew Soloff, Howard Johnson, Marvin Peterson, Tom Malone, Dave Bargeron, John Clark, Pete Levin, and now young Miles Evans. Drummer Adam Nussbaum and bassist Mark Egan became his regular rhythm section, and they, too, were soon able to anticipate the band's hairpin twists and turns as quickly as the veterans. Guitarist Hiram Bullock added a fire and intensity that was closer to Jimi Hendrix than any jazz guitarist ("Gil always said that I played *un*-guitar guitar," said Bullock, "whatever that means.") Chris Hunter, newly arrived from England, would strive to fill the shoes of one of his own influences, David Sanborn. Then there were Gil's friends and colleagues from earlier bands—like Johnny Coles, George Adams, Steve Lacy, Ryo Kawasaki, John Scofield, and Bill Evans. If one of the players could not make the gig, it was easy enough to find a substitute. Many times the subs just kept coming back, however. That could mean you lost your chair to the sub, but often it simply meant that Gil wanted you to move over and make room for one more player.

The allure of Gil's "just see what happens" attitude was never greater, and no one enjoyed the unpredictability of the band, the music, and the night ahead more than Gil himself. Yet, despite the party-like atmosphere of their sets, he did not treat the music as mere jam sessions. He and the band were intent upon making every tune a special experience. "He was committed," said Bullock, "but committed to the process of making music, as opposed to making a hit record or whatever. You're more committed to the fact that you enjoy it and you do it."

‡   ‡   ‡

In July 1983, Gil made a special appearance at New York's Kool Jazz Festival (formerly the Newport Jazz Festival). He performed with his band, and he was the subject of a major retrospective organized for the festival by jazz writer Gary Giddins. "At that point," said Giddins, "no other orchestra had ever played Gil's music. So what we decided to do was put together an all-star band that would play some of his classics in the first half—because *he* wouldn't play them anymore—and then in the second half, Gil would conduct his own orchestra." Among the all-stars were many who had played on the original sessions, including Lee Konitz (who served as the retrospective's music director), Gerry Mulligan, Bill Barber, Budd Johnson, and Johnny Coles. Gary Giddins:

> We did all of these wonderful Evans pieces, going from Thornhill up to the Miles Davis suites. Gil was very shy about it. At first, he was sort of troubled that we were going to do it at all. I remember he came over to my apartment, and we discussed it for a while. I told him the pieces I was thinking about—for example, I wanted to do "La Nevada" and have Budd Johnson play another great solo live—and so he got more and more into it. But the night of the concert, he didn't want to be around. So they put him in a private room upstairs, and I was told later the sound was turned all the way up on the speakers, and he just sat there quietly listening to the music. And he was thrilled. I think he had actually over the years had some doubt about whether it stood up. And at the intermission, he came downstairs and he was just elated, and he shook the hand of every single musician in the band.

The musicians were also delighted, as Gerry Mulligan concurred when I asked what it had been like to play the music again all those years later. "It didn't seem so long ago to me," he said. "No, because, listen—to me, a good piece of music is *always* a good piece of music, and I don't think about that it was written in '48 or something. I was glad to play those pieces again because I liked them. I liked playing them. So that's my feeling toward it, it was the pleasure of the music itself."

During the intermission, Lee Konitz suddenly decided that he and Gil should open the second half with a short duo set, to which Gil, surprisingly, agreed. Giddins was excited:

I SAID, "OF COURSE, that'd be incredible." So I walked out to introduce them. I introduced Lee, and Lee walked out and got his applause, and then I introduced the hero of the evening—and Gil was nowhere to be found. And the audience kind of laughed, so I did the introduction again—and he still wasn't there. Then I turned around and saw him standing there in the wings with his corncob pipe in his mouth. So I just kind of shrugged my shoulders and started to walk offstage, and when I got to Gil I said, "What the hell are you *doing*?" And he took his pipe out of his mouth and he said, "Sinsemilla—want some?"

☩   ☩   ☩

Shortly after the Kool Festival event, Gil flew back overseas, to Montreux, where his stay was successful and highly productive. His concert with the British group RMS went beautifully. Despite having had just a single afternoon to rehearse, the band and soloists appeared completely comfortable with Gil's charts, and the group played his music with enthusiasm and reverence. Gil, on electric piano, did not take any solos, but in his introductions, comping, and his backgrounds, he contributed actively and tastefully on every tune. This concert was also superbly recorded. In 1990, three tunes from the concert (Jimi Hendrix's "Stone Free" and "Little Wing" and Gil's arrangement of "Gone") were released by a British independent label, Last Chance Music, on the album *Take Me to the Sun: Gil Evans with RMS*.

Gil's Montreux concert with Billy Cobham was also recorded—in this case, on videotape. The film was originally produced as part of an educational video series that featured Cobham (also one of the producers of the series) playing with other big bands. The Evans-Cobham orchestra comprised Gil's regular players (Lew Soloff, Howard Johnson, John Clark, Tom Malone) together with several European and American players (notably vibraphonist Mike Manieri, and the Brecker brothers, saxophonist Michael and trumpeter Randy). Another of the Americans was Gil Goldstein, a young keyboard player and arranger who had been working in Switzerland with Billy Cobham. Goldstein, who would return a year later to New York and join Gil's band, was deeply affected by the experience of playing with Gil.

I LEARNED A LOT OF THINGS about playing, just from playing with him, that I feel I wouldn't have got in any other situation. We did a rehearsal for this gig in Switzerland, and it was a little bit unorganized. Gil would pass out a score, and a guy would be like, "What do I do with this?" And Gil just said, "Well, pick a line and follow it," and he was a little bugged. And I found myself really siding with Gil, like saying, "Yeah, this is the way we're *supposed* to do this." Because we had done a program with Louis Belson the same day, and I thought it seemed kind of dumb to be so *organized* in jazz and have all the music totally organized. And then we were about to do the concert, and I was pretty nervous, and Gil walked out with his hands over his head—like he had just won a fight, in that kind of way he used to do it—and it just felt so great. I felt like, "I'm going to play so *good* tonight."

The video shot at this concert—possibly Gil's only appearance on camera since 1959, when he conducted Miles's band—shows him in splendid sartorial form. Clean-shaven, with neatly trimmed hair, and wearing a smartly tailored navy pinstriped suit, he could easily pass for a bank executive—that is, until the camera tilts down, revealing the red sneakers and gray gym socks that were also fashionable at the time, at least for musicians. No one else on stage is dressed quite so sharply as Gil, but each is in top form musically. Despite any difficulties at the rehearsal, the band plays flawlessly and often reaches soaring and perhaps unexpected heights. Most of the solos are taken by Gil's own players—Howard Johnson ("Friday the 13th"), Lew Soloff ("Variation on the Misery," "Stone Free"), John Clark ("Waltz," "Stone Free"), and Tom Malone ("Stone Free"). The only exceptions are Randy Brecker, on "Copenhagen Sight," and Mike Manieri, featured on "Here Come de Honey Man" and on an extended improvised introduction to "Friday the 13th." Billy Cobham is a delight to hear (and watch) both on the high-energy vehicles ("Gone," "Stone Free," "Waltz") and also on Gil's subtler works ("Copenhagen Sight," "Variation on the Misery"), in which he brings to bear his full array of percussion instruments. Gil himself, who so often maintains the lowest profile on the bandstand, is clearly the leading figure throughout the evening. He is a principal soloist on acoustic piano on three tunes ("Copenhagen Sight," "Variation on the Misery," "Orange Was the Color of Her Dress Then Silk Blue"), and his comping—particularly on "Stone Free," played on his beloved Fender Rhodes—is authoritative and exuberant. He spends most of the night seated at the piano, rising occasionally to signal something, and except for an inaudible thank-you at the end of each tune, he does not say a word, either to the band or the audience.

✝   ✝   ✝

Gil did two more engagements that summer before returning home. The first was a recording project in Germany with another old friend, Airto Moriera. Airto's *Brazilian Spiritual Mass* was written for an eighty-six-piece orchestra, including jazz and symphony players and a vocal ensemble. In August, Gil returned to London to perform again at Royal Festival Hall. He also played with a pick-up band for a week at Ronnie Scott's, London's most famous jazz club. Here, he had yet another fateful meeting with an eager young musician—a singer and bass player in a rock and roll band called The Police.

IT WAS THE SECOND SHOW at Ronnie Scott's, and I plucked up the courage to go back and say hello and just introduce myself [to Gil]. He looked pretty strange. He looked nothing like he'd looked on album covers. He had this headband, and he looked like an old Indian, really. I said, "Look, you don't know who I am but I'm a rock singer and a big fan of yours." He said, "What's your name?" I said, "I'm called Sting," and he said, "Oh yeah, I know your song 'Walking on the Moon.'" And I couldn't believe that this *hero,* this revered giant, knew who I was—and not only that, he knew one of my songs. I said, "Well, what do you like about it?" And he said, "I really like the bass line. It's very simple, there's a lot of space in it." I was so thrilled that he knew that, I was on cloud nine, basically. And I said, "Well, I'd really like to work with you one day, Mr. Evans," and he said, "Well, maybe we will. Make me an offer . . . "

Sting did make him an offer, when they met up again a few years later, and Gil would accept it. In the meantime, though, they went their separate ways. Sting left The Police and established an even bigger career as a solo artist. Gil returned to New York to pick up where he left off at Sweet Basil, with the band everyone was now calling The Monday Night Orchestra.

✝   ✝   ✝

On his return from Europe, Gil went back to the studio with Miles to finish the last tracks for *Decoy*. Their last tune was "That's Right," for which Miles and John Scofield share the writing credits and Gil is listed as co-arranger with Miles. None of Gil's contributions on the other tunes is acknowledged. *Decoy* represents the historic, if inequitable reunion of Miles and Gil for one last album. Fittingly, the arrangement for "That's Right" is the album's high point. Like "Round Midnight"—the stand-out tune that Gil arranged (also without credit) for Miles's debut on Columbia in 1956—this arrangement, too, is simple, sparse, and infused with the clean, understated elegance that characterized so much of each artist's work both together and individually. It features a soft, relaxed synthesizer background for the blues theme, introduced by Miles, then stated in a guitar/saxophone unison, and followed by solos on trumpet and saxophone. "That's Right" is an unceremonious conclusion to one of jazz's greatest partnerships, but as the tune was wrapped, and as they packed up and left the studio that day, it is unlikely that either of them thought about ending anything. And for the rest of Gil's life, they would still hang out, they would remain in contact, and even though their lives were on different paths, the relationship would be as solid as ever.

MONDAY NIGHTS

AFTER THE *DECOY* SESSIONS, Gil returned his attention to Sweet Basil, where he played almost every week for the remainder of 1983 and into the following spring. In fact, during this period he did little else but the Monday night dates. At one point, there was a brief stint of Monday night dates at another club, Seventh Avenue South, but he returned to Sweet Basil (after Horst Liepolt agreed to pay him a modest increase) and settled in for an indefinite run. The money was still not great, but Gil, coming off his busiest run in years, was better off financially than ever before. Likewise, for most of the band, Monday nights were for pleasure, not profit. While many of the players had very lucrative careers, one exception was Chris Hunter, who had given up an active schedule in London and come to New York with the expectation of working full-time with Gil. "It was hard for me," Chris said. "I left everything behind and was just hanging out in New York, not doing a whole hell of a lot, but playing with him—that whole experience—was really so exhilarating, it was something I couldn't let go of. So it was a constant back and forth, wanting to be here [in New York] and wanting to be there [in London]." Chris did eventually establish himself in New York, but interestingly enough, he began to see a marked change in his attitude about the business:

> ONE OF GIL'S GREAT LESSONS was to go with it, go with the flow and not
> have these absurd concerns about career and prestige and all those ludicrous
> things that people seem to be consumed by. When I came from London, I
> would get really caught up in that—the corporate ladder of the musical in-

235

dustry. "Am I in the scene?" All bullshit. Once I dumped that, those kind of ridiculous feelings, I found that I actually became a lot more successful.

Working with Gil also had a great effect on Hunter's playing. "Because the band played so many different types of music, I realized that I was going to have to become efficient in a broad area. It really made me want to become familiar with the bebop repertoire, so actually I became really studious, in a much more retrospective way than before." Yet even as a musician acquired more knowledge, the challenge of playing in this band, Hunter emphasized, was to unlearn what you knew—to play not what you knew, but what you felt:

I THINK GIL JUST WANTED the whole experience to be a celebration—something that everyone would enjoy constantly. I mean, one of the things he would say would be, "Don't play anything unless you feel like playing"—stuff like that. It took me a long time to get the hang of it. One of the things that I found really frustrating when I first played in the band, you felt, "Hey this is a great moment to play a solo," and then you'd just never know what would be coming at you next. I mean, I'd get up and I'd play—anybody would get up and play—and then the rug would be kind of pulled out from under you—I don't know, just something that would defeat me totally. But now I think, what a great thing, you know—that's really the way everything *should* be.

Confronting the uncertainty of Gil's music, at first so disorienting to Hunter, was now the most fulfilling thing about playing it. Gil's approach had the same effect on Hiram Bullock:

AT THAT TIME, I'D BEEN in New York about five or six years, and I was very successful on the studio scene. And the studio scene was all about coming up with parts, coming up with the right part and playing it and being able to play relatively precisely—over and over at any given moment. And what we're talking about with Gil is exactly the opposite. You *couldn't* play the same part from night to night in a given section. You had to create all the time.

Just as you learned this music largely through osmosis, Chris told me, you got to know Gil—or about him, at least—less from his words than his presence. "He was a guy you kind of felt very close to, but you couldn't ever really get to *know* him. That was his mysterious thing. I felt that."

✦   ✦   ✦

For the first time in nearly fifty years, Gil had the opportunity to perform on a regular basis with more or less the same group of people. He enjoyed playing immensely, so much so that he seemed to have lost all interest in writing (just three new compositions in as many years and very few new arrangements). Even on the bandstand, he was much less concerned with leading the band than playing in it. John Clark:

> HE DIDN'T LIKE TO GIVE any directions. He didn't even like to call a tune. He would call a tune by playing a little bit of it on the piano and then he'd just wait until everyone figured out what tune he was playing. He didn't even like to count the tunes off—he would only do it in certain cases where he had to, where everybody had to start at the same time. But if we could start a tune by just sort of drifting into it, that's what he would prefer to do. And he used to call it a leaderless band.

"I play what I call cheerleader piano," Gil told CBC Radio Canada's Katie Malloch in a 1987 interview. "If I want the band to do some intensity, I'll play intense, or if I have a line or something that I want them to pick up, they'll pick it up—if they *want* to. They don't *have* to pick it up if they don't want to—and they don't have to *improvise* if they don't want to. That's one thing, we finally got it straightened out. Just because there's an open space for the whole band, you're not *required*—it's a duty-free band. That's the main thing." Gil also talked about this in his *Coda* magazine interview two years earlier: "The only thing I *don't* want to do is draw them into some kind of freedom that they're not really that interested in. That's why I say to them right away that I don't like duty; I don't want anyone to do me a favor. *Please* don't do me a favor."

Clearly, Gil told his musicians it was not about playing free—or nailing each note in the charts, or playing hard or soft or fast or slow—but simply about playing what you felt. "It was all built upon trust," said drummer Adam Nussbaum, "and people *giving* to the music, and letting the music happen, where the *music* was the guide."

> GIL WAS KIND OF LIKE the chef overlooking the big pot. When he would put the right combination of ingredients in, special things can happen. But

then again, sometimes a little too much of one thing? It might get crazy. Not enough of something? Throw it out of whack. But then there were those nights when everyone was zoned in to that *other force*. There might be twelve people in the band, but there's thirteen people up there, because the *music* becomes another entity on the bandstand. And when things are right, you're only aware of that. You're not aware of the elements involved in creating it.

Yet the fact remains that Gil exerted a tremendous influence over the band, no matter how slight his direction or his actions. "Other people would be bringing in charts," said Chris Hunter, "especially the last three or four years, I guess, but incredibly enough, even if there were other arrangers and tunes, the music was still his. He just seemed to cast a spell over the whole band, and they played differently than they did with anybody else."

✝   ✝   ✝

In early 1984, Gil took on a new project without the band—another duo recording—with soprano saxophonist Steve Lacy. It had been twenty years since Steve had recorded with Gil (1964's *Individualism* and on Gil's Kenny Burrell album). He lived in Europe for most of this period, but he had remained in contact with Gil and worked with him frequently. "Anytime I was in a place he was working, he would add me to the band," Steve told me.

WHETHER I KNEW THE MUSIC or not, he would ask me to play with the band. And that happened quite a few times. If I was in New York and he was playing, he'd say, "Okay, you're working tonight," and so there I was, working. This happened a few times. Over in Europe, the same story. He'd come with a band and if I was in that same town and I was free, he would recruit me, just like that. And it was always very gratifying, a very great honor and a pleasure.

Taking this date with Steve (they recorded one tune, "Bemsha Swing," for a Thelonius Monk tribute album) was much more about friendship than about playing. After his experience with Lee Konitz in 1980, which he found too technically demanding, it seemed unlikely Gil would ever have agreed to play another duo, except as a personal favor—and also, of course, because he adored Steve's playing. "Jesus, he can play," Gil told *Coda's* Don Lahey. "He has a range from the lowest note on the soprano, which is A-flat below middle C, to the top

A-flat on the piano. You can write any of those notes for him. A lot of times when you're improvising you can try a thing like that and maybe you can make it, but to be able to guarantee it—he can read it *and* play it. Fabulous."

Gil brought along another special friend on his next engagement, a tour of Japan. Jaco Pastorius was the Jimi Hendrix of the electric bass—a wild, explosive player and one of this instrument's first true virtuosi. He had released his debut album in 1976, but he gained far greater fame during his stint with Weather Report (1976–1982). After resuming a solo career, he performed with his own bands and also with many leading jazz and popular artists. For most of his adult life, however, Jaco suffered severe emotional problems—later attributed to manic depression—that were made worse by drug and alcohol abuse, which ultimately destroyed him. He would die in Florida in 1987, just thirty-six years old, as a result of injuries sustained after he tried to force his way into an after-hours club.

When Jaco signed on for the tour with Gil in 1984, he was already an international star (he toured Japan that same year with his own band), but he was also a longtime friend and admirer of Gil's and was eager to play with the band. A year earlier, Jaco had been one of the first to play with Gil when he started at Sweet Basil. And their relationship actually traced back to the mid-1970s, long before anyone had heard of him. Anita Evans remembered Jaco calling Gil, asking for advice:

> WHEN HE WAS AT HOME IN FLORIDA becoming a writer, he would call Gil all the time and ask, "How'd you do this, how'd you do that?" Sometimes Gil didn't want to be bothered and he'd hang up, but Jaco was persistent. He'd call back and say, "Wait, I just admire your writing so much and what you do," and Gil then would share with him. He was a real good teacher for him—sent him stuff, showed him stuff—and then when [Jaco's] album came out in '76, it was awesome. We suddenly heard who this kid from Florida really *was*.

The Japanese tour went smoothly and was unmarred by any of Jaco's infamous disruptive incidents. "When Jaco was doing the music, he was on the money, there was no problem," Anita recalled. "His problems were more before and after the gig. When it was time to do music, that was him, that was the definition of his life, to be able to be serious and concentrate on the music. So on that level they got along great. He had a very reverential attitude toward Gil, and Gil appreciated his talent and his playing. Gil didn't necessarily appreciate his *behavior,* although he was too cool to ever say anything about it."

Gil and Jaco did not play again after the tour, and none of their music was recorded, but Anita has fond memories of their time together. "I never had more fun with anybody in my life," Anita remembered. "He had a *great* sense of humor. It wasn't a longtime [collaboration], but it was very serious and very sincere and very much of the period." The attraction, of course, was mutual. "Absolutely," Anita said. "It's what kept Gil going, to orchestrate and compose around the sound of some great new innovator. So many of the great new innovators who emerged, those who could hear themselves in a Gil Evans orchestration, they'd beat a path to the door."

✝   ✝   ✝

Noah Evans, by now a full-time recording engineer at New York's Nola Studios, had also started to help out with the band's sound mix. Because of the band's blend of electric and acoustic instruments, it had always been a challenge to set up the equipment to achieve a proper sound balance. Then, once the band started playing, the sound levels had to be adjusted on an almost continuous basis—all, of course, with no prior warning as to what tune was coming up, who would solo, who'd play the ensembles, or how long they would play. "It's a lot harder than people think," Noah told me with a chuckle. "If you set it up in a way which you're already ninety percent there in terms of how you think it should be, you're gonna be in good shape when you're mixing it. But if you're in the mix and it's barely close to what you want, you're in big trouble." Noah's success at the mixing board made him a welcome addition. Even though he wasn't playing an instrument, Noah had an important contribution to make and a role in the band that both he and his father were happy to acknowledge:

> I REMEMBER WHEN I FIRST was actually able to do something—for instance, make the stage mix the way the guys wanted to hear it, and just even *caring* about it, you know? Just having someone there who can care about it and who understands the language—it was a good feeling, and I realized that I could be pretty valuable. And when I understood that Gil was proud of me, it was the best feeling in the world. Even though I wasn't doing exactly what he does, he was happy for me that I found something that I not only was good at but enjoyed doing. He could see that, he knew that, and that felt great.

Noah did the sound for as many of the band's New York gigs as he could, and then took time off from his engineering job during the summer. "I didn't do vacations when I worked at Nola," he explained. "I would save my time to go on tour with the band—that was the only way I could work it out." And so the family's summer tradition continued even as the boys became young men—with Miles in the trumpet section, Noah at the sound console, and Anita standing by, watching over the goings-on.

‡   ‡   ‡

Getting the right sound for a club date is one thing, but recording a live performance is quite another matter. Few musicians are satisfied with the results of their recording sessions; someone is always too high or too low in the mix, a little too close or too far from the microphone. Invariably, the best takes seem always to go unrecorded, or the tape runs out—and on and on the list of disappointments goes. Gil's players, without exception, insist that the spirit and energy of this band were never captured on tape. "The Gil Evans Orchestra on vinyl," Chris Hunter frowned, "it's kind of like watching opera on TV. You can't, really, you just *don't* translate very well." Some of the players will admit, albeit grudgingly, that the recordings that were made at Sweet Basil do come close, at least occasionally, to succeeding.

In August 1984 and again in December 1986, the band was recorded at the club by a Japanese label, King Records. The sessions were produced by King's Shigeyuki Kawashima and coproduced by Horst Liepolt. "Actually, it wasn't even my idea," Horst said. "It was King Records. They approached me, and said, 'Is it possible to record the Gil Evans Orchestra live?' They knew that they couldn't do it in a studio because it would cost too much money. And also, they wanted it the way the band sounds on a Monday night. A lot of Japanese fans loved it the way it happened there, and they wanted to get that feeling onto a record." Horst continues:

> IT WAS A REAL MEDITATIVE THING—he got on stage, everything was slow motion, he started to clink on the piano, and then it went for ten minutes, and slowly he set the pace, the feel, and then maybe the trumpets came in. Now, a lot of people would not call it a performance, like in a concert tour, but it happened. You hear an arrangement in progress. Not like a workshop, but like you develop things while you're playing at home. You don't come in with the finished thing—you come in with an arrangement which

has a couple of changes. And the band doesn't know the changes because you just made them, so he is developing while he is playing—and that's what's on the record.

The first sessions were recorded on two consecutive Monday nights, after which the tapes went back to Japan with the producer to be compiled. The result was two volumes (each of them released originally as a two-record set on vinyl) called *Gil Evans and the Monday Night Orchestra, Live at Sweet Basil.* It was released in Japan by the end of the year, but it did not reach North America until 1987. The music on the two double albums includes only two new arrangements—"Prince of Darkness," a Herbie Hancock tune, and "Snowflake Bop," written by Anita Evans, but the albums feature several of Gil's other arrangements that had been recorded previously in Europe or Japan but had never been made available to American audiences—notably, Gil's "London," his blues medley (his latter version comprises one original and three Charlie Parker tunes), and Thelonious Monk's "Friday the 13th." Among the other tunes are several of the band's signature pieces—two Mingus tunes ("Orange Was The Color Of Her Dress Then Silk Blue," "Good-bye Porkpie Hat"), Gil's "Jelly Rolls," his arrangement of "Gone," and three Jimi Hendrix tunes ("Voodoo Chile," "Stone Free" and "Up from the Skies").

Volumes I and II of *Live at Sweet Basil* are dominated by extended solos, but the ensembles (heard before, during, and after the solos) are every bit as exciting. The unison parts on "Blues in C," "Voodoo Chile," and "Prince of Darkness," for example, are played with effortless fluidity and grace, even as they fly along at breakneck speed. The Monday Night Orchestra versions of these tunes are vastly different than any that Gil had done before, even as recently as the 1980 two-album set, *Live at the Public Theater,* which include many of the same pieces. Most here are far longer, and all of them have the loose, relaxed feel that permeated every Sweet Basil set. Solo highlights include George Adams on "Stone Free," Howard Johnson and Hiram Bullock on the most raucous and hilarious version of "Voodoo Chile" ever recorded by any band, Chris Hunter on "Blues in C" and "Good-bye Porkpie Hat," and Pete Levin on "Parabola." Trumpeters Lew Soloff, Marvin Peterson, Shunzo Ono, and Miles Evans are featured (although the solos are not identified individually) on "Parabola," "Orange Was the Color of Her Dress Then Silk Blue," and "Blues in C." Gil himself is heard mainly in his cheerleader piano mode, but "Prelude to Stone Free" is a prime example of the piano introductions that he played to ease his way into a new set and lead the band, eventually, into a specific tune.

A final distinction of these recordings is that they capture what is undoubtedly the loudest Gil Evans band to date. Once again, his audiences seemed either to love it or simply could not tolerate it. Pete Levin:

> IF YOU COULDN'T HEAR YOURSELF quite so well, you'd play a little louder. And the guy next to you turns up, and the guy next to *him* turns up, then the horn players reach for their earplugs, get closer on their mics—so then the stage monitors get louder, so everybody *else* turns up, and the *drummer* plays louder—and you've got a real loud band.
>
> Gil liked the spirit of it, so he almost never said anything like, "Could we turn it down, please, it's too loud." In fact, he told me once he never wanted to say that to somebody individually, even when he thought they *were* playing too loud. Because he said, "Well, then they'll just sulk for the rest of the night," and he didn't want that to happen. So he would rather let somebody go off and play too loud if he thought the spirit was there.

Intolerable as the loudness or the long solos were to some ears, the Sweet Basil recording project became one of the most profitable ventures of Gil's career. For starters, Gil and the band were paid promptly (the very night the last session was done), and they were paid very well. "As it turns out, we got paid twice," Horst told me, "because the first sessions produced *two* double albums. We got the same money again for the band. It was a very good break; that was really big money then." In Japan, King Records also profited on the album. And, in turn, the success of the albums in Japan (and then in Europe) also had an immediate impact on the club itself, which drew substantial numbers of foreign visitors, especially from Japan. Horst was delighted and astonished by the response:

> THE MINUTE THE RECORDS started coming out, then it just went *crazy*. Because they had enormous publicity, they did a number on that shit in Japan, and they sold by the thousands over there. I mean it just exploded. It sounded to them like they're sitting at Sweet Basil. And if they haven't *been* to Sweet Basil, their friends who have been here say to them, "*Listen, it's like sitting in the club, baby, yeah.*"

As word spread across Japan and Europe, Horst Liepolt was soon talking with King Records about a Gil Evans follow-up record, which they did a year and a half later. King Records also did a live album at the club with Art Blakey, which led to several more records with Blakey's band. There would then be a Sweet Basil label to record and distribute their records, and even a new Japanese magazine, also called *Sweet Basil*. Horst and his partners realized that Sweet Basil had suddenly become the most talked-about jazz club in New York. And at the center of the action was a quiet, mild-mannered (now seventy-two-year-old) man who played there just once a week.

BUSTER'S LAST STAND

THE BUZZ CREATED BY GIL'S weekly Sweet Basil sessions sparked a new surge of offers and commissions, some of which Gil actually accepted. He had already started working without his band, but these projects were all with friends—Lee Konitz, Miles Davis, Steve Lacy, and Airto Moriera. And now there would be new people, new friends. The band, still his first priority, was booked into the future. Sweet Basil was essentially a permanent date, and he could also rely on at least one good tour of Europe or Japan every year. That left him plenty of time to accommodate additional work, but more to the point, he also had the inclination to do it.

The largest of these new commissions was for a film score he worked on in 1984–1985, which was his first soundtrack since the mid-1960s. *Absolute Beginners* is an offbeat musical that satirizes the emergence of rock and roll in the swinging London of the 1950s. It features rock star David Bowie, along with cameo appearances by several British-based pop and rock artists (Sade, Ray Davies, Style Council). Director Julien Temple, known previously as a music video and music documentary filmmaker, wanted Gil to create a jazz-based ambiance that was authentic to the period but that could also be juxtaposed with pop and jazz tunes of differing styles and more current eras. To capture the mood of the times, as well as the up-tempo pacing of the movie itself, Gil adapted his existing arrangements of two Charles Mingus tunes, "Boogie Stop Shuffle" and "Better Get It in Your Soul." No new writing was required for these charts, but he did write new horn arrangements for several of the pop tunes, together with an orchestral version of

David Bowie's title track. These horn arrangements had the interesting effect of tying together a disparate collection of songs to establish a more cohesive overall sound. Gil also contributed an original composition, "Va Va Voom," an energetic, tongue-in-cheek Latin Caribbean dance number—and also one of the lushest, most polished Gil Evans arrangements since perhaps *Quiet Nights*. "Va Va Voom" is all but lost in the film itself, and since the movie's soundtrack album has remained an obscurity, little of this music has been heard at all. This is especially unfortunate for die-hard fans of the "old" Gil Evans, who would have been pleased and surprised to see that Gil could still write as deftly as ever.

The music of *Absolute Beginners* is far removed from what Gil played on Monday nights, but it is not nearly as great a departure as his next project, which would be different from anything Gil had ever done. This was a commission to write arrangements for five tunes by a young Canadian saxophonist, composer, and part-time bandleader named Glen Hall. In addition to working with Glen on the charts, Gil also agreed to come to Toronto to conduct the orchestra (for three rehearsals followed by two recording sessions) at CBC Radio Canada's studio. By the time the band was assembled, Gil had also written parts for himself, and he ended up playing electric piano on every tune. Glen Hall first approached Gil in 1982, but the project did not begin until two years later, once the funding and logistics were in place. Gil's work started in November 1984 and continued both during and after his work on *Absolute Beginners*.

Initially, Glen's proposition seemed simple and straightforward. He wanted to do a big-band album, something he had never done before. He knew how much Gil could contribute to the music and, equally important, how much he could learn from him about arranging and orchestration. What he did not know was that Gil had been turning down such offers for the better part of two decades, nor was Glen aware of the style or the snail's pace at which Gil's work proceeded. Glen knew nothing about Gil except what he heard on his records. Gil, of course, knew virtually nothing about Glen Hall either, yet on the strength of little more than a couple of phone conversations, he decided to accept his offer. At first, Glen told me, Gil did not actually say yes, but then again neither did he turn him down. "I got a 'maybe' from him, and that was enough for me to start with."

Over the course of the next two years, Glen would call periodically to update him on his progress—his grant had come through, the CBC was on-board, and so forth—and to talk about the kind of music he envisaged. The original concept, Glen admitted, was ambitious but conventional, designed primarily to impress Gil and to "look good on paper" (that is, on arts grant applications), but the more he talked to Gil, the more Glen's writing began to change.

THIS WAS AT THE TIME when I was getting rid of the idea of having a big band and getting back to what it was that I really wanted to do. I had the feeling that Gil could sense that—like, "You're giving me this big-band stuff because you think that's what I'm interested in. But in fact, if I'm going to work with you, I'm only going to work with you on the basis that we're dealing with what *you're* interested in." I thought I was being straightforward, but I was probably being devious, and he knew it. And when I started to be more honest with myself, then he picked up on that. And then *he* would sort of gently manipulate the situation, too—to his own advantage and to *mine*. He really wasn't doing it for himself, I don't think. I wish I could give you a reason for that. To this day, I don't know. I think there are people—in this case, Gil—some people are sensitive to being able to bring out a potential in a person and have a capacity to help them develop it. It's an obligation they feel to themselves and to the person whose capacity they can intuit or can see. They feel that it's somehow an obligation for them to fill that need.

Glen is also convinced that Gil would not have worked with him unless he, too, was gaining from the experience. "Gil could see, somehow, that I had this need to have someone bring something out in me. And he felt that he could do that, and at the same time do something that was interesting to *him*. I mean, he wouldn't do it simply out of the goodness of his heart." In this instance, Gil was attracted by a collection of tunes that drew from Glen's studies in non-jazz and non-Western idioms, much of which was steeped in mysticism and ancient mythology. The music also featured an array of contemporary instruments (synthesizers, electric bass, and guitar) together with traditional instruments from Asia, Africa, and the Far East, many of which were new and exotic-sounding even to the ears of Gil Evans. The music is an elaborate mix of rhythms and percussion-based textures and colors—featuring vibes, marimbas, hand drums, crotales, log drums, tabla, mridangam, and many other instruments. The recording is also highlighted with a guest appearance by the acclaimed Canadian contemporary percussion ensemble Nexus.

And so Glen Hall became the latest to join that long procession of musicians whose life and music would be transformed by the Gil Evans experience. In Glen's case, this would include a drastic reevaluation of what exactly it is that arrangers do and how they do it.

Gil arrived in Toronto to meet with Glen in late November 1984. This, Glen assumed, was to be their only session together prior to rehearsing with the band and then recording, but Gil had other ideas. At his own expense (and at a cost far exceeding his arranging fees), he took it upon himself to return to Toronto from New York a week later—and again the week after that, and the week after that. So it went, into December and into the new year. (His visits were interrupted briefly in January, when he flew to London to finish up *Absolute Beginners*.) He usually stayed in Toronto all week—flying back Sunday night, so he could play Monday night at Sweet Basil, and then returning on Tuesday. During these trips, Gil stayed with some musician friends of Glen's. From about ten in the morning until four in the afternoon, Gil would sit at the piano while Glen played through sections of each tune, either on saxophone or guitar. Gil taped everything, whether they were playing, writing, or even just talking, after which he would spend the evening going through the tapes. He seemed to enjoy the process as much as Glen. "See you Tuesday," he'd say as he left to catch his Sunday night flight. Except for the headband, the moccasins, and the corncob pipe, he could have been mistaken as just a senior executive heading off for a business meeting in Manhattan.

The experience was obviously a significant one for Glen and nothing at all like what he expected. Far from playing the apprentice working over the master's shoulder, Glen found himself at the center of Gil's attention. "Gil kept asking me, 'What do *you* want? I came here to work on *your* music. You know it better than anybody else, so tell me what you want.'" Gil would sit and listen, humming quietly. "He would let time pass. He was deliberately *not* reacting to things. He showed me that time has its *own* way of dealing with creative material. And that only by allowing time to pass did things in Gil's music come about."

Therein, of course, lies the ecstasy and agony of the Gil Evans oeuvre. Inspiring as the process was to Glen the composer, it became increasingly stressful to Glen the project manager. The scheduled rehearsal dates were drawing closer, but Glen had yet to actually see anything on paper.

HIS PHRASE WAS, "Well, when I write music, I have to *swim around* in it for a while before I settle on anything." And that stuck with me, because he was swimming around in that material until the night before we had to go into the studio! He was *still* paddling around in that. And it dawned on me that he would *never* have finished writing that music if it wasn't for the fact that there *was* a deadline.

Late into the night before the first rehearsal, the last of the five arrangements still remained unfinished. "He'd say to me, 'Well, I don't know if I *like* this.' I'd say, '*I think it sounds great.*' I kept thinking of the Pope, looking up at Michelangelo in the Sistine Chapel—'When will thou be *done?*'" The last arrangement did get finished—just in time for the last of the band's three rehearsals. And for all the anxiety Gil might have caused, from the moment he entered the studio, his presence was at once calming, reassuring, and invigorating. He continued to make changes to the charts all through the rehearsals, but he also worked side by side with each of the musicians. When it came time to record, everyone was not only prepared but inspired. "Without question," Glen said, "Gil was the linchpin."

WITH VIRTUALLY NO EFFORT, he got everyone to do what they had to do. He was not up there flailing his arms around—although he *would* do that occasionally—he would sort of just stand up and signal different people into different sections of the tune. Instead of section two, he might decide to go into section three, so you really had to keep your eye on him. But the real work, the straw-boss stuff, was done at the piano. Gil's comping set the intensity with which these things would be played. The drums and bass, with Gil's comping, did everything as far as holding the structure, the feeling, all the things that make the music so alive, so organic.

The project culminated with a one-time broadcast over the CBC's national network. It would then take almost nine years for Glen to find a distributor to release this music on CD. The resulting album, *The Mother of the Book,* released in 1994 by the German label InRespect, ranks as one of the least visible of Gil's projects, but it contains some of the most interesting writing of his latter-day career. With the understated style and exquisite intricacy of his arrangements, it is the diametric opposite of the music of his

Monday Night Orchestra—precisely the reason that, for Gil, the work had been a challenge and a refreshing change of pace. The project had become a trial by fire, yet even before they finished recording Hall found himself talking to Gil about what they might do next. Gil seemed to be as receptive and enthusiastic about a new project as Glen was. It is that attitude that Glen remembers best about Gil Evans:

> I don't remember him really criticizing *anything*. He may have done that, but that's not what stuck with me. What stuck with me was his ability to find one gem in a mountain of slag. He could take it from Ravel or the Police or a violin concerto or three bars from a Fletcher Henderson arrangement—or anywhere. Gil had just gone out to see John Cage conducting an orchestra, and he talked about that with such enthusiasm, and he would get just as enthusiastic about listening to a Chaka Khan tune that was playing on the radio. I always remember him accepting things, valuing things. He'd go through the whole damn mountain to find one gem. He wasn't looking for the slag, he was looking for the gem. And he always came up with it.

☨   ☨   ☨

Gil did two more projects in 1985 without the band. In March, he sat in on Lew Soloff's debut album, *Hanalei Bay,* playing electric piano. This was followed by another film score commission, for *Insignificance,* directed by Nicolas Roeg. Gil's participation was limited to a single piece of music, which he recorded in one session, for which he hired Lew Soloff. "There was a scene that we did where he re-orchestrated—didn't change one note of it but re-orchestrated—part of Mozart's *Jupiter Suite,*" Soloff explained. "The second movement for brass and string bass—fourteen brass and string bass and improvising with a percussionist over it—and then I played some improvised trumpet over it."

There was no European tour that summer, but Gil did go to France with the band—for one night only. "They flew us all the way to Paris and back," Gil told *Coda's* Don Lahey, "just to play for an hour and fifteen minutes. We played in a new place called Le Palais de Sport in Bercy, and there were 16,000 people there. Can you imagine that?"

Gil's next project was another film score. This time his work was much more extensive, and it brought him together with another old friend, Robbie Robertson. "When I first met Gil," said Robbie, "I was always trying to find an excuse for how I could possibly do something with him."

THERE WAS A MOOD in his music and his arrangements that touched home for me. I was working on this album with The Band in 1970, and I had written this song called "The Moon Struck One," and I thought it would have been great for Gil and us to do it together. So I contacted him, we got together, we talked about it, we said that we were going to do it. Then the next thing I knew, he had to go to Europe for a tour, and one thing led to another, and I got side-tracked, and we never got around to it.

Fifteen years later, Gil's name came up again during a conversation Robbie had with Martin Scorcese, who was shooting *The Color of Money.* Scorcese had directed *The Last Waltz,* the celebrated music documentary film of The Band's farewell performance, and he and Robbie had become close friends. Robbie had also worked on two other Scorcese films, *The King of Comedy* and *Raging Bull.*

WE MET IN LOS ANGELES, Marty and I, and he explained that this film was the continuation of the story of *The Hustler,* and it takes place in and around Chicago. And he was kind of going on about this sleazy type of factor that it had—a very appealing factor for music. So I said it sounds like it should have some kind of a blues basis to it, just because of the Chicago connection and the pool hall connection—it just seemed natural. The problem was, I was in the middle of making an album, and I told Marty, "I can't make this album and do the music for this film at the same time, but if I *could* do it, what I would love to do is, I'd write the music and then ask Gil Evans to do the charts for me—meaning orchestration and arrangements, collaborating on the arrangements." And so I said, "I'd love to do this with Gil, and perhaps collaborate with Willie Dixon on some things as well." He said, "Jeez that would be *fantastic*"—and he very efficiently kind of ignored my saying that I wouldn't be able to do it. He just started talking about ideas, things that he needed for the film—and he got me so intrigued by it that the next thing I knew, all of a sudden we were into it.

After working out the logistics of doing his album (his first solo record since leaving The Band), Robbie's next priority was to see if Gil was actually interested. He called him in New York ("This is Gil Evans, the musician, *not* Gil Evans the casting director," said Gil's answering machine) and left him a message. "He called me back and he said, 'You know this song we were talking about years ago? Well coincidentally, I was just finishing up the chart on that.' And I thought to myself, I always heard that Gil wasn't famous for being what you'd call speedy but this is *outrageous*—you know, seventeen *years* or whatever it was. Anyway, it made me think, the fact that he was working on this piece of music, that this was definitely meant to be—we got an *omen* going for us, Gil. So anyway, we talked about doing it and he was completely into the idea."

The plan was that Robbie would stay in Los Angeles and continue recording. At the same time, he would work with Gil and Marty over the telephone and by exchanging packages of audio cassettes:

I WOULD WRITE STUFF, just rough sketches of things, and I would send them to Marty. I hadn't seen the film, so this was completely working in the dark. I had a script for it, but still, you can't write music to a script; you've got to kind of see it. And Marty's stuff usually has such a *look* to it that it means a lot. So I had to work in the dark. I would send Marty music, he would get a sense of what was working and what seemed like we should pursue, he would then send it on to Gil, and Gil would start working on the orchestration for these pieces. So this was the best technique we could use under the circumstances. Marty was in New York editing the film, and once in a while he would send me something to look at, not very much, and this was kind of *after* the fact anyway, after I had already submitted a bunch of stuff. Gil then was working on the stuff on his own, and we would talk on the phone about ideas, things to listen to, any clues we could possibly get.

Willie Dixon was in L.A., so I would get together with Willie. One day, he was trying to remember a melody, so he was whistling this piece of music that I was writing, and it had a nice quality to it, so I said we should send this to Marty, too. So I put this on tape and I sent it to Marty. Then, as it turns out, Marty started laying some of this stuff into the movie. And he laid this whistling in—it's the very first thing you hear when the film starts, Willie Dixon whistling this melody that I had made up. And he began to use some of the rough stuff that I had done, like a demo of the idea of something I was trying to get at. So then in some cases, Gil had to write specifically to the demo version of it.

Gil, in the meantime, was committed to a tour of France and Italy that summer, so he simply packed up his tapes and videos and brought them with him. "Even while I was on the road," he told Ben Sidran, "I had a VCR and a videotape of this movie *The Color of Money*. So I worked on that after the concerts at night." John Surman remembered helping him with some of the transcribing:

HE HAD A BUNCH OF CASSETTES—with lines, bits of a tune that he was writing down—so he had a stack of them, so I volunteered to give him a hand, transcribing a few of these things for him. Gil had a little keyboard, and at one point, he's stabbing away at the keyboard, and he says, "Damn, here I am again, playing D minor 9th. It *still* sounds the same, it's *always* going to sound the same, and I just gotta keep checking it." And it was lovely, just to see a man who had such a grasp of sonorities and everything—and *still* sort of went through the same processes as everybody else. He'd keep pounding away at it, and he'd say, "Damn, I *know* what that sounds like already, but I'm still doing it. I just can't make up my mind."

Gil had also enlisted more help for this project. Back in New York, Gil hired Maria Schneider, a young musician and composer who had been working for him as a copyist. *The Color of Money* was the first major project she worked on with Gil. Just as John Surman had marveled at the sight of Gil struggling away at the piano on a single chord, Maria soon saw, too, that Gil's writing was as finely detailed as ever:

WHEN WE WERE DOING *Color of Money*, I walked into the apartment one morning, and he was sitting at the keyboard, just hitting this little cluster. He was in his underwear. I walk in and he keeps hitting it and hitting it, he didn't turn around. It was at least twenty minutes of just changing a *note*. I mean, he was so detail-oriented, and you can really hear it in the arrangements he wrote.

Maria, soon to become an acclaimed composer, arranger, and bandleader on her own, counts Gil among her most important influences.

I WAS IN COLLEGE, in about 1980, '81, and I remember sitting in my room listening to *Svengali*, and I was looking at the picture of Gil, and I

was just thinking, "Wouldn't it be neat if Gil Evans actually took somebody on as an apprentice?" So then it was years later—I'd finished school,
moved to New York, and I was just working in copy offices, things like
that—and one day, this guy came in, Tom Pierson, who was a composer
and was friends with Gil. And he and I were just talking about music, and
he was asking me who my favorite writers were, and I was going on and
on about Gil Evans. And that night I got a call from him, and he said "Gil
needs somebody to do copy work, just help him organize his music and
everything."

At first, Maria was intimidated by Gil, but he quickly made her feel at
ease. So the working relationship, and the learning experience, began:

I FEEL MY MUSIC HAS BECOME freer and more open because of working
with him and seeing how he got that—but also just his attitude and just
the way he lived. Not that I will ever be as cool-headed as Gil, it's just not
in me, but that was so inspirational, to see somebody who didn't really let
that much get him frazzled. And his open-mindedness, that he loved so
many kinds of music, and that he loved so many things. Every time I was
there, there was some other book he was showing me—a book on African
masks, or face painting, or something—just showing me all these beautiful things. One day we saw a roach and he went off about how roaches are
really clean and they're really wonderful animals.

I think about that stuff all the time. That he was just like a child, you
know, just interested in so many things, and it never stopped. He said,
"You know, I feel like a kid, and sometimes when I look in the mirror and
I see that I'm an old man, I can't believe it, because I feel like a kid. It surprises me all the time. I feel just like I did when I was a kid. I'm still the
same, you know?" And that's the way he lived, too. I think he never really
lost that child. Who was it, Paul Klee or some other painter, who said
that's the definition of a great artist, that they never lose their child.
Maybe that's why Gil could change so much.

I admired Gil so much, but I was always very careful about the amount
of time I spent with him. Gil used to always say, "Why don't you just relax
and hang out a little bit?" After he was gone, sometimes I would think, I
should have spent more time—he *wanted* me to—but I was just so scared
of imposing. But by the same token, I think that that's what made our re-

lationship really good, because I didn't go overboard. But we got along really well. I'm the sort of person who is really uptight about deadlines and being really organized, and Gil was so—relaxed. So I think he found somebody who would keep everything tidy for him and make sure his deadlines were met. Gil was a slow writer anyway, from everything I've heard from everybody. I always wondered if it was maybe more as he got older that he slowed down, but I think he was always slow. And so when he'd get big projects, I would help him.

When Robbie arrived in New York to finalize the charts and prepare for the recording sessions, he and Gil agreed to work at his apartment:

I WENT UP TO HIS PLACE and the front buzzer didn't work, so you had to yell up to him. And he was on the top floor—I had to yell *"Gil, Gil!"* until he heard me. Then he would come to the window, and he would throw down the keys in a glove, so you could catch it and the keys won't hit you in the head. So he throws down the keys, and I go up to his apartment. And he has this funky apartment up on the top floor, and the elevator is broken, so you have to walk all the way up there. So I'm walkin' up, breathing and sweating, and I'm thinking, how can Gil do this all the *time?* And when we were working, they had sent something over to us—a piece of film to look at, that we needed to write something to—and when the guy brought the thing over, Gil *dashed* down the stairs to the delivery guy and dashed back *upstairs*—and I mean he wasn't even hardly *breathing* hard. And I thought, God, he's in *amazing* shape.

Gil might have been in great shape but not too surprisingly the charts were not.

LIKE I MENTIONED BEFORE, Gil wasn't famous for doing things real quickly. His work came when it came, and he needed to do some kind of processing in his mind and in his soul to get what he wanted out of his music. So when I got there, I found out that we were seriously behind schedule, and I said "What are we going to do, Gil, are we going to be able to make this happen in time?" And he was very confident. He said, "Oh, we'll make it. We've just got some work to do. You just got here and we haven't seen any of the film, so we've been working at a bit of a disadvantage, but we'll get there." And he seemed not too stressed about the situation, although we knew we needed to roll up our sleeves immediately, which we did.

Sure enough, once they started working together, the work did proceed smoothly and efficiently. All of the charts were finished just in time for the recording sessions. "Really, we had a job to be done and we did it, and we worked really really hard. We had some great talks, and some great meals in between, but they were just fleeting moments. We couldn't afford the luxury of reflection. Our whole thing was that we were under the gun."

On the first day in the studio, only one piece of music was completed. Robbie was concerned, but not alarmed:

I THINK, ON THE FIRST DAY of working together in a circumstance like this, if you get *something* on tape the first day, you're in good shape. Because it takes some discovery also, when you're mixing different worlds of music together. I don't come from his usual background, and he doesn't come from my usual background, or Willie Dixon's. Scorcese, he was there, and the producer and the people from the film, and everybody was trying to help us make sure that the stuff is going to sound right. We were working on this piece of music, and something about it was causing a complication.

The next day we went in, and by this time we had a little bit of a technique going. I worked with some of the rhythm people, Gil worked with some of the horns, trying different variations on instruments and sounds. We knocked off a few things the next day. We were finishing up the last piece, and everybody was getting a little tired—and Gil was a little tired because he had to stay up really late finishing up these things—and one of the musicians said, "At the end of this piece here, what do you want us to do—should we just vamp out?" And Gil said, "I refuse to resort to your lingo." And I thought, "Well, I'm glad *I* didn't ask this question." And he just meant, in my music, you don't just "vamp" on something, you know, but anyway it put a stillness over the room. And I thought it was wonderful. And the way he'd be sitting there and people would be playing along and he would stand up and he would just shake one of his hands very slightly—and everybody would go into this *sound*. They'd all start quivering what they were playing on the horns. It was beautiful, and it was lovely to see him *conducting* this thing that was being taken out of the air at that moment. He had some kind of unspoken language with these players. They got it completely what he was talking about, and if they didn't, believe me, he was quick to let them know. After this thing about the lingo, he said, "I don't know, do you think I'm getting old and crotchety?" And I said, "Well Gil, it's just your way of communication, and whatever you want to call it, I think it works."

In the commercial release of the film, most of Robbie's original music is heard only in fleeting passages, and it is interspersed with clips from a huge variety of other tunes ranging from Charlie Parker to Giuseppe Verdi to Eric Clapton, B.B. King, Muddy Waters, and many others. The soundtrack album includes three of Robbie's compositions and just over ten minutes of his music. "Don't Tell Me Nothin'" is his vocal feature for Willie Dixon. "Modern Blues" features Robbie on lead guitar playing over Gil's ensemble (harmonica, electric piano, and brass). Gil's work is most prominent on "The Main Title," which plays over the movie's opening credits and again at its conclusion. It features Robbie's wordless vocals over an elaborate full orchestra arrangement.

There was one more tune gleaned from these sessions. Right after Gil and Robbie finished recording, Robbie left for Dublin, Ireland, where he was recording the last tracks for his album. Along with his own music, he also took two Gil Evans arrangements that had not been used. One of these showed up on his new record as "Testimony" (for which Gil's arrangement is credited), and the second was written later by Robbie as a guitar instrumental but not recorded:

ON THE TAPES I WAS SENDING to Marty and Marty was sending to Gil, there were two pieces of music that were on the tape kind of by accident. It was confusing, and Gil had written two charts for things that weren't necessarily stuff that he needed to do. So since he had written them and we were there, we thought, well we'll lay them down on tape. And this one we put down, we really liked it a lot. I liked the horn riff that had come out of this thing. I was going to do some recording with the band U2 for my first album, and we had talked about—once again—an experimentation in music, mixing worlds together and all this kind of stuff. And I took over this horn thing Gil had written. It was just a horn thing and the bass drum, and we played to Gil's horn chart. On the tape, I just kept the bass drum and Gil's horn section, then we recorded the rhythm section and I sang on it with Bono.

The resulting song, "Testimony," may well be the first tune ever written backwards—beginning with the horn tracks instead of finishing up with them:

THIS IS A VERY UNUSUAL thing to do. You usually do the rhythm and then the strings and everything as an add-on, but you don't ever do the rhythm chart *after* the fact. And it wasn't done to a click track or anything like that, so it was a little tricky following this piece of music around. But we just had a *great* time—in Dublin, playing this Gil Evans real New York flavor and New York *attitude* in these horns—and *recording* this on the song I was in the process of *writing*. I didn't even have the song *written*, really. We were just picking up the pieces on the way.

After I did this and I mixed the album, I was in New York and I wanted him to hear what we had gone and done with this thing, so I was playing the album for Martin Scorcese and Gil Evans. It was just the two of them there, and I played them the whole album. So it was fantastic for Gil then to come back and hear what this turned out to be. So he was amazed at what it turned out to be, and I really enjoyed playing this album for him and Marty together. And we had talked about doing some *other* stuff together. We were kicking around some ideas, and this was just the *beginning*. And that was the last time I saw him . . .

‡   ‡   ‡

In December 1986, The Monday Night Orchestra recorded what would become two more albums in King Records' series of live recordings at Sweet Basil. Gil had already used most of his regular tunes on the previous two double albums, but these sessions featured ten songs—all but one of them ("Little Wing") new to this band's repertoire. "At that point," said Tom Malone, "in order for us to do any more recording, we had to have some more arrangements, and it wasn't a real prolific period for Gil as far as cranking out arrangements. At that period in his life, he just did something when he felt the urge to do it, and otherwise didn't. So it was more or less up to the people in the band." On the first album to be released, *Bud 'n' Bird,* only the title track was Gil's arrangement. "There were five tunes on that CD," Tom told me, "and I arranged two of those. I arranged 'Nicaragua Blues' and 'Half Man, Half Cookie,' the Bill Evans tune. John Clark arranged his song ["Groove from the Louvre"], and Mark Egan arranged the other one, his song 'Illuminations.' Gil got credit for arranging all five tunes, but in fact he only did one of the arrangements on that particular album." For once in his life, at least, Gil was credited for more than he did on a record instead of less.

The second album (*Farewell,* which was not released until 1992) features four tunes, three of which (except for saxophonist Bill Evans's "Let the Juice Loose") are Gil Evans arrangements—John Clark's ballad "Your Number," Gil's "Waltz" (formerly called "General Assembly" and also known before that as "Time of the Barracudas"), and another ballad, Jimi Hendrix's "Little Wing." Each tune features several extended solos, along with some of this band's most exciting ensembles and group improvisations on record. "Waltz," for example, may well be the most successful and interesting of any of Gil's own reinvented tunes. It recalls the great driving theme of the original 1964 version, now played in waltz time, and veers off into several wildly abstract ensemble variations. "Waltz" also provides the best solos of this set—by Chris Hunter and Bill Evans on saxophones, Pete Levin on keyboards, and a guest appearance (his last on record with Gil) by Johnny Coles on flugelhorn.

Many of the solos are long and meandering, yet none of them feels excessive or self-indulgent. And there is tremendous interplay amongst the players in the improvised ensembles and in the embellishments they add to the solos. On "Let the Juice Loose," this is accomplished with great artistic flair and with considerable humor and mischief. On "Little Wing," some of the most fascinating group improvisations (and truly exquisite music) are going on not only within the solos but also behind them.

These two final Sweet Basil albums show the Monday Night Orchestra at the height of its creative powers. Now heading into its fourth consecutive year at the club, the band was cohesive, relaxed, and more adventurous than ever. "There was no wrong note in Gil's band," Tom Malone recalled. "Especially during these freely improvised sections—there was no way to play a wrong note. I think at one point or other everybody tried every note that was possible. And it was a great state of mind to be in, where any note was acceptable."

The band's operating guidelines had always been this loose, said another veteran, Dave Bargeron, and yet the music was never as unstructured as it sometimes might have seemed:

> THIS EXERCISE OF PLAYING with Gil is *not* taking away all the rules and setting up completely new ones, like free jazz was in the late '60s. It's not that. This is relating in your own personal way to whatever the core of this is that's going on. That's quite different. There are some organizing elements of this that pull you in and help you along. There is usually a mood that's played on, if nothing else. There are usually chord changes, there is usually some kind of set context that the tune is about. There are organizational factors that are a step more organized than just playing free jazz. You're encouraged to play as freely as you can *against* this core. That's the deal.

Ultimately, what Bargeron refers to as the core of this music was Gil himself, no matter who was playing or what they did, even on the arrangements he did *not* write. "Half Man, Half Cookie," for example, was written by Bill Evans and arranged by Tom Malone, yet Gil's treatment of those charts makes it uniquely his. "I had Tom Malone arrange it for me, and for the band," Bill said. "It actually had a beginning and an end like a regular arrangement. Then Gil came in, playing just one section of the tune, and then he kept repeating it, and the band started picking up on that. It came out kind of weird, but it just turned into this whole other thing—the *Gil* version of the tune, you know?" And so the signature sound remained. The same thing applied to the Gil Evans version of the re-orchestrations Maria Schneider wrote for him—and to the cues the band got from Lew Soloff rather than Gil, and to the charts that Gil Goldstein or Pete Levin helped him organize. In the charts Gil did write, there was no mistaking his still unwavering attention to detail. Maria Schneider:

> THE NATURE OF THE MUSIC was a little different, but I don't really think his basic technique of writing was really that different. It was just not as full-blown, and I think it was intentional, it was the sound he wanted. I think he wanted more of the rhythm section dominating the solos, just a freer sound—but *within* that free sound, a lot of details. And the orchestration was very fussy and very Gil. Some people got the idea that Gil's

sound toward the end was just improvised and it was whoever was in the band—but those little things really added the character, and those little details he was *fussy* about.

As ever, what Gil lacked in quantity he made up for in the quality of his writing. "Bud 'n' Bird" is not only the strongest tune in the new collection but also one of his best compositions ever. Gil's homage to Bud Powell and Charlie Parker offers up a latter-day interpretation of his great mentors' virtuosity as well as his own bebop arrangements for the Claude Thornhill band—highlighted here by an explosive unison chorus played at warp speed by the whole band. It was that kind of music, not just the improvisations, that Bill Evans, like so many of the players, wanted to hear—and to play:

> HE COULD STILL WRITE amazing charts if he wanted to. I remember we did one rehearsal, and he said he wrote two or three new charts, and he wanted to try them out. The voicings were incredible, everybody was speechless after we heard the songs—and we never played them again. Every time we'd ask Gil about them he'd forget what they were. But he could do it when he wanted to—highly structured, harmonic arrangements. Every note is there for a reason, you know? They're like *Sketches of Spain* music. As intense as that, where they *weren't* free, and everyone was reading a part from beginning to end. And we'd finish and go, "Gil, that was a *great* arrangement." "Oh, well, thanks—I have another one." He'd throw it down, we'd play that, and we'd finish, going like, "*Wow*," but then we'd never see them again.

✢   ✢   ✢

Now in its third year, Gil's Monday night date (plus a full week every Christmas) were as popular as ever. "The Sweet Basil's crowd, I always called that the Grateful Dead of jazz," said Hiram Bullock. "Really, a total cult thing. People would show up there and the weirder the man played, the more they loved it." A great deal of the band's appeal was the ever-present sense of anticipation about who would be playing and what would transpire on the bandstand. Now there were increasing numbers of people coming for the celebrity-watching. Miles Davis came in just once, but that visit generated the most delicious rumors (and wonderful block-long line-ups) for months on end.

Among the famous non-jazz visitors, Mick Jagger had been spotted several times at the club. It was believed that he wanted Gil to collaborate with him on something, too, but according to Anita, it wasn't in the cards. "Gil was just doing something else at the time," Anita said, "and Gil didn't change his plans for anything like that. He didn't care that it would have been a lot of money. So it wasn't personal, Gil liked [Jagger] okay—he was just busy thinking about something else at the time."

For Sting, on the other hand, the timing worked out perfectly. He had taken up residence in New York earlier that year, and he spent many of his Monday evenings at the club. "I started to go to Sweet Basil just as a member of the audience," Sting told me. "It was great to go there and see him organizing this motley crew. He filled that room with a wonderful gentleness, and yet it was powerful. I knew some of the guys in the band, and I met Gil again, and he said, 'How ya doin'? You want to sing with us?' I said, 'I'd love to. What am I going to sing?' He said, 'I don't know, sing *something.*' I said, 'Why don't we do one of the Jimi Hendrix arrangements?' And he said, 'Sure.'"

GIL WAS VERY COOL. You would expect someone as established as Gil Evans to be set in his ways—"*This* is what it is, it's not this, it's not this, *this* is how you do things." Gil wasn't like that. He was really creative about it—I think that's the word, he was a creative guy. And being creative is, you have to throw the rules away sometimes, and I think it's one of the things that Gil encouraged. So anyway we sorted it out, I did a little rehearsal—and we did "Little Wing" and "Up from the Skies." This was pretty much just Gil's arrangements, and I sang the song over the arrangements and played some guitar. It was pretty easy, sort of just thrown together. And it was great, it was really good. So then I said I'd like to put one of these tracks on my next album. And he said, "Sure."—Almost anything you suggested to Gil, he would say, "Yeah." He was very open to new ideas. So we got the band into the studio in New York—and we recorded *both* numbers actually, very long, twenty-minute versions of these songs, which we eventually edited down.

Only one of these tunes, "Little Wing," made it to Sting's new album *(Nothing Like the Sun),* and it was edited to such an extent that Gil's presence is just barely visible. At the same time, however, even before the record was released, Sting's collaboration with Gil generated considerable attention. "These gigs at Sweet Basil set off some sort of chain reaction," Sting said. "People heard about this thing. And these festival organizers in Italy heard about it and thought, great, this is a gold mine here. We'll just add Gil Evans with Sting, and we'll get enormous numbers at our jazz festival. And it worked."

Sting and Gil agreed to do a concert, and Sting commissioned Gil to write band arrangements of some of his tunes. In the meantime, he went to Montserrat, in the Caribbean, where he was recording his album. "I just suggested the tunes," said Sting. "I sent the recordings to him, and when I got back everything was done. All the arrangements were done. I just had to sing on them, so it was pretty easy for me." The new arrangements were relatively straightforward, designed primarily to enhance Sting's songs through the orchestrations. "He wasn't this kind of person that would just dress something up just to say he'd done something. If something was working, he'd leave it. Which is another lesson—less is more."

Maria Schneider was hired again as Gil's principal assistant on this project. Working under Gil's direction, she had become much more active in the scoring itself. "Over time, Gil and I worked so much together, and it started to turn into, 'Will you re-orchestrate this for a different instrumentation for me?' He would guide me, tell me what he had in mind. He'd say, 'Well, for the bass line in this tune, use bass clarinet, tuba, and then over here, do whatever you want.'" Working with Gil was also something of a mixed blessing. "It was a little frustrating, because everything was always so last minute. I never really felt I could do the job that I wanted to do—it was always kind of a panic."

Gil was doing less writing now, not for any lack of vigor so much as a shortage of time. At the same time that his writing workload began to grow, he also embarked on the heaviest touring schedule of his career. In April 1987 (in the midst of preparations for the Sting concert), he took the full band to England, where he performed a seventy-fifth birthday concert at London's Hammersmith Odeon Theater (recorded by BBC Radio). In June, he brought the band to Canada, for his first-ever performances there—at Montreal's International Jazz Festival (which was recorded for a radio feature by CBC Radio Canada) and also at the Toronto Jazz Festival. Just days later, he went to Italy for his concert with Sting, and afterwards, he stayed on at the festival and played every night, from midnight until two or three or four in the morning, for another full week.

Much of this music was eventually released on CD. Music from the London concert came out in 2000 as a two-CD set, as part of BBC Music's *Jazz Legends* collection. Excerpts from the Sting concert at the Umbria festival were released in 1997 *(Strange Fruit: Sting and Gil Evans)*. And music from the band's club engagement at the Umbria festival was released in 2000 and 2001, respectively, on two separate volumes *(Gil Evans Orchestra Live at Umbria Jazz 87)*. Each of these recordings has excellent recording quality and captures the excitement of the still-inventive, challenging Gil Evans band. They played intensely, yet with poise and style and grace, not so much working at these charts as toying with them, in the manner of great athletes whose feats appear effortless.

For the London concert, Gil invited some of his favorite guest soloists: Steve Lacy (featured on Mingus's "Boogie Stop Shuffle"); George Adams (featured in a unique match-up with Hiram Bullock and Dave Bargeron on "Orange Was the Color of Her Dress Then Silk Blue"); Gil's longtime British colleagues John Surman (featured on a superb, freshly minted arrangement of the Sting tune "Murder by Numbers") and tenorist John Weller (featured on "Bud 'n' Bird" along with Chris Hunter and Lew Soloff); and Airto Moriera (on vocals and percussion on "Solo"). Also featured is a tune by keyboardist Delmar Brown, "Sometimes"—originally an unaccompanied synth/vocal tune, to which some of the players had gradually started adding improvised backgrounds.

The touring schedule was brutal, even for musicians half Gil's age, yet his vitality seemed in no way diminished. At the London concert, his piano is heard steadily if not prominently throughout the duration of the two-hour concert. When I saw the band two months after this, in June 1987 in Toronto, Gil took the stage looking frail and alarmingly thin, but once he sat down to the piano, he became as animated and spirited as the music itself.

✢   ✢   ✢

In Perugia, the concert with Sting was played before an audience of 30,000, the largest Gil had ever played. "We played in a football stadium—the Gil Evans Orchestra with me," Sting said. "We did arrangements of some of my songs, and the songs I'd done with Gil, and it was very successful. It was televised, and everybody raved about it. And for me it was a great honor, to be performing in such a public arena with Gil Evans."

I THINK WHEN YOU MEET musicians of that age, it's always inspiring, because I'm in a particularly transient, ephemeral kind of form. Rock and roll—whatever I do—you know, you start when you're eighteen and then you try and be eighteen for the rest of your life. If anything, when you see a musician like Gil, you say, "Yeah, I want to be playing music when *I'm* seventy-six." And I don't want to be pretending I'm seventeen. I don't want to be wearing a corset and a wig, you know? Or satin trousers. I want to be my age. And I think to meet and to work with musicians of that caliber—one, it's great, you learn a lot just by osmosis, being with them, but it's also inspiring. It makes you realize that music doesn't end at twenty-five. New things don't stop occurring to you if you're in the right frame of mind. He really was a great archetype. He was the *youngest* old man I've ever met.

Following the concert, the band remained at Perugia and played for a week at San Francesco al Prato, the abandoned ruins of a fourteenth-century cathedral, which had been converted temporarily into a jazz cabaret. It was a magical environment, with warm and enthusiastic audiences every night, both in the church itself and in the open fields outside the building. Gil had a full eighteen-piece band, plus his own keyboards. He also had the luxury of playing a full week without having to travel and set up the equipment every night. To all of the musicians I spoke to, this was one of the most enjoyable and fulfilling dates the band had ever played. The comfortable atmosphere is evident throughout the recording. Along with the standard repertoire (Mingus, Hendrix, and original Evans material), Gil was still adding new material—including "Orgone," written by Gil in 1980 but rarely performed since then, and an elaborately orchestrated arrangement of a Pete Levin tune, "Subway," which features a barrage of synthesizers and a performance art–styled vocal by keyboardist Delmar Brown.

Delmar had played with Gil just over a year before this tour. He remembered how inspiring it was just to see Gil, let alone play with him. "He made *me* feel even younger. He was one of those guys that you wanted to go and hang out with. The vibe was cool. If he'd be sitting there, people would just naturally congregate." Increasingly, though, Gil was nowhere to be found until it was time to go on stage. "One time, when we were in Perugia," said John Clark, "I saw him during the day and I said, 'Hey, how are you? What are you doing? Are you having any fun?' He said, 'All I do is sleep.' He'd go to the gig—I mean he really loved the gig, he loved to play—but he said, 'I don't have the strength to do anything else. All I do is go back to my room and fall asleep until it's time to go play again.' That's the way it was." Yet Gil kept bouncing back—ready to play, ready for the next gig. Delmar Brown:

> Everybody knew he was up in age, but he was going pretty good for quite a while there. I mean, we called him Iron Man. This cat would go on the *road,* man, he was into going on the road with the cats. He got kind of sick now and then—you know, at that age you get sick sometimes and then you get well again—then he'd be out here, ready to go on tour. If Gil was alive now, he'd still be ready to go on tour. He'd say, "Aw, I can't sit down, I gotta get up," you know? He'd always want to work, he'd always want to play. He always used to say he feels better when he's playing, he always feels better. Whenever he felt sick or a little low, he would play. He said he always felt bad. That's why he always wanted to play.

‡   ‡   ‡

From Italy, Sting had returned to Montserrat to finish his record, and he invited Gil to join him. "I just basically gave him a holiday," said Sting:

> HE WAS THERE FOR TWO WEEKS, not really to do anything except just be a sort of presence. And he came into the studio. I remember having a problem with one of the arrangements, where the saxophone player, who was Branford Marsalis, couldn't get this phrase right, that I had written. We tried and we tried and it was still not happening. I mean, I don't write very well for saxophone, this is why the problem was happening. But Gil said, "Can I speak to you?" And he took me outside and he said, "Look, you're concentrating on this note, B flat, and it's the note before the B flat that's causing the problem—change that." And he showed me the notation. So we went in, we did exactly what he said—and it worked. And I thought, "Well, Gil has just paid for his holiday." And the fact is, he didn't sort of stop the session and say, "No, you're doing it wrong." He took me out privately. It was this private little fatherly session.

‡   ‡   ‡

Back in New York, in August 1987 Gil went into the recording studio once again—this time for a new project with Helen Merrill. It was a make-up date of sorts, for a project that had been initiated two years earlier by Helen's record company. "They wanted Gil and me to do an album again,"

Helen explained. "We started two years earlier, but Gil really had slowed down enormously. They came up with the idea of redoing the same music in modern technology, and that's what we did. I would have preferred that we did new material, obviously, but . . . Except we added two songs. One is 'Summertime' and the second one is a Japanese folk song, but that one, it was not appropriate to the album, so we cut it out."

When Gil met with Helen before the sessions, he seemed to her to be bright, cheerful, and ready to go to work.

> WE KNEW EACH OTHER at different points in life, and when we met he said, "Helen, would you believe, I'm solvent? I have money in the *bank*." Gil would talk like a little boy, you know? He had money in the bank—and that he worked with Sting, he thought that was so wonderful. So he remained very young. He was like a little boy when he came to my house, like he probably was when he was twelve. He didn't change. And he'd always speak like a little boy, but with the wisdom of a wise, wise man.
>
> Miles and he had a very special relationship, and during the time that Gil came to my home, he spoke a great deal of Miles. Some very funny stories and some not so funny, and we were laughing and crying the whole night talking about these things. And he did tell me one story—you know, Miles loved him as a father, and he was in Spain and he called Gil up and he said, "Gil, are you all right? I had a terrible dream, that you were sick and that you were dying." And Gil said, "No, I'm *fine*, Miles." Miles was really that close to him, and he was so frightened of losing him.

The resulting album was called *Collaboration*: *Helen Merrill and Gil Evans*. Gil Goldstein assisted Gil in transcribing and re-orchestrating the original arrangements, and he played on the album along with fellow band members Lew Soloff, Chris Hunter, Dave Taylor, and Shunzo Ono. Gil also called in two old friends who played on the 1956 album—Harry Lookovsky and Danny Bank—as well as other longtime colleagues he had not played with for many years—Phil Bodner, Jimmy Knepper, and Joe Beck. Helen told me that Gil also proposed to invite Steve Lacy, specifically to play on "Summertime."

> WE DIDN'T REALLY HAVE Steve Lacy in the budget, but we knew he was coming to New York, and typical of our mischievous ways, we said,

"Let's hire Steve for this." So we invited Steve to come to the recording
session to play, without telling the producer. Meanwhile, the producer
is already having a heart attack—he was gray, we were both gray—because
we were way over budget, so when the producer saw Steve Lacy he almost fainted. But Gil said, "Don't worry." He had Indian moccasins on,
and he had hundred dollar bills stuck in the moccasins. He said, "I
brought the money for Steve, it's right here!" That's Gil. Of course I
wouldn't let him pay for it, and it was paid for by the company eventually. But he knew Steve's solo belonged there. Yeah, he was special, very
special. Very young.

‡   ‡   ‡

In the same month of the Helen Merrill recording, Gil went into the hospital for a hernia operation, and by mid-September he was back on the road.
He took his band to Brazil—his first visit to this country—to play a series of
concerts in Rio de Janeiro and São Paulo. Many in the band were worried
about Gil's condition, but the tour proved to be well organized and went
smoothly. Gil himself, back into Iron Man mode, was as resilient as ever.
Airto Moriera described a telling incident that took place between Gil and
Hermeto Pasqaul, one of Brazil's leading jazz artists.

HERMETO IS VERY WELL KNOWN. He's notorious for playing long sets.
He plays like five hours and doesn't stop. And the people, they leave, they
go home—and all of a sudden there's ten people there instead of a thousand—and he's still playing. But it was a festival, and it was a very tight
schedule, because it was too many bands in one night. This was in Rio, and
Hermeto played before us and then we closed. So Hermeto was supposed
to play forty-five minutes and he played an *hour* and forty-five minutes.
And Gil was in the audience, he was sitting there applauding, right?
Going, "Yeah! Yeah!" Everybody was very nervous, because Gil was old already, and they'd say, "Oh, Hermeto's making Gil Evans wait, this is terrible," and they were looking for Gil, and meanwhile I knew where Gil was,
because he told me, "If they look for me, I'm out there in the audience,
I'm going to have to listen to this." So finally Hermeto finished, and we
went on at one-thirty in the morning—and then we played for two hours.
So then, two days later, we played São Paulo, which was the end of the festival and the last day. Gil said, "Okay, I don't want to close this time, I

want to play before Hermeto, because he plays too long." So everybody said, "Okay Gil, whatever you want." So we went on and we played for *three and a half hours.*

Noah had accompanied Gil to Brazil, and upon their return to New York, he and Miles decided that they needed to spend more time with Gil. This time he did not return to his job at Nola.

HE NEEDED HELP, physical help. Miles was there as well, and we would just basically take care of errands and stuff for him. Miles tended to do more of the music stuff, like get stuff from the copyist or alphabetize the book for Mondays or like those kinds of things. But he really did start to need help, which wasn't something that we were used to. Even though he was a much older father than most people have, he always was physically very capable and physically very strong. We weren't really *used* to him needing any sort of assistance.

✝   ✝   ✝

Gil was not accustomed to needing help, either. Despite his sons' concerns, he was back on the road, with Anita. Less than a month after the Brazil tour, they traveled to France, where they commenced one of Gil's most arduous tours ever. From late October to mid-November, he played throughout Europe with Lumière, an orchestra led by French composer and bandleader Laurent Cugny. This project had been initiated by Cugny in early 1986, after Gil had met with him in New York for a series of interviews for his book, *Las Vegas Tango: Une vie de Gil Evans.* Cugny then called Gil a few months later from Paris to see if he might consider playing with his band.

Gil sent Cugny a set of his Monday Night Orchestra arrangements, which Cugny adapted for his band. They also played some of Cugny's own material and Cugny also wrote slightly modified arrangements of some of Gil's earlier classics, including "La Nevada." After Gil heard this arrangement, Cugny wrote that, to his great relief, Gil complimented him on his work.

Two days after his arrival in Paris, the tour began—twenty-one concerts across France, Switzerland, Germany, Holland, and Italy, all in less than four weeks. During this time, the band also did two recording sessions (Novem-

ber 3 and 26), which resulted in two albums, *Rhythm-a-ning* and *Golden Hair.*
After the final recording session with Lumière, Gil recorded with another
French orchestra—l'Orchestre National de Jazz, under the direction of
French composer Antoine Hervé. They recorded Gil's arrangement of "Orange Was the Color of Her Dress Then Silk Blue." As he had done throughout his tour with Lumière, on this recording Gil conducted and played electric and acoustic piano.

‡   ‡   ‡

Gil had been away with Laurent Cugny for five straight weeks, most of
which was spent either traveling or performing. Yet before returning home,
he attended to one more piece of unfinished business. This was another collaboration with Steve Lacy—two days in a studio (November 30 and December 1)—in which they recorded as a duo. Steve Lacy:

> WE HAD TALKED A NUMBER of years ago about making a record together,
> where I would be featured and he would write some arrangements,
> where I could use the members of my band and all that. Instead, that duo
> record happened, just because it could. In other words, we didn't do what
> we *wanted* to do, we did what we *could*. That duo record was sort of a
> sketch toward a possible more elaborate recording collaboration that just
> never happened, because he died. Anyway, it wasn't meant to be or some-
> thing, it was just a dream.

The resulting album, *Paris Blues,* features three Mingus tunes ("Orange
Was the Color of Her Dress Then Silk Blue," "Good-bye Porkpie Hat," and
"Reincarnation of a Lovebird"), one of Gil's tunes ("Jelly Rolls"), and one of
Steve's ("Esteem"), and the title track, written by Duke Ellington. Ironically,
Paris Blues is the only recording Gil made of an Ellington composition, and
this might well have been the first time he performed his mentor's music
since the days when he used to transcribe it for his first band, more than fifty
years earlier. The relative prominence of Gil's playing goes far beyond his
more usual role as accompanist. "That was one reason I really wanted to do
it," Lacy explained, "because I had never heard a record where he was shown
to full advantage as a pianist. And that's why I knew the duo would be a good
thing for *him* to do."

GIL AND I USED TO PLAY together for practice all the time. He would rent a studio, we'd get a drummer and a bass player and we would play. This went on for several years. He wanted to work on his chops, he thought he was an inadequate piano player. He always had a complex, because he was intimidated by the other cats who had more technique than he did—but he *was* a great piano player. And the proof, well, the proof is on his first record, *Gil Evans Plus Ten*—he plays the most beautiful piano solos I ever heard—very brief, but very succinct. But on *Paris Blues* he really gets a chance to stretch out, for the first time, I think.

Gil's playing is in fact the great surprise of this album. He had established his unique sound years earlier, but his playing was usually heard quite sparingly—in his introductions, his solos (usually very brief), and his comping. As Lacy recalls, the vigor and energy of Gil's playing is all the more impressive given the state of his health.

GIL WAS VERY ILL already at that time. He was not well. It was touch and go, because he was not feeling well a few days before then, and it was possible that we would have to cancel the whole thing. I didn't know until the day itself that he felt well enough to do it. So it was lucky that he did feel well enough to do it for two days. But he was not well at all, he was already ill. I didn't want to impose on his health, but he said, "No, I'm okay today, let's go." Then that was it. It was difficult for him. We had to stop every now and then, but he was beautiful. He had such an indomitable spirit and such a youthful zest. And he had a *ball,* and you can hear it, it's very *joyful* the way he plays. It's not gloomy at all. It's right in the record, you can *hear* it. It was a powerful experience, man—very moving, very emotional . . .

✦   ✦   ✦

On Gil's return to New York, Anita and the two boys decided to take him to Florida for a much-needed rest and to escape from a particularly harsh winter. "I had this friend in Soho," Miles recalled, "and he said, 'Miles, I hate Florida, but the one place I like is Sanibel Island.' And it was beautiful—sunny and really nice. The four of us—my mother, my father, my brother—we went down and it was beautiful. And that was the last one we went to."

Then it was time for Gil's annual weeklong Christmas date at Sweet Basil. It was during this gig that Noah remembers seeing the age in his father's face. His father always had white hair, he had always looked thin if perhaps not gaunt, but it struck Noah that this was the first time that Gil actually looked to him like an old man.

> YOU'VE GOT TO UNDERSTAND, every Monday Gil would *walk* from 76th Street down to the village, to Sweet Basil. So I mean, I never questioned his physical capability. But there was this one time, he came into the club and I saw that he kind of almost stumbled a little walking in, and I noticed that, and I noticed that he wasn't moving as strongly and surely as he usually does. I think that's when I first started to notice that something was happening, but even at that point, I just kind of wrote it off—maybe to the cold weather and him having a cold.

In January 1988, Gil went into the hospital for prostate surgery, a common and normally routine operation, to correct blockage of the urinary tract caused by swelling of the prostate gland. But following the operation, Noah recalled, there were complications: "They gave him this thing called a spinal, it's a form of anaesthesia. I believe it's injected directly into the bottom of the spine. At any rate, after that he was not the same, he was never all there after that. There was always just a little bit of a—almost a dreaminess about him. He never really recovered from that."

"They fucked me up!" Gil told Horst Liepolt over the telephone. "'Jesus Christ,' he said, 'very soon you're going to have to have that done to you, too. Get the *best*.'" Gil had called to tell Liepolt that he was going to Mexico for a rest and that he was not sure when he would be back to play again. Even then there was still work that he wanted to do before leaving. In February, he met with British guitarist Ray Russell, with whom he had recorded at the 1983 Montreux Jazz Festival. Gil worked on three tunes with him in a studio in New York. On two of these—Gil's "The Pan Piper" and Russell's "Sketches of Gil"—Gil's electric piano was overdubbed on Russell's existing masters. These tunes were released (in Europe only) on Ray Russell's album, *Why Not Now*. Gil also recorded Charles Mingus's "Good-bye Porkpie Hat," which was included on another European album by Ray Russell and the group RMS, along with the other tunes they had recorded with Gil in 1983 at Montreux. "Good-bye Porkpie Hat" is a duet. It features an excellent performance by Ray Russell on guitar, but as with *Paris Blues,* it is Gil's playing, on electric piano, that will be remembered.

Gil's solo on this tune is one of his best ever, and it is the last recording he made.

⁺   ⁺   ⁺

The trip to Cuernavaca was supposed to have been a working holiday or, at the very least, Noah Evans remembered, another of the rest-and-relaxation breaks he had taken Gil on many times before:

> IT WAS ACTUALLY my Mom's initiative, through Maxine Gordon, Dexter Gordon's wife. And they knew of a place down in Mexico, in Cuernavaca, through Charles Mingus. They had a whole team of naturalists there—women that were doing everything from acupuncture to nutrition, body work, and just a whole regimen of stuff that we thought would be just perfect. It was the first time he had gone to Mexico, but it wasn't the first time we had gone to warm places. Gil always loved nature and outdoors and warm weather, so that was something that didn't need any convincing.
>
> So that was really what happened. We just were going to go down there for a recharge—hibernate through the winter and charge up for the summer tours that we had booked. We had Perugia again, we had Sicily, some other places. But that was really it. And I was going to go down for the first month, and then I would come back after Miles came down for the next month. We were going to switch off back and forth, and then once it got warm again, he was going to come back up, resume the Mondays, and then go into the summer tour.

Gil also brought down tapes and music that he intended to work on. One of the arrangements he had with him was Robbie Robertson's tune, "The Moon Struck One," which had taken Gil some fifteen years to get around to writing, and then another two years to actually finish. The tune premiered a year later, in a concert by the Gil Evans Orchestra, but Gil was not there to hear it.

There would be no recharge on this trip, no resurgence of energy. In Cuernavaca, Gil got weaker, not better, and his health began to deteriorate rapidly. Noah discovered that Gil had not taken any of his post-surgery antibiotics:

> HE TURNED INTO A KID—like a kid would spit out something that they don't like. They're like, "Eewww" or "Gross" or something. It was like

that. He'd make that face, where you make that face . . . eewww—when you don't like the way something tastes—then he'd just spit out the pills. So we would have to do what he used to do with me, when we were kids—he used to stick penicillin and stuff in oranges, and stuff that we would eat. I remember a couple of times, we caught him. [As kids, we] were like "phooey" and we'd spit it out, and then he'd have to sneak it into something else. But it turned into us having to do that to him.

Worse still, Noah told me, Gil was soon unable to eat. "He got to the point where he couldn't really get food down, because his throat was kind of closing off. He could get fluids down, but he couldn't really eat anything of any substance. Then he started getting really weak, but we couldn't build up his strength because he couldn't eat, so it was this vicious circle. At that point, we had to get him into a hospital."

Noah took Gil to the local hospital, and then he called his brother in New York. The plan was that Miles would join them later, but Noah told him to come right away. "Also what was happening, I was getting tired. I had been close to twenty, thirty days with maybe just half-hour, hour chunks of sleep here and there. If he slept for an hour at a time, that was a lot. I wasn't the sharpest myself, because I wasn't getting a whole lot of sleep. So I called Miles and I said, 'Look, I'm not really sure here, I'm starting to get a little something here, I'm not exactly clear. I think you should come down.'"

MILES GOT INTO MEXICO City and then our friend Larry, who's a sax player down there, picked him up and drove him down to Cuernavaca—about a two-hour drive if there's not a whole lot of traffic. Miles came into the room—it was about four or five o'clock in the morning, somewhere in that time frame—he walked into the room, I gave him a hug, I said "Good to see you," "How's Gil doin'?" "Oh, he's doin' all right, you know—you wanna say hello?" "Okay." So then Miles put down his bags, and he went over to the bed. I went to shake him a little, to wake him up, let him know Miles was here—so I shook him, he didn't wake up. I was shaking him a little harder—he didn't wake up. And Miles came over and he was shaking him, didn't wake up. Then next thing you know, we're *really* shaking him, and he's not waking up. Now at that point, you should know—if we were in a different state, we would have known right away—he's gone. But we didn't know, so we kept trying to revive him or wake him up at first. And then we started to realize, Okay, he's not waking up.

We got the nurses in there and they said, in Spanish, they were trying to tell us he was gone. They were just shaking their heads, and they weren't going to do anything. So me and Miles threw them out of the room and we were pounding on his chest and shaking him. I don't know if you've ever held a dead body, a body that doesn't have life in it, but it's just this kind of rubbery thing that just flops around. But we were definitely in huge denial and we weren't going to stop. So we were pounding his chest and I mean, I don't know, trying to do stuff.

He was gone. And we didn't know it, and we weren't at all willing to accept that.

Gill was seventy-five years old. It was March 20th, the vernal equinox, the first day of spring, and one day before Noah's twenty-third birthday. Noah Evans, no longer denying his father's passing but still in shock, remembered the walk that morning from Gil's room to find a telephone:

WHAT DO THEY CALL the area where they keep brand new babies that are just born? There's an area of the hospital that I had to walk through to get to the pay phone to call my Mom. Gil had just passed away, and there were all these moments-old, hours-old babies, a dozen of them or something like that. It was a really kind of profound experience . . .

Then I got on the phone with my Mom and told her what happened, and then the next day we had to deal with the cremation. Thank God, Maxine Gordon was down there, because she not only spoke Spanish but she dealt with a lot of the details, which I was absolutely incapable of dealing with, because at that point I was totally numb. I couldn't do anything. I could walk and I could see, I could speak, but I was just numb. Nothing made sense to me. So thank God for the support around us; otherwise, how would we have dealt with all the post-mortem stuff? I couldn't deal with that.

But poor Miles. He came down and—I'm telling you, during that month, however many days that was, all Gil had to do was make a little sound and—snap—I would wake right up. "What is it? What do you need?" So I know if he had made a sound that I would have woken up. So he went quietly and he went, at most, a half an hour before my brother came down. Now, how hard was that on him compared to me? I can't even imagine. That would have to have been devastating. To this day that's devastating.

✛   ✛   ✛

The news of Gil's passing seemed devastating to practically everyone who knew him. It was obvious that he had been working far harder than he should have been, yet it seemed that he had been thriving on the excitement, even as it wore him down. People had widely varying ideas about what had driven Gil during these last months and years: Was he oblivious to death? Did he see it coming? Noah Evans, even though he was closest to Gil at the end, can only speculate like the rest of us.

I DON'T KNOW if he had this feeling like, "Wow, I've got to do these things," or "These are the things I want to do because, you know, I'm on the way out." Did he know that? Did he think that way? He was working and traveling as hard as a twenty-year-old would—and the answer to that is, I don't know. The only thing I can say is that he didn't say that or share that with me, or with any of us. He wasn't always the greatest at sharing what was going on with him, and his feelings.

To the very end, Noah said, Gil's innermost thoughts and emotions would remain a mystery, even to his own family:

IT'S THE WEIRDEST THING in the world. You'd feel so close to Gil—I'm talking about people who were in the band. When Gil passed away, I would talk with them and they were worse than *me*. For them it was like losing a dad, a brother, a son, whatever it was—losing a family member—and they were heartbroken. Miles Davis, Pu, the people I talked to that were devastated by it was amazing. But at the same time that they felt so close to him, and thought of him as a father or brother, they didn't really know a whole lot *about* him. It's a weird thing, how the two can coexist at the same time. I don't know how he managed to do that. He managed to make people feel very secure, very comfortable, very loved—like they were the most important people in the world to him. But at the same time, he didn't really share that much of himself, what was going on with him, his feelings, or

how he thought about things. In later years, I blamed myself for that somewhat, because I wished that I were more active or more aggressive in seeking out some of these things—What was your childhood like? What was
your mom like? What are you thinking *now?*—anything . . .

It has been suggested that in his final months and years, Gil had accepted
more work so that he would have more money to leave his family. This might
be true to some extent, Miles Evans told me, but then again, Gil continued
to turn down projects, however lucrative they might be, if the people or the
music were not to his liking. In the summer of 1986, for example, he reput-
edly turned down a six-figure offer for a project with pop singer Barry
Manilow, while at the same time he signed on for Helen Merrill's project,
which paid less than one-tenth of Manilow's offer. "It wasn't about him not
being able to make the money," said Miles. "It was about his integrity. He
wanted to do the music that *he* wanted, and he did not want to sell out, even
if Barry Manilow or musician X had a quick hundred grand or two hundred
grand for him. That's just the way he was. And it was an amazing thing that
he could actually do that."

And there were more and more projects coming up that Gil *did* want to
do. That's why he worked as hard as he did, Miles believed:

> GIL MIGHT HAVE SEEN the end at hand, that could have been one of the
> elements, but he continued to grow and develop over the years, and his
> work was *never* done. And things just started to *click* then—the stuff that
> he did with Sting was very well received, the stuff with Robbie Robert-
> son, he worked with David Bowie at that point—all these people that he
> started working with. And with all that happening, of course he would
> find music that he *wanted* to be involved with.

Apart from such commissioned works, there was more work with the
band and with his own music. Howard Johnson had just spoken to Gil about
reintroducing more of his earlier arrangements—not necessarily to displace
the newer material but rather to balance it:

> THIS IS NOT A PERIOD I was very warm to, the last few years. I was
> mostly there in support of Gil as a person and a musician and my friend,
> but I wasn't into that way of playing—mostly because it de-emphasized

the arrangements. He wanted to emphasize his bandleader thing and do a sound that other bands didn't have through that. He said that too much of a fuss had been made over his arrangements. One of the last times I really talked to him at length, in the early part of 1988, I told him, "You know, you can't go around saying people make too much of a fuss over your arrangements, because you're like one of the world's leading arrangers. It's just a simple fact that you ought to get really used to, and that that's one of your strengths that you're not *using* in this band. And even if the band stays like that, I would like to see some of that high-quality stuff come back into it." And he said that he had just done a thing with Ben Sidran [September 1986, for his National Public Radio series, *Sidran on Record*], where he had been interviewed while listening to those arrangements, and he said he was pretty happy with what he had heard. He had kind of forgotten the work that had gone into it, and the results, and he thought it was pretty nice. So he thought that maybe he *would* begin to emphasize arrangements more. And I said, "Well, you'd make me real happy if you do that, because that's really the thing that I signed *on* for, you know?"

Gil had talked about this in the summer of 1986, during his get-togethers with Helen Merrill, in this case focusing on a new recording project:

WE HAD LONG TALKS about his music. I said, "What do *you* want to do, Gil?" He said, "All I want to do is an album of my *own* music." I said, "Do it, Gil, go for it." And I thought about getting hold of Miles, to sponsor it, and I knew I could get record companies to sponsor it—his own album, for himself. The most moving thing to me was, he called up all the record companies and got all his out-takes and all his old things, and he took all of that to Mexico with him, and he was working on that album at that time. That moved the hell out of me, because he took it at face value—and of course we could have gotten him a record date, no question about it— of his own music. So he didn't expect to die. So we can be angry. We *can* be angry, yeah . . .

George Russell talked to Gil not long before he went to Mexico. They, too, had spoken about the next project, but it quickly became apparent that Gil was not well:

WE WERE SUPPOSED to do a "battle of bands" at the Village Gate. I called him and told him that he'd have to get himself together. I thought I was cheering him up, but he didn't respond to that at all. That's not what he wanted to hear. So I almost felt like I'd said the wrong thing, you know? He didn't want to talk about the business. I'd had more experience at being ill than he had, so I think he wanted to be consoled, in a sense. I should have known—you don't cheer somebody up in their last days talking to them about the music business. I hope he doesn't hold it against me . . .

Many of the people I talked to felt badly about their last words with Gil—regretful, remorseful, terribly disappointed that they never got to tell Gil how much he meant to them. We can be angry, perhaps—for the great music that was not to be, for all the new projects that went unfinished—yet this is how it should be, George Russell offered, for this is how artists live and how they die:

I THINK HE WAS still searching, and as *all* of the innovators who pass on are doing, dying in the *midst* of their creation, in the *midst* of their creative life . . .

Epilogue

The example of great and pure individuals is the only thing that can lead us to noble thoughts and deeds.

—ALBERT EINSTEIN

MEMORIAL

IT IS EASTER SUNDAY, April 3, 1988, and five hundred people have crowded into St. Peter's Lutheran Church in New York City. They are here today not to celebrate Easter but to pay their respects in a memorial service for Gil Evans. He had died fourteen days earlier, less than a month before his seventy-sixth birthday. The service, in words and in music, honors an artistic legacy—the achievements of a career spanning more than fifty years of arranging, writing, and performing music—and it pays homage to the passing of an illustrious member and dear friend of the jazz family.

Reverend John Gensel, New York's official jazz pastor, has presided over congregations like this one since 1960. He modeled this ceremony on the traditional New Orleans funeral—in this case, keeping the music inside the church rather than marching his procession down Lexington Avenue. Reverend Gensel has led services for many of jazz's most revered artists—Duke Ellington, Thelonious Monk, Bill Evans, John Coltrane—and for many others less widely known. All of them are special people, says the Reverend, for musicians are among "the privileged people of God." It will be less a somber affair today, more an affirmation of life—all the more appropriate, says Reverend Gensel, that for Gil Evans it should take place on Easter Sunday, "a day which celebrates life like no other."

Then of course there is the exuberance of the music that will fill the afternoon: a final bow to the maestro, one last set, a celebration of the gifts bestowed on us by this musician's musician. These would include personal tributes—Cecil Taylor playing unaccompanied piano; Joe Beck on acoustic guitar; Emily Mitchell-Soloff, unaccompanied harp; Delmar Brown performing his solo piece, "Sometimes," always a personal favorite of Gil's. And then there is Gil's own music: his elegantly detailed arrangements for the famous 1940s chamber group—"Boplicity" and "Moondreams," performed with original nonet members Gerry Mulligan, John Lewis, Bill Barber, and Lee Konitz. A spirited selection of arrangements is played by the band that Gil had led to the very end of his days—"Bud 'n' Bird," "Good-bye Porkpie Hat," and stretching back three decades, concluding with "La Nevada." The band is led today by Miles Evans, who would continue to lead the band from that day to the present, and many of these same players would remain with him.

Through all of this music, we catch a glimpse of the *many* lives of Gil Evans—a phenomenon due less to the longevity of his career than to its diversity. Many careers are as long as Gil's was, but who else covered such a range of territory? Who else's work predates the swing era and moves so adeptly from Louis Armstrong and Fletcher Henderson to Maurice Ravel and Manuel de Falla, from Lester Young and Charlie Parker to Igor Stravinsky and Jimi Hendrix? Who else but Gil Evans made synthesizers and electric guitars as intrinsic to his sound as his beloved French horns and tubas? Who else could embrace so many idioms, explore so many different ideas, and create from them his own singular voice?

The music played on this Easter Sunday is all over the map—how could it be otherwise?—and so is the seemingly incongruous mix of people in attendance. Gathered here are some of the oldest and youngest of his friends and admirers. Mostly they are musicians—music people, music "types" of every stripe: beboppers, rockers, traditionalists, revolutionaries *et al*. Not all of them share Gil's interest in the full span of these musical genres, but each shares a personal connection to Gil that transcends any of their differences. "I've always thought of Gil Evans, the musician, as a national treasure," says John Simon, fellow musician, composer, and today's master of ceremonies. "But for me to have had the privilege of knowing him, Gil, the man, was a *personal* treasure." Variations on this thought are expressed by everyone who speaks today. "Each time that I would see Gil it would be an *up*," John Simon continues. "I don't know what there was about the man, but even when things were down, I would walk away from the meeting feeling lifted."

It's not just that Gil was special, we hear time and again, but that he was *outstandingly* special, "unlike anyone I've ever met in my life." Nor is it that he was seen as a demigod; rather, it was his humility, his utter lack of egotism, his openness to others, that drew people to him like a magnet. Gerry Mulligan called him Svengali—a perfect anagram for Gil Evans by name, and a perfect analogy for the Gil Evans touch—for Gil seemed able to make everyone sound better than they ever had before. He could take the most temporary aggregations—session players hired just for the gig, guest soloists sitting in for a single tune—and turn them into a supremely unified entity. Like a Pied Piper of the jazz world, he could summon the very best musicians of the day to drop everything and join his parade. Much of the allure of his music, if not its principal historical significance, was in the way he created his sound by blending together, yet still preserving, the individual voices of each performer. Not even the seasoned veterans were used to anything this challenging or rewarding. "Play what *you* want to hear, not what you think *I* want to hear," he would tell them. Be honest with yourself, use your *own* voice, trust your *instincts*—these were pretty much his only rules. In the end, Gil would usually say, he'd simply led the life of a working musician, paying his dues, trying to get by as best he could. But with his music and by his example, Gil Evans has inspired generations not to chase the Pied Piper but to follow their hearts. Few individuals in this world have left us with greater, nobler thoughts and deeds than these. Fewer still had such a wonderful time along their way.

LAST WORDS FROM THE MUSICIANS

GIL GOLDSTEIN

I think of him walking into Sweet Basil, just kind of relaxed, strolling in and getting a cup of tea, and sitting down at his electric piano. But Gil was an incredibly hard worker, and he wasn't *just* a relaxed kind of guy. That always hits me when I take a look at some music of his. I know, as an arranger, how hard it is to get something to that level. It's not something that you can just kind of bang out. It's something you really have to sit and churn over. It's won from pretty hard work and a lot of dedication. That's really the way I think of Gil—as somebody who had a vision and was lucky and hard-working enough to get it realized.

Gil said to me once that that was his religion. He said he would wake up in the morning and say, "God, I hope I'm lucky today." But it was lucky in that he was so *prepared* for luck to happen that it just was bound to happen. Like if you think about him meeting Miles Davis, and just the way his life went and opened itself up for him to do the kind of stuff he did. It's some kind of combination of the luck of existence and just being an incredibly hard-working guy.

HERBIE HANCOCK

Gil Goldstein sent me some copies of piano reductions of some of that music—there's "My Ship," there's "The Duke," there's "Gone," there's

"Maids of Cadiz" and "Summertime." I went right to the piano, because that music meant so much to me. When I heard the *Miles Ahead* album, that really changed my whole outlook on music, it really changed my life. So as soon as I got 'em, I ran to the piano and started trying to play to these things. You would have thought I was having an orgasm: "Oh!" "Ah!" "Oooo"—and things like, "Fuck! How in the hell did he *do* this?" And I learned. It's funny, too, because I can definitely see how much Gil has influenced me. Because I look at these chords and now I know what they *are*. Years ago I didn't know. Now I know, but still—like I'm looking at this thing "The Duke"—there are *still* new lessons for me to learn. And I know a lot about chords, believe me. I've studied that, 'cause I love harmony. And there are little secrets here that I didn't know. And it's amazing the way this stuff is constructed. Just looking at it, just playing it on the *piano*, without the different colors, it's amazing. And then with the records— with the instruments that these things were *designed* for—that just blows you away.

BILL EVANS

One thing is to capture the different phases and just keep it in mind that he wasn't affected by this. He's affected people on the whole planet. He's part of a small group of people that will actually affect people in a thousand years. They'll be playing Gil Evans arrangements. But he remained the same—no ego, no material things, he wasn't interested in money. He'd just kind of float through time. Aside from the music, just the way he was should be what's remembered too, because that's a lesson in itself. He was just so laid back and so non-material. I mean, we'd be walking along and he'd see a cat, maybe in the stairwell of a building. He'd stop and say something like, "Have you ever thought about how carefree a cat must be in the summertime when it's really warm out?" I mean he would just come out with these things . . .

One time he said, "I was at the store today and I really got a shock." And I said, "Why, what happened?" He said this little kid came up to him and said, "Boy you're old." And Gil said, "I never thought about it until the kid said it. Old . . . I don't even know what that means." That's what he said, and he was actually shocked. Everyone always had the feeling that Gil would never die because he was so young. In his mind he never aged.

STING

I don't think he ever lost that feeling of being the kid who learned to play the piano, the wonder of music that you get when you first pick up an instrument. The longer you play, the further away from that magic you can get—it becomes a chore, a duty, it becomes second nature, and you don't think about it. I don't think Gil ever lost that sense of wonder. If he were alive today he'd still have it. I think that's his legacy. He never lost that sense of child-like wonder about music, even though he knew so much— that there's still more, that you can never ever understand the whole thing, that it's limitless.

KENNY BURRELL

First of all, I think what we call *jazz* will some day be measured and identified as the most important music of the twentieth century—just because of its influence, its power, its innovative qualities, its cultural connections, the method, the complexity, the artistic achievement, the highly technical and psychological requirements for musicians—as we look back in earnest, and with a search for truth. And then, given that, we will look at Gil Evans as one of the most important *contributors* of this most important music. If we're just going to focus on jazz, we say, Well, Gil Evans was one of the most important people in jazz—certainly, without question—but I'm saying something else. I'm saying that when the truth be told, he will be one of the important musicians of the twentieth *century*—period.

SUSAN EVANS

I remember going up to his apartment and he'd be having dinner with Anita and Miles and Noah, and sometimes he wouldn't even realize I was in the apartment. And I understood I should just join in and have some food. Then he'd go over and plunk at the piano, not necessarily to rehearse or anything, and I'd join in. Then he'd leave, he'd have some errand to do and wouldn't even say good-bye, kind of—is "amorphous" the right word? Somehow that word is coming to me. I'd take from him, he'd get things from me. That was the essence of our relationship, even on a personal level. There was no real beginning or end to the communication with Gil. It would just kind of flow in and out.

ADAM NUSSBAUM

He kept his mind open to everything. I think that was something I really learned a lot about from him—to always keep your mind open, to all kinds of music. Because there's validity in everything. There's only good and bad, and he'd be listening to everything, like pop tunes—if a song was a good song, it was a good song, it didn't matter what it was. Like Willie Nelson—Gil liked his phrasing. And it taught me to be more aware—look at what's there, not at what's *not* there. And that's a good attitude to have in life, too.

DAVID SANBORN

Gil was uncompromising without being an asshole about it. Gil wanted his music to be successful, but *he* didn't want to be successful. In other words, he didn't try to write music that he thought would be successful. He wrote what he felt. And his music was him. It was an expression of who he was. There was continuity of person and creation, and I've never been around somebody where I've experienced that kind of continuity of being—from anybody. Gil's music was him; he was his music. And it was like the music was alive—it was messy and beautiful and delicate and crude, just like *life* is. And it made a lot of people uncomfortable. They wanted him to keep on doing *Sketches of Spain,* they wanted him to *do that thing.* And he wrote some incredibly beautiful music in his later years—music that was an evolution of the same kind of artistic thought that went into *Sketches of Spain,* that went into *Porgy and Bess.* He wrote music that was as sophisticated and involved and as meaningful as any of the music that he wrote during what people like to call his golden period. It had meaning, it had depth, it had character, and so did he.

JOHN SURMAN

When people talk about Gil Evans they mean *Sketches of Spain*—they don't mean George Adams playing "The Meaning of the Blues," not really. But for me, I would hope that there'd be some respect for the direction that he took later on in his career. It's notoriously difficult to capture the spirit of those improvisational things on record. That's the ethereal nature of improvisation, I'm afraid—that those of us that are really fascinated by pure improvisation are always caught within a trap—it's over as soon as it's done. Some of the *point* of what happens is like, you're there and you're hearing this stuff and you're *feeling* this music evolve. And I think that's really the joy of it.

Playing with Gil, you couldn't really wait to get to work—you couldn't wait to get there and get on with it. You never knew what was going to happen, but you knew that something *fantastic* was going to happen. And it always did, one way or the other, and I miss him like hell, I really do.

INTERVIEWS
CONDUCTED
BY AUTHOR

All interviews took place in person except as noted; (*) indicates interviews by telephone.

Note: Quotes throughout the text are from the author's original interviews as shown below; other interview sources, as indicated in the text, include magazines and publications as listed in the following bibliography.

ABERCROMBIE, JOHN . . . . .25 JUNE 1991, TORONTO

AVAKIAN, GEORGE* . . . . .13 FEBRUARY 1993

BARGERON, DAVE . . . . .8 APRIL 1991, NEW YORK

BECK, JOE* . . . . .17 SEPTEMBER 1992

BROWN, DELMAR . . . . .23 MARCH 1992, NEW YORK

BULLOCK, HIRAM* . . . . .9 JUNE 1992

BURRELL, KENNY . . . . .5 APRIL 1991, NEW YORK

BUSHLER, HERB* .23 MARCH 1992

CARISI, JOHN . . . . .9 DECEMBER 1990, NEW YORK

CARISI, JOHN* . . . . .3 FEBRUARY 1992

CLARK, JOHN . . . . .11 DECEMBER 1990, NEW YORK

DIEDRICK, RUSTY* .30 MARCH 1992

EVANS, ANITA . . . . .7 APRIL 1991, NEW YORK

EVANS, ANITA* .19 SEPTEMBER 1992

EVANS, BILL . . . . .11 DECEMBER 1990, NEW YORK

EVANS, MILES* .29 NOVEMBER 2001

EVANS, NOAH . . . . .7 JULY 1992, NEW YORK

EVANS, NOAH* .6 NOVEMBER 2001

EVANS, SUSAN* . . . . .26 SEPTEMBER 1992

FADDIS, JON . . . . .4 JULY 1991, MONTREAL

GENSEL, REVEREND JOHN* . . . . .12 FEBRUARY 1992

GIDDINS, GARY* . . . . .2 APRIL 1999

GILBERTO, ASTRUD (VIA EMAIL) . . . . .15 APRIL 2001

GOLDSTEIN, GIL . . . . .10 DECEMBER 1990, NEW YORK

HALL, GLEN . . . . .26 AUGUST 1992, TORONTO

HANCOCK, HERBIE* . . . . .18 MARCH 1992

HARPER, BILLY . . . . .27 JUNE 1992, TORONTO

HOROWITZ, DAVID* . . . . .23 MARCH 1992

HUNTER, CHRIS . . . . .11 DECEMBER 1990, NEW YORK

JOHNSON, HOWARD . . . . .8 APRIL 1991, NEW YORK

JONES, ELVIN . . . . .24 MAY 1991, TORONTO

KONITZ, LEE . . . . .21 JANUARY 1989, TORONTO

LAPORTA, JOHN* . . . . .27 MARCH 1992

LACY, STEVE . . . . .29 APRIL 1990, TORONTO

LEVIN, PETE . . . . .9 APRIL 1991, NEW YORK

LIEPOLT, HORST . . . . .5 MARCH 1990, NEW YORK

LIEPOLT, HORST . . . . .8 APRIL 1991, NEW YORK

MACERO, TEO* . . . . .FEBRUARY 1992

MALONE, TOM . . . . .9 APRIL 1991, NEW YORK

MAXWELL, JIMMIE* . . . . .20 MARCH 1992

MAXWELL, JIMMIE* . . . . .23 MARCH 1992

MAXWELL, JIMMIE* . . . . .27 MARCH 1992

MERRILL, HELEN . . . . .SEPTEMBER 1990, TORONTO

MORGENSTERN, DAN . . . .5 MARCH 1990, NEWARK, NEW JERSEY

MORIERA, AIRTO; PURIM, FLORA . . . . . .26 MAY 1992, TORONTO

MUCCI, LOUIS* . . . . .20 MARCH 1992

MULLIGAN, GERRY . . . . .8 DECEMBER 1990, CONNECTICUT

MULLIGAN, GERRY* . . . . .23 MARCH 1992

MULLIGAN, GERRY* . . . . .6 APRIL 1993

NUSSBAUM, ADAM . . . . .25 JUNE 1991, TORONTO

PEACOCK, GARY . . . . .5 JULY 1992, MONTREAL

ROACH, MAX . . . . .26 APRIL 1992, TORONTO

ROBERTSON, ROBBIE* . . . . .14 SEPTEMBER 1992

RODNEY, RED* . . . . .12 AUGUST 1992

RONEY, WALLACE . . . . .24 MAY 1992, TORONTO

RUSSELL, GEORGE . . . . .8 JULY 1992, CAMBRIDGE, MASS.

RUSSELL, GEORGE* . . . . .23 JULY 1992

SANBORN, DAVID . . . . .6 APRIL 1991, NEW YORK

SCHNEIDER, MARIA . . . . .6 JULY 1992, NEW YORK

SCHULLER, GUNTHER . . . .8 JULY 1992, NEWTON CENTER, MASS.

SCOFIELD, JOHN . . . . .16 NOVEMBER 1991, TORONTO

SHORTER, WAYNE* .5 FEBRUARY 1992

SOLOFF, LEW . . . . .11 DECEMBER 1990, NEW YORK

STING . . . . .4 MARCH 1990, NEW YORK

SURMAN, JOHN . . . . .5 JULY 1992, MONTREAL

WILLIAMS, TONY* .6 DECEMBER 1991

BIBLIOGRAPHY

BOOKS

Chambers, Jack. *Milestones: The Music and Times of Miles Davis.* Toronto: University of Toronto Press, 1983.

Collier, James Lincoln. *Benny Goodman and the Swing Era.* New York: Oxford University Press, 1989.

Cugny, Laurent. *Las Vegas Tango: Une Vie de Gil Evans.* Paris: P.O.L., Collection Birdland, 1989.

Davis, Miles, with Quincy Troupe. *Miles: The Autobiography.* New York: Touchstone/ Simon & Schuster, 1989. Quotes reprinted with the permission of Simon & Schuster. Copyright © 1989 by Miles Davis.

Gitler, Ira. *Swing to Bop: An Oral History of the Tradition in Jazz in the 1940s.* New York: Oxford University Press, 1985.

Horricks, Raymond. *Gil Evans.* New York: Hippocrene Books, 1984.

Murray, Charles Shaar. *Crosstown Traffic.* New York: St. Martin's Press, 1989.

Schwartz, Charles. *Gershwin: His Life and Music.* New York, Indianapolis: Bobbs-Merrill, 1973.

Shapiro, Harry, and Caesar Glebbeek. *Electric Gypsy.* New York: St. Martin's Press, 1991.

Sidran, Ben. *Talking Jazz: An Oral History.* New York: Da Capo Press, 1995.

Simon, George T. *The Big Bands.* New York: MacMillan, 1971.

Simon, George T. *Glenn Miller and His Orchestra.* New York: T.Y. Crowell, 1974.

Wade, Graham. *Joaquín Rodrigo and the Concierto de Aranjuez.* England: Mayflower Enterprises, 1985.

Walker, Leo. *Wonderful Era of the Great Dance Bands.* Garden City, N.Y.: Doubleday, 1964.

MAGAZINE ARTICLES, INTERVIEWS

Down Beat
Nat Hentoff. "The Birth of the Cool." May 2, 1957.
Nat Hentoff. "I'm No Granddaddy: Gil Evans." May 16, 1957.
Marc Crawford. "Miles Davis and Gil Evans: Portrait of a Friendship." February 16, 1961 (reprinted February 1994).
George Hoefer. "Gil Evans: The Early Years of Learning." February 25, 1965.
Leonard Feather. "The Modulated World of Gil Evans." February 23, 1967.
Don DeMicheal. Concert review (Whitney Museum, New York). August 6, 1968.
Excerpts from articles listed above used with the permission of Down Beat *magazine.*

Coda Magazine
Don J. Lahey. "Gil Evans: Out of the Cool." August 1985.

Metronome
Dave Soloman. "Jazz Is Popular Music: Dave Solomon Interviews Gil Evans." June 1961.

Guitar World
Bill Milkowski. Interview with Gil Evans. March 1988.

Village Voice
Howard Mandel. "Evans Above." July 26, 1983.
Gary Giddins. "The Scene Changes." April 5, 1988.

International Musician
Martha Sanders Gilmore. "Gil Evans." November 1972.

Musician
Mark Rowland. "Miles Davis Is a Living Legend and You're Not." March 1987.
Jerome Reese. "Teo Macero." March 1987.

ADDITIONAL INTERVIEWS CITED

Helen Armstead Johnston. Unpublished interview with Gil Evans, Jazz Oral History Project. Conducted for Smithsonian Institution of Performing Arts, with support from the National Endowment for the Arts, Washington, D.C., November 11 and December 12, 1972 (Transcript courtesy of the Institute of Jazz Studies), Rutgers University.

Charles Fox, BBC Radio 3. Interview with Gil Evans. August 1983 (as featured on "Gil Evans 75th Birthday Concert," BBC Music *Jazz Legends* series, 1996).

Katie Malloch, CBC Radio Canada. "Jazz Beat." June 1987.

ALBUM LINER NOTES

Claude Thornhill

Best of the Big Bands [Columbia WCK 46152], Will Friedwald

Miles Davis

Birth of the Cool [Capitol Jazz C2–92862], Pete Welding; Special Note by Gerry Mulligan

Miles Ahead [Columbia CK 40784], George Avakian

Porgy and Bess [Columbia CK 40647], Charles Edward Smith

Sketches of Spain [Columbia CK 40576], Nat Hentoff

Gil Evans

Great Jazz Standards [Capitol–Pacific Jazz Series CDP 7 46856 2], Dave Baker

New Bottle, Old Wine [Capitol–Pacific Jazz Series CDP 7 468552], (probably) Michael Cuscuna

Out of the Cool [MCA Records–Impulse IMPD–186], Tom Stewart (1961), Michael Cuscuna (1996 reissue)

Into the Hot [ABC–Impulse A9], Nat Hentoff

The Individualism of Gil Evans [Polygram–Verve 833 804–2], Gene Lees (1964), Michael Cuscuna (1988 reissue)

Where Flamingos Fly [A&M Records–CD 0831], John Snyder (1981 reissue)

The Gil Evans Orchestra Plays the Music of Jimi Hendrix [RCA–Bluebird 8409–2–RB], Stephanie Stein (1988 reissue)

There Comes a Time [RCA Victor–Bluebird 5783–2–RB], Fernando Gonzales (1975), Ed Michel (1987 reissue)

Gil Evans Live at the Public Theater, Volumes I and II [Evidence Music ECD 22089, ECD 22090], Elliot Bratton (1994 reissues)

Farewell: Gil Evans and the Monday Night Orchestra Live at Sweet Basil [Evidence Music ECD 22031], Stephanie L. Stein and Robert P. Crease (1992 reissue)

Gil Evans Orchestra Live at Umbria Jazz 87, Volumes I and II [EGEA–UJ EUJ 1001, EUJ 1002], Paolo Occhiuto, with translations by Iain Adams

INDEX

Abercrombie, John, 289
Absolute Beginners, 244
Adderley, Julian "Cannonball," 97
American Federation of Musicians (AFM), 25–26, 46
American Society of Composers, Authors, and Publishers. *See* ASCAP
Armstrong, Louis, 6, 7
arrangers
  Gil's skill as, 8
  importance of, 1
  role in bringing unity and cohesion, 87
ASCAP (American Society of Composers, Authors and Publishers), 24–26, 46
Avakian, George
  interview with, 289
  Johnny Mathis and, 80–81
  Miles Davis and, 86, 91
avant garde jazz, 118–119

Bach, J. S., 34
"Barbara Song, The," 137, 139
Bargeron, Dave
  on Gil's role in the band, 185–186
  interview with, 289
  on playing with Gil, 259
  at Westbeth Cabaret, 185
Bartók, Béla, 34, 127
Beck, Joe, 289
Berk, Idaho, 5
big bands
  breaking up of, 46–47
  decline of, 45–46

"Bilbao Song," 117
"Bird Feathers," 97
Birth of the Cool
  album, 50, 73, 85
  Miles Davis Nonet, debut, 69–71
  Miles Davis Nonet, formation, 63–66
  Miles Davis Nonet, participants, 67–69
  Miles Davis's role in, 60–63
  post-war renaissance of arts, 59–60
  recording sessions, 71–73
Bitches Brew (Miles Davis), 220
Bloch, Ernest, 34
"Blues for Pablo," 87
Blues in Orbit, 174–177
Bob Hope Show, 16–17
Boplicity, 65
Borden, Bill, 21
Brass Ensemble of the Jazz and Classical Music Society, 86
Brazil tour, 267–268
Brazilian Spiritual Mass (Moreira), 232
Briggs-Evans Band. *See* Gil Evans Orchestra
Brown, Delmar, interview, 289
Bud 'n' Bird, 257–258
Bullock, Hiram, 235, 289
Burrell, Kenny
  Guitar Forms album of, 146–148
  interview with, 289
  last words, 286
Bushler, Herb, interview, 289

Cal-Neva Club, 11
Capitol Records, 73

Carisi, John
  on Gil's mystical quality, 55
  Gil's respect for writing of, 124–125
  hired by Claude Thornhill Orchestra, 38–39
  interview with, 289
  on motivation to play music, 59
  as writer of "Israel," 65
Carnegie Hall Concert, 198
Casa Loma Orchestra, 9–10
CBC Radio Canada, xiii, 33
chamber jazz approach, 65
childhood years, Gil Evans
  introduction to jazz, 6
  parents and nomadic lifestyle of, 3–6
  sound sensitivity, 8
Clark, John
  on Gil's role as band leader, 187, 236
  interview with, 289
  on response of Japanese audiences, 208
  on touring with Gil, 207–208
Classics in Jazz (Capitol Records), 73
Claude Thornhill Orchestra
  arrangements for, 39–41
  Gil's role in, 36–37
  hiring new talent, 38–39
  last period of, 44–45
  low-register sound of, 42–43
  popular tunes of, 44
  reforming of, 35–36
  at Rendezvous Ballroom, Balboa Beach (CA), 19
  Shribman circuit, bookings, 19
  sound of, 38–39, 63
Coleman, Ornette, 118–119
Collaboration: Helen Merrill and Gil Evans, 265–267
Color of Money, The, 249–257
Columbia Records, 85
Concierto de Aranjuez (Rodrigo), 108–110
"Concord," 137

dance halls, decline of, 46
"Davenport Blues," 105

Davis, Miles
  Bitches Brew, 220
  collaboration with Gil, 49–50, 62–63, 106, 224, 233
  declining health of, 221
  Decoy, 223
  first meeting with Gil, 61–62
  on Gil's ability to write music, 89
  Gil's attraction to sound of, 62, 88
  heroin habit of, 73
  Japan tour, 224
  method of working with Gil, 223
  money attitude, contrasted with Gil's, 151–152
  personal relationship with Gil, 60–61, 221
  quintet, 150
  refusal to work with Teo Macero, 127
  resistance to free jazz, 125
  response to challenges of Gil's music, 113, 116
  Star People, 222–223
  at Sweet Basil, 260
  trumpet tone of, 88
de Falla, Manuel, 34, 107
death of Gil Evans, 273–278
Decoy (Miles Davis), 223
Diedrick, Rusty
  Gil's arrangements and, 24
  interview with, 289
  joining up with Gil, 20–21
  post-war scene and, 35
Directions (Miles Davis), 170–171
disc jockeys, 46–47
Don Redman band, 8
Dream of You (Merrill and Evans), 81
Dreamland Ballroom, Stockton (CA), 11
drugs
  55th Street and, 53–54
  Gil's use of pot, 162–163, 220
  hard, 75
  heroin habit of Miles Davis, 73

"El Matador," 196
"El Toreador," 136

electric instruments, first concert use, 166–167
"Eleven," 198
"Ella's Speed," 94
Ellington, Duke, 6
English tour, 224–225
Ennis, Skinnay, 15–17
entertainment tax, 32
Europe tours
  final, with Laurent Cugny, 268–270
  first, 205
  jazz market alive in, 206
Evans and Konitz duo, European tour, 219–220
Evans, Anita
  age difference with Gil, 132
  author's meeting with, ix
  as business manager, 157, 205–206
  on Gil's devotion to his children, 156
  Gil's first meeting with, 129–130
  on Gil's openness to listen to everything, 194
  on Gil's relationship to musical innovators, 239
  help given author, xiii
  interview with, 290
  separation from Gil, 213–216
Evans, Bill, 285, 290
Evans, Gil, life milestones, 28–34
  Anita, first meeting, 129–130
  Anita, separation from, 213–216
  army period, 26–30
  birth/childhood/family of, 3–6
  childhood years, 3–6, 8
  death of, 273–278
  devotion to his children, 156
  family trip to Florida, 269–270
  hernia operation, 267
  Lillian Green, end of marriage to, 121
  memorial service, April 3, 1988, 281–283
  name change Green to Evans, 174
  Noah and Miles, births of, 135
  prostate surgery and recuperation, 271–275
  Westbeth move, 180
Evans, Gil, music
  as arranger, 8, 82
  attention to detail, 111
  balance between order and chaos, 182–183
  breaking music rules, 183
  career accomplishments, ix, 173
  classical influences of, 33–34
  Claude Thornhill, collaboration with, 18–24
  Claude Thornhill, split with, 44
  collective nature of, 105
  commitment to music-making process, 229
  conducting style, 90
  demands on other musicians, 112
  emphasis on living spirit in, 55
  as established orchestrator, 33
  George Russell, relationship with, 57
  greatest music of, 85, 141
  Hollywood politics and, 128–129
  income from, 119–120
  influences on, 107, 161
  interest in classical repertoire, 33–34
  interest in texture, 216
  Jimi Hendrix, relationship to music of, 192–193
  leadership style of, 185–186
  Lester Young and, 29–31
  living spirit in music of, 145
  Miles Davis, contrast with, 89
  Miles Davis, relationship with, 233
  music charts of, 169
  openness to listen to everything, 193–194
  re-composing others' tunes, 40
  record labels of, 119
  relationship to his own music, 83, 177
  respect of other musicians, 112
  role in the band, 236
  as skilled selector of musicians, 138
  song orientation of, 182

sound palette of, 115
submerging of self in music, 165
use of synthesizer, 178–179
writing style of, 248
Evans, Gil, personal qualities
    attitudes on therapy and self-discovery,
        163–165
    drug use, 162–163
    gentle softness, 137–138
    money attitude, contrasted with Miles
        Davis, 151–152
    money, unconnected to, 130
    personality of, 8–9, 13–14, 55–56
    preference to work with friends, 81
    religious and spiritual views, 9, 180
    way of deflecting and eliminating
        bullshit, 204
    work ethic, 146
    youthful attitude of, 253
Evans, Miles
    birth of, 135, 148
    debut as trumpet player, 225
    interview with, 290
    music interest of, 215
Evans, Noah
    birth of, 135
    on Gil's death, 273–275
    on Gil's lack of sharing, 275–276
    on Gil's need for physical help, 268
    interview with, 290
    studio career of, 214
    success at mixing board, 239
Evans, Susan
    on Gil's youthful quality, 207
    interview with, 290
    last words, 286–287
    on personal quality of Gil's band and
        music, 175

Faddis, John, 208–209, 290
Farewell, 258
Fender Rhodes electric piano, 171–172
55th Street, basement room
    1947–1949, 50–51

Charlie Parker as roommate and visitor,
    53, 54–55
drug use and, 53–54
gathering place for musicians, 49–52
Gerry Mulligan as roommate, 52–53
Gil's influence on others, 56–58
Gil's move out, 70
religious and philosophical exchanges at,
    55–56
Filles de Kilimanjaro (Miles Davis), 170–171
film scores
    Absolute Beginners, 244
    The Color of Money, 249–257
    Insignificance, 249–257
Five Spot, Charles Mingus band at, 152
flamenco, origins in Sketches of Spain, 108
Flower Power, 158–165
    Haight Ashbury music scene, 158–159
    Jimi Hendrix at Monterey Pop Festival,
        159
    Motown Records, 158
    plagiarism in music business, 159–161
    Robbie Robertson, revolution in the air,
        159
formaldehyde bands, Evans on, 154
Free Jazz. See avant garde jazz
fusion band, Montreux concert, 230

"General Assembly," 175
Gensel, Reverend John, 290
Gershwin, George, 98, 101
Giddins, Gary, 290
Gil Evans and the Monday Night Orchestra,
    241, 242
Gil Evans Live at the Public Theater, 217–218
Gil Evans Orchestra
    Benny Goodman's influence, 12–13
    Bob Hope Show radio contract, 16–17
    Casa Loma Orchestra influence, 9–10
    contract with Victor Records, 13
    engagements of, 10–11, 14–16
    hiring of Claude Thornhill, 17
    instrumentation of, 168–169
    musical influences on, 7–8

nucleus of players of, 184–189
original music of, 9
Skinnay Ennis and, 15–17
swing years, 7–17
Gil Evans Orchestra, Live at Umbria Jazz 87, 263
Gil Evans Plays the Music of Jimi Hendrix, 191, 198–200
Gil Evans Plus Ten
    personnel of, 93–94
    Prestige Records, 85
    production of, 93–95
Gilberto, Astrud, 148–149, 290
Gillian Music, 120
Glen Island Casino (NY), 19–21
Golden Hair, 269
Goldstein, Gil
    affected by playing with Gil, 231
    interview with, 290
    last words, from, 284
Goodman, Benny, 12–13
Grace, Lillian. *See* Lillian Green
Grammy Award, 1960, best jazz composition, 114
Grammy nominations
    Guitar Forms, 147
    The Individualism of Gil Evans, 141
Great Jazz Standards, 104, 105
Green, Ian Ernest Gilmore. *See* Evans, Gil
Green, Julia (McConnachy), mother, 3–6
Green, Lillian (Grace), marriage to, 74–75
Greenwich Village, family life in, 155–156
Guggenheim writing fellowship, 173–174
Guitar Forms (Burrell), 146–148

Haight Ashbury, music scene in, 158–159
Hall, Glen
    collaboration with, 245–249
    interview with, 290
Hammersmith Odeon Theater, London, 262
Hancock, Herbie
    on Gil's personal qualities, 133
    interview with, 290
    last words, 284–285
    use of Fender Rhodes by, 172

Harper, Billy
    first meeting with Gil Evans, 152–153
    interview with, 290
Harvey, Laurence, 131
Hawkins, Coleman, 30–31
Henderson, Fletcher, 12
Hendrix, Jimi
    Gil intrigued by music of, 189
    with Miles Davis, 189–190
    at Monterey Pop Festival, 159
    two album proposal by, 190
Heyward, DuBose, 98
Hollywood, Gil's distaste for, 128–129
Horowitz, David
    interview with, 290
    joining the band, 178–179
"Hotel Me," 136
Hunter, Chris
    changes in attitude toward business, 234–235
    interview with, 290
    on playing with Gil's band, 226

"I'm a Fool to Want You," 127
improvisation
    attraction to great improvisers, 77–78
    quality in written music, 97
Impulse recording, 116–118
Individualism of Gil Evans, The
    "Barbara Song, The" 137, 139
    "Concord," 137
    "El Toreador," 136
    Grammy nomination for, 141
    "Hotel Me," 136
    "Las Vegas Tango," 136–137
    "Nothing Like You," 140
    "Proclamation," 139–140
    "Spoonful," 137
    "Time of the Barracudas," 137
Insignificance, film score for, 249
Into the Hot, 124, 125
Israel, 65

Japan tour, 209, 224

jazz
  avant garde jazz, 118–119
  as featured act, 41–42
  loss of stature, 47, 76

jazz suite, 87

"Jelly Rolls," 196

Johnson, Howard
  collaboration with Gil, 154–155
  interview with, 290

Jones, Elvin
  collaboration with Gil, 110–111
  on Gil's leadership qualities, 106
  interview with, 290

Jones, Philly Joe, 79–80

Jones, Quincy, 130

Jordan, Louis, 47

Kennedy Center for the Performing Arts, 206

"King Porter Stomp," 97

King Records, 258

Konitz, Lee
  Claude Thornhill Orchestra hires, 37–38
  duo with Gil that did not happen, 230
  interview with, 290

"La Nevada," 105, 117

Lacy, Steve
  duo recording with, 237
  on Gil's ability to lock onto sound, 95
  interview with, 290
  life-altering experience of, 94
  Paris Blues, 269–270

Lake Tahoe (CA), engagements, 10

"Lament," 87

LaPorta, John, 78, 290
  on Gil's arrangements, 39–40
  records, mass market for, 46

"Las Vegas Tango," 136–137

Le Palais de Sport concert (Bercy, France), 249

leadership style, 14, 236

Levin, Pete
  on Gil's interest in texture of music, 216
  on Gil's leadership qualities, 217
  on importance of intuitiveness of players, 187
  interview with, 290
  joining up with Gil, 184

Liepolt, Horst
  on band's performance, 240–241
  interview with, 290
  part owner of Sweet Basil, 227–228

"Light My Fire," 159–161

listeners, new generation of, 192

Little Wing, 210

Live at Carnegie Hall, 122–123

"Love in the Open," 174

Lydian Chromatic Concept of Tonal Organization, 57

Lynch, Ruel, 12

Macero, Teo
  editing work of, 102
  interview with, 290
  Miles's refusal to work with, 127

"Maids of Cadiz," 87

Malmo, Sweden, recording engagement, 209

Malone, Tom
  freedom and challenge of playing with Gil, 187
  interview with, 290

"Manteca," 97

marijuana, 54

Mathis, Johnny, 80–81

Maxwell, Jimmie
  on Gil as roommate, 50–51
  on Gil during swing years, 13–16
  on Gil's difficulty delivering arrangements on time, 76
  influence of Gil on, 7–9
  interview with, 290

MCA (Music Corporation of America), 13

"Meaning of the Blues," 87

memorial service, April 3, 1988, 281–283

Merrill, Helen
    Collaboration: Helen Merrill and Gil Evans,
        265–267
    on desire to work with Gil, 81
    interview with, 290
Miles Ahead
    concept of, 86–92
    content of, 87
    editing techniques used for, 91
Miles Davis Nonet
    Basie, Count, comment on, 69–70
    collective consciousness of, 68
    Evans, leader in spirit, 69
    forming, 63
    musicians involved, 67
    recording session roster, 68
    Royal Roost, billing at, 69
    voicing of, 64
    writer versus instrumentalist, 64
Miles in the Sky (Miles Davis), 170–171
Miller, Glenn, 19
Mingus, Charles, 152
Minton's Playhouse, Harlem, 30–31
Monday Night Orchestra, The
    Bud 'n' Bird, 258
    concerts, 249, 262
    Farewell, 258
    Golden Hair, 269
    as the Grateful Dead of Jazz, 260
    King Records recordings, 240–243,
        257–260
    loudest band to date, 242
    Mick Jagger's visits, 261
    new name of Gil's band, 232
    Rhythm-a-ning, 269
money
    contrast between Miles and Gil, 151–152
    Gil unconnected to, 130
    limited income from royalties, 119–120
Monk, Thelonious, 82
Monterey Jazz Festival, 153, 262
Montreux concert, 230
Montreux Jazz Festival, 209
Moog synthesizer, origin of, 178

"Moon Dreams," 65–66, 72
More Music from the Legendary Carnegie Hall
        Concert, 1987 album release, 123
Moreira, Airto
    Brazilian Spiritual Mass, 232
    on Gil breaking musical rules, 183
    interview with, 290
    on sense of freedom in Gil's band, 181
Morgenstern, Dan, 78–79, 290
Mother of the Book, The, 248
Motown Records, 158
Mucci, Louis, 35–36, 40–41, 290
Mulligan, Gerry
    Claude Thornhill Orchestra hires, 37
    on decline of big bands, 45–46
    on Gil's piano playing, 77
    as Gil's roommate, 52–53
    interview with, 290–291
    on Miles Davis Nonet, 63
    rehearsal scene in New York, 45
music
    blending jazz and classical, 113–114
    folk and popular themes, 107
    Gil's emphasis on living spirit in, 55
    importance of musicians' enthusiasm for,
        106
    role of emotions in, 170
    Schuller on integrity in Gil's, 58
    as single unified entity, 118
Music Corporation of America (MCA), 13
musicians
    as artists, not entertainers, 60
    classically trained, 112
Musso, Vido, 12
"My Ship," 87
mystical understanding, Carisi description
        of, 55

"Nana," 196
National Public Radio, xiii
New Bottle, Old Wine
    content of, 96
    improvisational quality in writing of, 97
    Julian "Cannonball" Adderley on, 97

as object lesson in recomposing, 96
    players on, 97
New Thing. *See* avant garde jazz
New Wave, 150
New York Kool Jazz Festival, 1983, 229
New York Town Hall concert, 222
Nexus, recording with, 247
Nolan, Kenneth, 197
nonet. *See* Miles Davis Nonet
"Nothing Like You," 140
Nussbaum, Adam
    interview with, 291
    last words, 287
    on letting music be the guide, 236–237

OKeh Records, 20, 21, 23–24
"Once Upon a Summertime," 126–127
Out of the Cool, 116–118
    content of, 117
    music, as single unified entity, 118

Palomar Ballroom, Los Angeles (CA), 11–12
"Pan Piper, The," 108
Paris Blues (Lacy), 269–270
Parker, Charlie
    arrangements for, 76
    erratic nature of, 63
    as featured act, 41–42
    as Gil's roommate, 53
    Mulligan's description of, 54–55
Pasqual, Hermeto, 267–268
Pastorius, Jaco, 238–239
Peacock, Gary, 291
Petrillo, Jimmy, 25
plagiarism, in music business, 160–161
Porgy and Bess
    background to album, 100
    DuBose Heyward and, 98
    editing album, 102
    George Gershwin and, 98, 101
    movie production of, 100
    musical content of, 103
    stereo recording, challenges of, 102
    success of, 103
    theatre production of, 99

Porgy, best-selling novel, 98
Priestess, 210
"Proclamation," 139–140, 174
prostate surgery, 271
psychiatrists, as attitude salesmen, 204
Purim, Flora
    connecting with Gil, 180–181
    on Gil's spirituality, 180
    interview with, 290

Quiet Nights, 127

racism, 31–32
radio ban, ASCAP, 24–25, 46
RCA Victor releases
    Gil Evans Plays the Music of Jimi Hendrix,
        198
    There Comes a Time, 201–203
re-composing
    genius for, 87
    object lesson in, 96
recording ban, 1942, 25–26, 46
records, mass markets, 46
Redman, Don, 8
"Remember," 94
renaissance of arts, post-war period, 59–60
Rendezvous Ballroom, Balboa Beach (CA),
    11, 19
retrospective, New York Kool Jazz Festival,
    229
Rhythm-a-ning, recorded in Europe, 269
rhythm and blues, 47–48
RMS concert, video recording of,
    230–231
Roach, Max
    52nd Street scene, 31–33
    interview with, 291
    jazz as featured act, 41–42
Robertson, Robbie
    collaboration with Gil on *The Color of
        Money*, 249–257
    on Gil's leadership qualities, 255–256
    interview with, 291
    on revolution in pop music, 159
rock and roll, impact of, 118–119

Rodney, Red
  on challenges of playing for Gil, 41
  Claude Thornhill Orchestra hires, 38–39
  interview with, 291
Rodrigo, Joaquin, 108–110
Roeg, Nicolas, 249
Roney, Wallace, 291
Round Midnight album, 85
"Round Midnight" (Thelonious Monk), 82
Royal Festival Hall, London, 210, 232
Royal Roost
  billing at, 69
  first engagement at, 67
royalties, limited income from, 119–120
Rugolo, Pete, 71
Russell, George
  interview with, 291
  *Lydian Chromatic Concept of Tonal
    Organization*, 57
Russian composers, 34

"Saeta," 108, 110
Sanborn, David
  Gil wrote his life, 194
  influence and attitude towards life, 203
  interview with, 291
  joining up with Gil Evans, 186
  last words, from, 287
  on trusting instincts, 204
Schneider, Maria
  coming in contact with Gil, 253
  on Gil's being detail-oriented, 252
  interview with, 291
Schuller, Gunther
  on Gil's personality, 58
  on importance of arrangers, 1
  interview with, 291
  low-register Thornhill sound of, 42–43
  third-stream movement, 114–115
Scofield, John
  interview with, 291
  joining band, 222–223
Scott, Ronnie, 232
Seventh Avenue South, 234
Shelly's Manne-hole, 153–154

Shorter, Wayne
  as close friend of Gil's, 128
  interview with, 291
  on role of emotion in music, 170
Shribman, Charlie, 19–20
Shribman, Cy, 19–20
Sidran, Ben, 6
singing stars, popularity of, 46, 48
"Sister Sadie," 117
Sketches of Spain
  blending jazz and classical, 113–114
  content of, 108, 114
  Elvin Jones's orchestration of march,
    110–111
  flamenco origins of, 108
  folk and popular themes in, 107
  Grammy Award, 1960, 114
  Manuel de Falla and, 107
  Miles's demands on musicians, 112
  Miles's transcendent experience with, 113
  musicians, classical training of, 112
  recording dates, 111
  response of critics, 114
Skinnay Ennis Band, 15–17, 18
"So Long," 175
"Solea," 108
Soloff, Lew
  on creativity in playing with Gil, 188
  interview with, 291
  on sound of now, 195
soloists, choosing own entry points, 210
"Song #1," 126
"Song #2," 126
"Song of Our Country," 108
"Spaced," 174
"Spoonful," 137
"Springsville," 87
St. George Church, New York City
  recording, 209–210
Star People (Miles Davis), 222, 223
stereo recording, challenges of, 102
Sting
  collaboration with Gil, 261–265
  with Gil in Montserrat, 265
  interview with, 291

last words, 286
Ronnie Scott's meeting with, 232
Stockton (CA)
    childhood in, 6
    swing years in, 8–11
"Straight, No Chaser," 105
Strange Fruit: Sting and Gil Evans, 263
"Stratusphunk," 117
"Summer Night," 126–127
"Summertime," 198
"Sunken Treasure," 117
Surman, John
    coming to work with Gil, 226
    on Gil's grasp of sonorities, 252
    interview with, 291
    last words, 287–288
Svengali, ix, 197–198
Sweet Basil
    players at, 228
    success of, 243
swing years, 7–17
synthesizer, 178–179

Taylor, Cecil, 125
Taylor, Creed, 124
Tempo, review in, 15
"Testimony," 257
therapist, Gil's experience with, 163–165
There Comes a Time
    huge band on, 201
    players on, 201–202
Thornhill, Claude
    cross-country tour, 21
    death of, 45
    early career of, 18–19
    Gil's collaboration with, 22–24
    Gil's split with, 44
    Glen Island Casino and, 19–21
    Glenn Miller and, 19
    leadership of Claude Thornhill Orchestra
        by, 41
    navy enlistment of, 26
    personnel changes, 20

record contract of, 20–21
Skinnay Ennis Band and, 17–18
sound of, 22
"Thoroughbred," 174
Time of the Barracuda (play), 131–132
"Time of the Barracudas," 137
tours, not all work, 206
Trianon Ballroom, Seattle (WA), 14–15

U.C. Jazz Festival, 167–169
Uptown Ballroom, Portland (OR), 15

van Gelder, Rudy, 93, 137
"Variation on the Misery," 175
Victor Hugo's, Hollywood (CA), 15–16
Victor Records, 13
Village Vanguard
    fill-in band Monday nights, 189
    jazz scene at, 30
vocal work, arranging for, 75–76
voicing
    definition of, xi
    of Miles Davis Nonet, 64

"Wait Till You See Her," 127
Westbeth Cabaret, playing at, 185
Westbeth, move to, 180
"Where Flamingos Fly," 117, 195–196
Whitney Museum Concert, twelve piece
    band, 166
"Will of the Wisp," 110
Williams, Hank, far outselling jazz, 47
Williams, Tony
    diverse musical interests of, 150–151
    interview with, 291
World War II
    effects on music business, 26
    entertainment tax implications, 32
    New York jazz club scene, 30–32

Young, Lester, 29–30

"Zee Zee," 196, 198

Printed in the United States
R3250500001B/R32505PG79123LVX1B/1}

9 780306 809453